Forms of
Contention

Forms of Contention

INFLUENCE AND THE AFRICAN AMERICAN SONNET TRADITION

Hollis Robbins

THE UNIVERSITY OF
GEORGIA PRESS
ATHENS

Credits for previously published material appear on pages 245–246 and constitute an extension of this copyright page.

© 2020 by the University of Georgia Press
Athens, Georgia 30602
www.ugapress.org
All rights reserved
Designed by Kaelin Chappell Broaddus
Set in 9.75/13.5 Skolar Latin by Kaelin Chappell Broaddus

Most University of Georgia Press titles are
available from popular e-book vendors.

Printed digitally

Library of Congress Cataloging-in-Publication Data

Names: Robbins, Hollis, 1963– author.
Title: Forms of contention : influence and the African
    American sonnet tradition / Hollis Robbins.
Description: Athens : The University of Georgia Press, 2020.
    | Includes bibliographical references and index.
Identifiers: LCCN 2019053562 | ISBN 9780820356945 (hardback) |
    ISBN 9780820357645 (paperback) | ISBN 9780820356952 (ebook)
Subjects: LCSH: American poetry—African American authors—
    History and criticism. | Sonnets, American—History and criticism.
    | American poetry—19th century—History and criticism. |
    American poetry—20th century—History and criticism.
Classification: LCC PS153.N5 R535 2020 | DDC 811/.0420996073—dc23
LC record available at https://lccn.loc.gov/2019053562

FOR *Skip Gates*

CONTENTS

PROLOGUE   1

CHAPTER 1. Tracing Tradition and Influence   7

CHAPTER 2. Suffering, Love, Bondage, and Protest   32

CHAPTER 3. Antecedents (1768–1889)   72

CHAPTER 4. Periodical Sonnets from Dunbar to McKay, 1890–1922   103

CHAPTER 5. Anthologies and Canon Formation, 1923–1967   132

CHAPTER 6. Power Lines: The Black Aesthetic and the Black Sonnet   169

ACKNOWLEDGMENTS   191

NOTES   195

BIBLIOGRAPHY   223

PERMISSIONS CREDITS   245

INDEX   247

*Forms of
Contention*

PROLOGUE

On a warm March evening in 2018 I drove to Duke University's Nasher Museum of Art in Durham, North Carolina, to see Natasha Trethewey give the inaugural John Hope Franklin Lecture. I was eager to hear Trethewey speak and to speak to her. I was at that time a fellow at the National Humanities Center working on this book on the African American sonnet tradition. Trethewey's name was everywhere in my early drafts as one of the best sonnet writers in this century's resurgence of sonnet writing. I had read Trethewey's 2006 Pulitzer Prize-winning collection, *Native Guard*, and marveled at her crown of sonnets in the voice of a black soldier watching over imprisoned white Confederate soldiers during the Civil War:

MARCH 1863

I listen, put down in ink what I know
they labor to say between silences
too big for words: worry for beloveds—
My Dearest, how are you getting along—
what has become of their small plots of land—
did you harvest enough food to put by?
They long for the comfort of former lives—
I see you as you were, waving goodbye.
Some send photographs—a likeness in case
the body can't return. Others dictate
harsh facts of this war: The hot air carries
the stench of limbs, rotten in the bone pit.
Flies swarm—a black cloud. We hunger, grow weak.
When men die, we eat their share of hardtack.

I wondered about her influences and why, in reviews and interviews, Trethewey always characterized her use of the sonnet form as something unexpected for a black poet, something that still had to be explained, 120 years after Paul Laurence Dunbar began publishing sonnets. Trethewey's sonnet, with its "small plots of land," seemed as familiar to me as the grim 1940s Alabama sonnets of Margaret Walker or the "small room" sonnets of Gwendolyn Brooks.

Trethewey's reading at Duke was moving: she recited poems and spoke about her family and her early years in Mississippi. She touched on her use of the sonnet form, a "received European form," and spoke of using the master's tools to dismantle the master's house, as Audre Lorde put it. The audience was transfixed.

I asked the first question after Trethewey finished and the applause died down. I said that I loved her work and her reading. But why was she was still characterizing the sonnet as a form received from white poets? Given the long list of African American sonnet writers—I counted them off on my fingers: Paul Dunbar, James Corrothers, Leslie Pinckney Hill, Claude McKay, Countee Cullen, Sterling Brown, Gwendolyn Brooks, Margaret Walker, Robert Hayden, Rita Dove—how many sonnets have to be written before someone will say she received the form from a black poet? How long until a poet says she received the sonnet from Natasha Trethewey?

Trethewey was silent for a long moment and then said, quietly, "You're right I can't say that anymore. I received the form from Gwendolyn Brooks." She spoke about Brooks, very movingly, and then paused, contemplative. Nobody asked any more questions. The audience got up and moved to the lobby. I spoke to Trethewey near the podium and she thanked me, but there was a tension between us too. My question pointed to a difficult truth in African American poetry: that too many ancestors have been forgotten. Too much nineteenth- and twentieth-century poetry was banished from the black poetry canon in the 1960s because it was too "traditional." The erasure of these poets long meant the erasure of their legacy. It is only with the emergence of digital technology to recover the wealth of literature published in African American newspapers during the first half of the twentieth century that we can finally see the extent of what was ignored and overlooked.

In the lobby afterward I spoke with the poet Nathaniel Mackey, with whom I had discussed my interest in sonnets at lunch at the National Humanities Center a month before. Mackey had posted on his Facebook page, "All these years reading Baraka's *Preface to a Twenty Volume Suicide Note* (1960) I never noticed there's a sonnet in it ['The turncoat']. Many thanks to Hollis Robbins, who's writing a book on the African American sonnet, for clueing me in." In the lobby, Mackey was wry. "I knew what you were going to ask the second you stood up," he said. "But I've never written a sonnet and I never will. You can put that in your book."

Some African American poets who write sonnets acknowledge their influences openly. "I've learned different things from different people," Marilyn Nelson wrote to me. "The 'old dead white guys,' of course, like the Romantics and Victorians, and Elizabeth Barrett Browning, Edna St. Vincent Millay, Claude McKay, Robert Frost, Marilyn Hacker...This is just off the top of my head. My model for the heroic crown of my Emmett Till poem was Danish poet Inger Christensen's Sommerfugl Dalen / 'Butterfly Valley.'" I was pleased she included McKay. But a complete genealogy of influence from Dunbar to McKay to Brooks and Hayden to Baraka to Trethewey or Nelson has not been fully traced until now. After spending nearly ten years writing this book and reading the long-lost sonnets of the newspaper archives, I see the deep impress of the older poets on the newer.

From the beginning, African American poets have influenced each other. Although Phillis Wheatley acknowledges Ovid, Shakespeare, Milton, and Pope as her literary forefathers, she also points to Terence, the black poet, and Jupiter Hammond points to her.[1] While Wheatley's studied engagement with the meters, forms, and tropes of neoclassical British poetry and her liberal use of classical, mythological, and biblical allusions established the African American poetic canon within a European poetic tradition, she also saw herself as within the tradition of black poets.

Forms of Contention: Influence and the African American Sonnet Tradition tells the story of African American sonnet influence: who wrote sonnets and when, who published sonnets, who praised and who opposed the form, who wrote about them critically, how sonnets were included in anthologies, how sonnets have been in and out of fashion, and how sonnet writers contended with each other. The story of the sonnet's appeal to African American poets from the nineteenth century through the tumultuous twentieth and into the twenty-first, even as sonnet writing remained a vexed pursuit for black poets, for black poetry anthologizers, for Black Arts advocates, and for black studies academics, is rich and surprising. Scholarship on black sonnets is only beginning to catch up with the continued output of black sonnets over the past century and a half, particularly in the post–Black Arts years. "Criticism has always lagged behind creation," William Stanley Braithwaite observes. "When it does catch up it begins to pound with the guns of orthodoxy; it brings precedent and tradition as tests, and not finding the progressive era of new art adhering to the fundamentals of a past period, it fails to understand the impulse and aims of the new conceptions and embodiments."[2]

Historically, academic study of African American literature has focused on four concerns: the historical and economic conditions of production and publication of black literature; the political and cultural importance of black literature in America; genres of and trends in black literature; and the nature of the literature as reflective of the black experience. A literary history of African American sonnets engages with these concerns but also opens up a fifth conversation: auxiliary genealogies of influence for Black Aesthetic production that foreground form and promote new conversations about form generally: how exactly it enables participation and protest, the overthrow and undermining of aesthetic expectation.

The list of sonnets by African American poets reaches back to Wheatley, begins to grow in the last decade of the nineteenth century, flourishes in the twentieth century, and resurges again in the twenty-first. With the exception of Dunbar, the first wave of sonnets by black poets in the late nineteenth century tended to be respectful and conventional in form, devoted to respectable and conventional themes. But under Dunbar's influence, scores and perhaps hundreds of political sonnets on race and race violence were published by black poets in the 1910s and 1920s. From the 1930s to the 1950s, black poets responded to modernist and racial pressures by breaking down and breaking out of form, *signifying* on each other's sonnets. Some experimented with sonnets and some rejected sonnets. At no point in the history of African American poetry have poets not read each other's formal sonnets, sonnet epics, and sonnet cycles on African American stories.

In 1967 Amiri Baraka addressed the Fisk University Second Black Writers' Conference and called for a new Black Aesthetic that eschewed traditional European literary forms. Perhaps not coincidentally, in the same year, Harold Bloom, the most influential scholar of influence, began writing *The Anxiety of Influence* (published in 1973) as a "response to the burgeoning Age of Resentment, the acclaimed Counter-Culture."[3] Bloom's theory of poetry is the story of poetic influence, "of intra-poetic relationships." Bloom claims that every poem "is a misinterpretation of a parent poem," though he never seems to have considered the question of a parent *form*.[4] Poets form each other, which means, in practical terms, that strong young poets must "wrestle" with their poetic forebears in order to "clear imaginative space" for fresh new poetry.

Both Baraka and Bloom characterize in their own ways a sort of master-disciple relationship of poetic apprenticeship. Both acknowledge that the master's hand leaves a mark. Were the spokesmen of the Black Aesthetic to acknowledge Bloom, they might well agree with his account of influence; they might recognize in Bloom's argument an acknowledgment that any new aesthetic necessitates not a distortion or revision or perversion or challenging of poetic inheritance but a wholesale rejection of the legacy. Baraka's call for new black forms acknowledges that it is difficult for poets not to write in the shadow of tradition. Poetry is inalienable from poetic tradition; poetry is a technique of engagement with cultural inheritance. All poets are in some way contending with tradition.

In 1922, launching the anthologizing movement in African American poetry, James Weldon Johnson called for specifically African American forms:

> What the colored poet in the United States needs to do is something like what Synge did for the Irish; he needs to find a form that will express the racial spirit by symbols from within rather than by symbols from without, such as the mere mutilation of English spelling and pronunciation. He needs a form that is freer and larger than dialect, but which will still hold the racial flavor; a form expressing the imagery, the idioms, the peculiar turns of thought, and the distinctive humor and pathos, too, of the Negro, but which will also be capable of voicing the deepest and highest emotions and aspirations, and allow of the widest range of subjects and the widest scope of treatment.[5]

Bloom might claim that African American sonnet writers, in revising and distorting the form, in making it their own, have misunderstood the poems and poets that have come before. But a refusal is not a misunderstanding. If tradition, as Henry Louis Gates, Jr., defines it, is a "repetition and revision of shared themes, topoi, and tropes, a process that binds the signal texts of the black tradition into a canon just as surely as separate links bind together into a chain,"[6] there is both a tradition of African American sonnets and a genealogy of African American sonnet influence.

Ralph Ellison argues that "while one can do nothing about choosing one's relatives, one can, as an artist, choose one's 'ancestors.'"[7] African American sonnet writers have clearly seen in the sonnet tradition a literary past that speaks to the black experience, a past involving shackles, desire, protest, memorial, the possibility of play and subversion, and a long genealogy of practitioners. Larry Neal, in his 1970 essay "Ellison's Zoot Suit," argues that it is possible to extend one's vocabulary and memory in a variety of manners as regards one's literary ancestors; the music of Coltrane and Sun Ra, for example, indicates a synthesis and rejection of Western musical theory, "just as aspects of Louis Armstrong's trumpet playing indicated, in its time, a respect for the traditional uses of the instrument, on the one hand, and, on the other, to the squares, it indicated a 'gross defilement' of the instrument."[8] We have to understand our role as synthesizers, Neal suggests, creating new visions out from under the weight of Western experience. Literary history requires engagement with the problems of public perception. Few scholars ask why white poets write in the sonnet form; the answer comes best from sonnet writers themselves: the sonnet is the valued coin; the sonnet is permanence; the dead leaves of the past are ever present to be overwritten, signified upon, contended with. Dunbar showed us how.

In her foreword to Langston Hughes's *New Negro Poets, USA* (1964), Gwendolyn Brooks laments that

> poets who happen also to be Negroes are twice-tried. They have to write poetry, and they have to remember that they are Negroes. Often they wish that they could solve the Negro question once and for all, and go on from such success to the composition of textured sonnets or buoyant villanelles about the transience of a raindrop, or the gold-stuff of the sun. They are likely to find significance in those subjects not instantly obvious to their fairer fellows. The raindrop may seem to them to represent racial tears—and those might seem, indeed, other than transient. The golden sun might remind them that they are burning.[9]

For Brooks, sonnet writing is in competition with "solv[ing] the Negro question" even though "poets who happen also to be Negroes" are likely to write sonnets of significance. And indeed, significant sonnets have been written, as Trethewey acknowledges. Although they were long lost, with the recovery of so many black newspapers in the era of digital humanities, they are found again. This is the story of their influence.

CHAPTER 1

Tracing Tradition
and Influence

If you were to read through the entire corpus of African American poetry—all two and a half centuries of it, from the widely anthologized to the long forgotten—you would find thousands of sonnets, suggesting that something about the sonnet form resonates with black poets. Since emerging in twelfth-century Italy, the sonnet has been used to voice suffering, spiritual transcendence, the pain of bondage, memorial, outrage, and political dissent. While only a handful of sonnets by African American poets were published before Emancipation, black poets turned in earnest to sonnet writing at the end of the nineteenth century amid growing violence and a sharp increase in lynching. The sonnet form was soon taken up by Paul Laurence Dunbar and Claude McKay as a platform for protest poetry as well as for every other topic and purpose, from urban life to King Tut. With its venerated status, its genteel appeal for editors and publishers, and its comfortable fit at the bottom of a newspaper column, the sonnet form was the single most popular form for African American poets in the first half of the twentieth century.

Patterns began to emerge. Scathing antilynching sonnets began to appear in print in the early decades of the twentieth century, notably after the Red Summer of 1919. New Negro sonnets appeared in the 1920s. Protest sonnets appeared again with the resurgence of lynching in the 1930s and again after soldiers returned from World War II, notably in the work of Gwendolyn Brooks. Black sonnet writers read each other's work, borrowing and challenging tropes of dignity, urbanity, and a necessarily "upward" climb. Even during the Black Arts movement of the 1960s as the sonnet faded as a fashionable poetic form, African American sonnet

writers continued to write and publish sonnets on love, poverty, returning soldiers, and the sonnet itself as a curiously productive form. By the
twenty-first century the sonnet has clearly become a black poetic form:
black poets have come to dominate the form, writing the contentious history of African Americans into the form, as recent work by Elizabeth Alexander, Terrance Hayes, Natasha Trethewey, Tracy K. Smith, and scores
of other black sonnet writers demonstrates.

Yet African American sonnet writers too rarely acknowledge the long
history of black sonnets or the ways that a century's worth of sonnets
have influenced the new sonnet explosion. Trethewey emphasizes the
sonnet form as a received "European" form rather than acknowledging
the influence of Brooks's sonnets. The sonnet is rarely seen as either particularly appropriate or influential within the field of African American
poetics. Why? Why did black poets from Dunbar onward begin using the
form? How did African American sonnet writers come to transform the
form? What is it about the sonnet that made the form so persistent and
influential for African American poetics? The answers are formal and political.

Long before W. E. B. Du Bois, the fourteen-line sonnet, with its questioning octave and responding sestet, could be seen as a formalized double consciousness. Sonnets require two voices, two perspectives, two warring ideas.[1] Sonnets simultaneously accommodate and enable the "double
trouble" of the black writer who, as Hortense Spillers argues, must speak
both to a dominant culture and a natal community.[2] Drawing on the work
of Henry Louis Gates, Jr., on the rhetorics of internal division, the sonnet
might be considered the free indirect discourse of black poetry.[3] While
the standard lyric speaker in the European tradition is a unified poetic
voice (with, of course, many exceptions), the sonnet speaker offers a divided self, a voice in argument with itself, polyvocal possibilities. The African American sonnet speaker is often doubly divided, arguing internally, politically, and aesthetically.

The complex dispute that the sonnet form enables—challenging, as it
does so, racist notions of blackness as illiterate and ahistorical—embod-
ies and expresses the essential conflicts of the black experience in America. While the sonnet emerged from Renaissance traditions that privileged transcendent spirit over "enslaved" or bondaged flesh, the black
sonnet insists that fetters and blackness can be both metaphysical and all
too real. Abolitionist poets in eighteenth- and nineteenth-century Britain and America embraced John Milton's transformation of the sonnet

for political protest a century earlier. Sonnets protesting war, labor conditions, and race politics remained popular on both sides of the Atlantic into the twentieth century.

Yet recognizing the centrality of the sonnet to black poetry has been difficult largely because the form was denounced as inappropriate, imitative, and even "untrue" for African American expression.[4] In the 1920s the sonnet was denigrated by both modernists and black poets as too white, too "genteel," too European for modern use. In 1927 Langston Hughes wrote that "[c]ertainly the Shakespearian sonnet would be no mould in which to express the life of Beale Street or Lenox Avenue."[5] During the early Black Arts movement, Amiri Baraka (then LeRoi Jones) dismissed the idea of writing sonnets, and Larry Neal endeavored to destroy the poetics of double consciousness altogether.[6] "Some slaves excelled at 'Sonnets,' 'Odes,' and 'Couplets,'" Ishmael Reed observes acidly, "the feeble pluckings of musky Gentlemen and slaves of the metronome."[7] In 1970 Gwendolyn Brooks acknowledged the pressure to try new forms: "I have written many more sonnets than I'm sure I'll be writing in the future."[8] Ten years later, Brooks stated more decisively: "[N]o more sonnets....I'm not going to burn up any of those I've written, but I just feel that Blacks should be trying to develop some Black styles for themselves."[9] And in 1984 critic Gary Smith "naturally" wondered why black poets "were drawn to the European sonnet—a four-hundred-year-old, genteel literary form that traces its roots to the sixteenth century Italian sonnet—as opposed to folk forms more native to the black American experience, such as the antebellum sermon, folk songs, blues, and spirituals."[10] The sonnet was seen as too calcified.

Accordingly, patterns of influence have been hard to see. When Brooks capitulates to criticism for using the "white" and "European" sonnet form, she does not defend her work as firmly in the tradition of Dunbar, Alice Dunbar-Nelson, Leslie Pinckney Hill, McKay, Cullen, Sterling Brown, and Margaret Walker, whom she read and admired. Trethewey has only begun to acknowledge Brooks and the broad and deep tradition of black sonnets that forms the basis of the recent sonnet flood. Criticism of the sonnet was understandable in a generation of scholars determined to foreground the distinct voices of black poets. "Structurally speaking," Stephen Henderson argues, "whenever Black poetry is most distinctly and effectively *Black*, it derives its form from two basic sources, Black speech and Black music."[11] Given efforts to articulate the resistance of black poets to European poetic influences, the black sonnet was more easily seen solely as evidence of white influence than as an engagement with older black sonnet writers.

Further, influence has been difficult to see because most sonnets by black poets were published only once and rarely anthologized. The growth of periodical studies and the new availability of black newspaper archives have revealed a very different picture than was previously known of sonnet flourishing from the early twentieth century through the 1960s. In making the case for the persistence and influence of African American sonnets, I look at a much broader pool of poetry than has been generally available: hundreds of sonnets by well-known and virtually unknown poets that were published in the black press from the nineteenth century onward. Sonnets that slowly dropped out of circulation over the decades—by Dunbar, James Corrothers, James Edward McCall, Hill, Carrie Clifford, Marcus B. Christian, and many others—can finally return to academic study. Demonstrating the influence of these sonnets may help overcome resistance to the sonnet form for African American poetics.

Perhaps the most influential voice opposed to black sonnets was June Jordan, whose landmark 1986 essay, "The Difficult Miracle of Black Poetry in America: Something Like a Sonnet for Phillis Wheatley," begins with the claim: "It was not natural." Jordan argues that a black slave woman should not have taken the European poetic canon as her model:

> It was written, all of it, by white men taking their pleasure, their walks, their pipes, their pens and their paper, rather seriously, while somebody else cleaned the house, washed the clothes, cooked the food, watched the children: probably not slaves, but possibly a servant, or, commonly, a wife. It was written, this white man's literature of England, while somebody else did the other things that have to be done.[12]

Jordan suggests that Wheatley was writing in the wrong country, in the wrong language, in the wrong idiom, in the wrong form; Wheatley would have been a better poet without the influence of white poetry, without the English poetic tradition, without iambic pentameter.

Jordan notes that nonetheless Wheatley managed to write "sometimes toward the personal truth," but consider the lines she quotes as evidence of "truth," from "Thoughts on the Works of Providence":

> Say what is sleep? and dreams how passing strange!
> When action ceases, and ideas range
> Licentious and unbounded o'er the plains.[13]

The phrase "passing strange" is spoken by Othello, who enthralls Desdemona with his tales: "She swore, in faith, 'twas strange, 'twas passing strange."[14] Wheatley seems to suggest a kinship with Shakespeare's imaginative Moor. But Jordan wishes Wheatley had written in her native tongue. "Consider what might meet her laborings, as poet, should she, instead, invent a vernacular precise to Senegal, precise to slavery, and, therefore, accurate to the secret wishings of her lost and secret heart?" For Jordan, affinities with the white Western tradition are a problem:

> And as long as we study white literature, as long as we assimilate the English language and its implicit English values…as long as we, Black poets in America, remain the children of slavery, as long as we do not come of age and attempt, then, to speak the truth of our difficult maturity in an alien place, then we will be beloved, and sheltered, and published.

Black poets write sonnets because they will be beloved, sheltered, and published, Jordan concludes, with some palpable sadness.

And then Jordan offers her own poem, "Something Like a Sonnet for Phillis Miracle Wheatley":

> Girl from the realm of birds florid and fleet
> flying full feather in far or near weather
> Who fell to a dollar lust coffled like meat
> Captured by avarice and hate spit together
> Trembling asthmatic alone on the slave block
> built by a savagery travelling by carriage
> viewed like a species of flaw in the livestock
> A child without safety of mother or marriage
> Chosen by whimsy but born to surprise
> They taught you to read but you learned how to write
> Begging the universe into your eyes:
> They dressed you in light but you dreamed with the night.
> From Africa singing of justice and grace,
> Your early verse sweetens the fame of our Race.

"Something Like a Sonnet" simultaneously embraces and contends with the Shakespearean sonnet form, resisting regular meter and offering trochees rather than iambs at the beginning of most of the ten-syllable lines. The poem tells the story of a young African girl "coffled like meat" who dreamed and wrote sweet verse. The meter seems to be dactylic tetrameter rather than pentameter; the girl is skipping along, "flying full feather," dressed in light, blithely resisting pedestrian iambic pentameter. Indeed, Jordan demonstrates why African American poets were drawn to the sonnet form: it allows and perhaps welcomes artistic subversion, the dramatization of resistance and escape.

Jordan draws on the sonnet form as an instrument of literary protest even as she *signifies* on the sonnet form, to use Gates's term for deliberate refiguration and transformation of literary convention. Black poets from Wheatley to the present have studied the canonical texts of the Western tradition; consequently, for Gates, "black texts resemble other, Western texts" to a certain extent and are "double voiced in the sense that their literary antecedents are both white and black."[15] Jordan signifies on the sonnet form as a matter of both tradition (in her refusal of the Petrarchan convention of idealizing her subject, to be addressed in chapter 2) and form (in her resistance to iambic pentameter), demonstrating what Gates calls "the black rhetorical difference."[16] Jordan performs here what black sonnet writers since Dunbar have done: she makes the sonnet her own, even while insisting that it is not a natural form for a poet of African descent.

Clearly some cultural forms, such as the English language, or drama, or the novel, are adopted by African American writers without pressing concern for origins. And consider T. S. Eliot's famous remark that "[i]mmature poets imitate; mature poets steal; bad poets deface what they take, and good poets make it into something better, or at least something different."[17] Why not say that Dunbar, McKay, Brooks, Hayden, Baraka, and Hayes stole the sonnet form and made it different and better? The sonnet in the hands of black poets has been so dynamic, flexible, and modern that it is as much a black form as jazz is. Setting aside questions of cultural appropriation allows patterns of African American sonnet influence to emerge.

One of the most celebrated African American poems, McKay's "If We Must Die," is a sonnet. Published in Max Eastman's socialist monthly the *Liberator* in July 1919, a summer that saw some two dozen violent race riots, eighty-three lynchings, and hundreds of meetings of the Ku Klux Klan, "If We Must Die" speaks to the outrage of black World War I veterans who fought for the United States in Europe and returned home to the stark reality of segregation and racism in America:

> If we must die, let it not be like hogs
> Hunted and penned in an inglorious spot,
> While round us bark the mad and hungry dogs,
> Making their mock at our accursed lot.

If we must die, O let us nobly die,
So that our precious blood may not be shed
In vain; then even the monsters we defy
Shall be constrained to honor us though dead!
O kinsmen! We must meet the common foe;
Though far outnumbered, let us show us brave,
And for their thousand blows deal one deathblow!
What though before us lies the open grave?
Like men we'll face the murderous, cowardly pack,
Pressed to the wall, dying, but fighting back!

"If We Must Die" calls for resistance to violence in an environment of violence. The power of McKay's sonnet—Shakespearean and yet with modern diction—is the tension between the measured lines and rhyme, the poetic phrases and the brutal words, the combination of enjambments and one exclamation point in the octave and the more deliberate and determined pace of the sestet. "If We Must Die" is a defiant call to action. The rage of the poem is made more potent by the tension of the sonnet form straining to contain it.

McKay's sonnet reaches beyond the particular crisis of race violence in 1919 America; it is a universal cry of defiance. The opening phrase evokes the famous Saint Crispin's Day speech of Shakespeare's *Henry V*, when the outnumbered English troops ready themselves for battle against the French:

If we are mark'd to die, we are enow
To do our country loss; and if to live,
The fewer men, the greater share of honour.
God's will! I pray thee, wish not one man more. (*Henry V* 4.3)[18]

Readers of Du Bois's journal, the *Crisis*, may have also heard echoes of his famous mocking September 1911 editorial, "Triumph," protesting a brutal lynching and calling on black Americans to prepare for a day of reckoning: "We have crawled and pleaded for justice and we have been cheerfully spit upon and murdered and burned. We will not endure it forever. If we are to die, in God's name, let us perish like men and not like bales of hay."[19] Others hear echoes of Rupert Brooks's sonnet "The Soldier" (1915), which opens, "If I should die, think only this of me."[20]

McKay's sonnet was immediately reprinted in nearly every black newspaper and church bulletin across the country; it was quoted at the end of sermons and has since been included in nearly every anthology of black poetry ever published. Yet "If We Must Die" has always fit uneasily in the African American poetic canon and anthologized despite its "incongruous" form, as James Weldon Johnson put it.[21] McKay's sonnet is never considered "representative" of influential black poetry the way, for example, Langston Hughes's free verse is. June Jordan doesn't mention McKay.

Within black poetic criticism, "If We Must Die" inaugurated the "although" tradition in writing about African American sonnets. Phrases such as "although they are sonnets," "while the sonnet form may seem surprising," and "while he happened to use this outmoded form" appear in nearly every review of McKay's poetry. For example, James Oppenheim, editor of *Seven Arts*, praises McKay's racial poetry, "though traditional sonnets in form."[22] Gary Smith argues that McKay's poem succeeded in galvanizing a poetic tradition "in spite of its traditional form."[23] The "although" seems designed to reassure the reader that the sonnet is exceptional and unexpected, even while McKay's sonnets became widely influential for generations of black poets.

From the beginning, McKay's critics found his use of the sonnet form for political protest odd. William Stanley Braithwaite disparaged McKay in 1924 as a "violent and angry propagandist, using his natural poetic gifts to clothe arrogant and defiant thoughts."[24] Benjamin Brawley claimed in 1927 that McKay's poetry "is successful because it not only has something vital to say but because it also shows due regard for the technique of versification. The favorite form is the sonnet, and within the narrow confines of this medium the poet manages to express the most intense emotion."[25] Eleanor Chace argued in 1940 that McKay was "[t]oo powerful to confine his voice to racial subjects" and that "[s]omewhat incongruously, he uses the sonnet form for his angriest outbursts," such as "The Lynching."[26] Decades later, Nathan Huggins criticized McKay in 1971 for not mastering "arbitrary restraints of form" well enough, for "strangling" his emotional experience: "McKay resorted to form which he could not manage and vagueness which obfuscated and blunted his statement."[27] None of these criticisms speak to McKay's influence on generations of African American sonnet writers.

One key obstacle for critics in seeing McKay's sonnet as influential for African American poetry is that "If We Must Die" does not proclaim its allegiance to any race or nation, though Gunnar Myrdal in *An American Dilemma* prints the poem in its entirety as evidence of race solidarity.[28] The poetic speaker states only that "we" kinsmen will be noble in the face of dogs, monsters, and murderous cowards. Its "racial spirit," if any, is a matter of elements external to the poem itself. Worse, to some, McKay refused the mantle of "Negro poet" explicitly: "'If We Must Die' is the poem that makes me a poet among colored Americans. Yet frankly I have never regarded myself as a Negro poet," McKay told an interviewer in 1955. "I have always felt that my gift of song was something bigger than the narrow, confining limits of any one people and its problems. Even though many of my themes were racial, I wrote my poems to make a universal appeal."[29] Indeed, James Emanuel remarks that it is hard to imagine "any Jew who remembers Belsen and Dachau and Auschwitz...could read the poem without profound identification with the desperate heart of its author."[30] Seeking a universal audience, McKay published many of his sonnets in the *Workers' Dreadnought* rather than the black press.[31]

Curiously, the person said to be most influenced by "If We Must Die" was Winston Churchill, who (it is claimed) read the sonnet aloud in Parliament during the Battle of Britain without remarking on the race of its author. Melvin Tolson, reviewing McKay's *Selected Poems* in 1954, leads with the tale of how Churchill "snatched" the poem "from the closet of the Harlem Renaissance, and paraded in it before the House of Commons, as if it were the talismanic uniform of His Majesty's field marshal."[32] Another claim has U.S. senator Henry Cabot Lodge reading the sonnet ceremonially into the *Congressional Record*. Other apocryphal accounts put the poem in the uniform pocket of a dead British soldier during World War I and on the wall of an Attica prison cell after the 1971 uprising. Lee Jenkins has shown decisively that there is no record of McKay's sonnet in the speeches of Churchill or Cabot Lodge, nor in the *Congressional Record*, but the poem was dangerous enough to be censored by the Justice Department and denounced "inflammatory and seditious."[33] Tolson wryly observes that McKay's most famous sonnet is simultaneously claimed and closeted by the black poetry tradition.

"If We Must Die" is rarely celebrated for its influence or considered a significant advance of a black sonnet tradition that began nearly two decades earlier, with Dunbar's startling "Robert Gould Shaw" (1900), which asked, in the context of Jim Crow race violence and lynching, whether Shaw's sacrifice to the Union cause was in vain. Without knowledge of the wealth of sonnets by African American poets in the first half of the twentieth century, a generation of critics was not able to see patterns of influence across the landscape of African American sonnets from Dunbar through Pickney Hill to McKay to Marcus Christian to Brooks to Robert Hayden's "Frederick Douglass," for example. Blyden Jackson seeks to place McKay on the borders of the African American poetry tradition as a "more roughly masculine" Shelley who employs this "stanzaic form...of English Heritage" in a manner that "ties him to the second-generation Romantics, immediate ancestors of the Victorians into whose world he was ushered as that world faded into its Edwardian afterglow."[34] Similarly, Dudley Randall labels the efforts of black poets to write formal verse as writing "as whites for a white audience": "In the Harlem Renaissance, Countee Cullen wrote under the influence of Keats and Housman, and Claude McKay wrote sonnets in the tradition of Wordsworth and Milton....Only Langston Hughes and Jean Toomer, one by his use of colloquial black speech and blues form, and the other by his employment of new images and symbolism, were abreast of the poetic practices of the day."[35]

The possibility that Dunbar could have influenced Cullen or McKay is not considered, nor does Randall note that Brown, Walker, Hayden, Tolson, and Brooks especially wrote dazzling sonnets that evoke the sonnets of McKay, Dunbar, Hill, Cullen, and others.[36] Eugene B. Redmond calls McKay "the first black poet to make sustained use of the sonnet as a political/racial weapon"; in his words, McKay should be credited "for turning this 'white' form into a vehicle of protest, love and race pride." All previous sonnet writers are erased as Redmond continues: "[I]n no other quarter, before or since McKay, does a black poet persist—infusing blues and tragic irony—with the sonnet."[37] This was simply not true then and it is certainly not true now. Sonnets were always written, the newer bearing a trace of the older.

Occasionally the African American sonnet has been recognized as important. In a 1976 *Black World* essay on black sonnet writers from the 1920s, the poet James Emanuel argued that black poets who know well "the stifling underside of racial experience, from indestructible roaches to lying textbooks to lying cops to lying employment interviewers to lying real-estate men," saw the sonnet as offering multiple ways for dealing with the "psychic brutalities" of being black in America:

(1) an evasion of, or indifference to, racial claims on the artist;
(2) poetic emotional discipline in the midst of relative environmental chaos;
(3) an insistence that worldwide cultural tradition remain a stabilizing guide for the artist; or

(4) a faith that the beauty and dignity of the sonnet form can express any controlled human emotion, or a programmatic axiom for a people.[38]

The sonnet form was a tactic or a means to a particular end, Emanuel argued; it balances or mediates poetic content. *Use* it. And Emanuel did: his own sonnet, "Freedom Rider: Washout" (1968), anthologized by Henderson (but not identified as a sonnet), is discussed in chapter 2. But Emanuel's pro-sonnet intervention into black poetry debates—though he too was drawing solely on the available anthologies—was an exception. Over the next several decades the sonnet would continue to be critiqued for being too white, too genteel, too dignified, and too dignifying.[39] In 2002 Arnold Rampersad describes Langston Hughes's attempt to write sonnets as "peculiarly regressive."[40]

Recent scholarly debate about the narrative and nature of African American literature, notably Kenneth Warren's questioning of the foundations of what we know as "African American literature"—whether it would have been "a literature" as such without Jim Crow—and Gene Jarrett's exploration of how African American literature "represents" the race, revolves around questions of coherence.[41] Some semblance of coherence—and exclusion—is a precondition for disciplinarity, for theorizing the totality of African American literature, as well as for assessing whether the totality "represents the race" in any particular way. McKay's "If We Must Die" has never been said to represent African American poetry, though it certainly could, particularly as a "first," given its role in desegregating the American sonnet tradition as the first and often only black sonnet to appear in anthologies of important American sonnets.

After the disappearance of Jim Crow, Warren asks, "Would the true contours of black difference finally shine forth?"[42] Henderson wonders about "difference" in the context of the sonnet specifically, asking what distinguishes "a Claude McKay sonnet from a sonnet by Longfellow? Is the difference a quality that is common to all, or only to a representative number of Black sonneteers?"[43] The notable difference is influence. Demonstrating the influence of Dunbar, McKay, Brooks, and many other African American sonnet writers on later generations is the goal of this book. I argue that African American sonnet practices have developed into a distinct and discernible tradition: sure-footed, politically astute, dynamic, steeped in black history and community, steeped in sonnet history, well versed in sonnet orthodoxy and play, self-consciously double-

voiced. Understanding the African American sonnet influence compli-
cates our understanding of the African American literary tradition.

Recent work by Timo Müller, Evie Schockley, Jon Woodson, and Keith
D. Leonard begins to tell important stories about the place of the sonnet
form in African American poetry, about canon formation generally, and
about questions of form and culture over time. Over the years scholars
have taken note of patterns in African American sonnet writing, notably Emanuel, Marcellus Blount, Antonella Francini, and Therese Steffen.
But these scholars, though well versed in European sonnet traditions, focus on individual poets or poems, not on the creation of an African American tradition, or, as with Michael Bibby, they simply note clusters of
sonnets.[44] And often these scholars too participate in the "although" tradition. When Blount writes, "Contrary to what one might expect, historically the sonnet has been a form of revision and rebellion," he assumes
a point of view about the sonnet on the part of his reader. The "although"
gesture perpetuates the idea of the sonnet's inappropriateness and creates space for scholarly intervention to address why a black poet might
use the form "[e]ven though the sonnet's origins as a literary form are
located within the discourse of elite white men of the thirteenth century."[45] Blount overlooks all black sonnets and all black sonnet writers
up to the moment under scrutiny. The position frees scholars from the labor of apprehending a tradition of extraordinarily good African American sonnets for more than a century.

I approach black sonnets as if their authors knew exactly what they
were doing in crafting their sonnets—including, of course, occasionally
playing on expectations that the sonnet form was inappropriate.[46] Some
of the most notable African American sonnets—by Brooks especially—
are invested in maintaining ambivalence about the sonnet form. Focusing on sonnets allows me to sidestep long-standing questions of essentialism or what is "natural" in African American aesthetics. If sonnets
are nobody's property, they are also not in anybody's blood or ancestry.
Poetic form is by definition not natural. "Writing poetry is an unnatural
act," as Elizabeth Bishop put it.[47] I am also sidestepping the biographies,
personal politics, and what Redmond calls the "intense feelings and positions" of scholars and critics of black poetry, to the extent I can, to focus
on the sonnets themselves.[48] There have been enough excellent studies
of the key personalities involved in the creation of the African American
poetic canon and Redmond is a good place to start. I grapple with the his-

torical criticism of the sonnet's appropriateness for black poetry because this criticism provokes important questions about the sonnet as a form through which black poets contend with the broader poetic tradition. The sonnet might be seen as particularly effective against white bourgeois culture that might see the sonnet as "its own." Black sonnet writers certainly use the sonnet form for grating and antagonistic purposes.

What do we see when we look at African American sonnets over time, written in particular moments, always against trends, drawing on each other? Do African American sonnets partake of the rituals of black signification that Gates, Zora Neale Hurston, Hughes, Larry Neal, and others have identified in the past century,[49] or do they stand apart, a hybrid or bastard tradition? Anthony Appiah suggests that it is possible to see sonnets, constrained by conventions of rhyme and meter, as simply "systems."[50] I argue that the sonnet's systemetized double-voicedness lends itself to political protest and ability to articulate a dialectic of physical and metaphysical. Dunbar first realized this, as has every African American sonnet writer since.

Certainly it is indisputable that by the twenty-first century, black poets dominate the form by taking advantage of its capacity for multivoicedness and drawing on the black sonnet tradition that has been ever growing and expanding. If the sonnet was ever considered white property, it is not anymore. Consider Marilyn Nelson's sonnet, "Like His Gouged Eye" (2005), for instance, which bears witness not only to Emmett Till but also to the compensations of sonnet writing about the African American experience:

> Like his gouged eye, which watched boots kick his face,
> we must bear witness to atrocity.
> But we are whole: We can speak what we see.
> People may disappear, leaving no trace,
> unless we stand before the populace,
> orators denouncing the slavery
> to fear. For the lynchers feared the lynchee,
> what he might do, being of another race,
> a great unknown. They feared because they saw
> their own inner shadows, their vicious dreams,
> the farthest horizons of their own thought,
> their jungles immune to the rule of law.
> We can speak now, or bear unforgettable shame.
> Rosemary for remembrance, Shakespeare wrote.[51]

Nelson's Italian (or Petrarchan) sonnet is part of a larger project called "A Wreath for Emmett Till," composed of a series or "crown" of sonnets in which the last line of one sonnet becomes the first of the next. The fifteenth one is made up of the first lines of the fourteen previous. "Like His Gouged Eye" is the fourteenth in the sequence.

Setting aside all metaphors of property or the influences of particular sonnets, how should we think about what the sonnet form brings to this poem? What is the relationship of the sonnet form to the poem? Perhaps the form is its DNA: both its blueprint and its inheritance. Nelson builds her poem on the Italian scaffolding, with its tradition of praise from afar and its resistance to resolution, and alludes to Shakespeare's many memorializing sonnets about words that remain after persons are gone. Nelson's poetic speaker is plural: "[W]e must bear witness"; "People may disappear, leaving no trace, / unless we stand before the populace." The sonnet's strict laws contrast with the "jungles immune to the rule of law" inside the lynchers' heads. The rules bring protection. Nelson has said the constraints of the form, the need for meticulous focus on her craft, kept her at a safe distance from the brutal and heartbreaking subject matter. "A Wreath for Emmett Till" sits in the long tradition of sonnets about lynching that begins with Robert Southey during the slave trade (chapter 3) and continues through abolition and Jim Crow, with heartbreaking sonnets by Hill, McKay, and Yusef Komunyakaa. The sonnet structure is essential, as are all the sonnets on lynching that came before.

Consider too John Murillo's third sonnet from "Renegades of Funk" (2010):

> The ghosts. The angels. Holocausts. The need
> To shake these shackles, filled songs in our bones.
> As if, at twelve, we knew all this, we named
> Our best moves free: to break and pop-lock, blood
> And bruises marking rites. We'd gather, dance
> Ourselves electric, stomp and conjure storm,
> Old lightning in our limbs. We thunderstruck
> maroons, machete wielding silhouettes,
> Reject the fetters, come together still
> Some call it Capoeira, call it street-
> Dance. We say culture. Say survival.
> Bahia's berimbau or Boombox in
> The "Boogie Down": a killing art as play,
> An ancient killing art to break us free.

Even without hearing Murillo's speaking voice extending vowels in words like "need" and "bones," one can see and hear how the poem asks to be spoken as rap, recited emphatically. Stomping, dancing, limbs, and capoeira (an Afro-Brazilian dance tradition) announce the sonnet's intention to tease and subvert the form's traditional iambic pentameter. Murillo's poem signifies and contends with the sonnet form in its invocations of shackles and fetters and in playing at killing ancient art to break free, only occasionally gesturing toward rhyme. The sonnet form is not external to "Renegades of Funk" but rather is simultaneously its topic and its structural principle: the sonnet is the "killing art" with which Murillo's poem plays.

June Jordan is not wrong to claim that readers and critics invest form with an identifiable ethnicity, ideology, or mood, that sonnets are generally considered highbrow and dignified rather than rustic and unlettered. All poetic forms "carry affinities and expectations," David Caplan observes.[52] Because so many thousands of black sonnets were gone for so long, sonnet affinities remained a matter of whiteness and privilege. Sonnets were granted the class status Du Bois evokes with "I sit with Shakespeare and he winces not."[53]

Putting the question of black sonnet influence aside, it is instructive to ask where exactly, in fourteen lines of iambic pentameter, would privilege, class, and culture reside? Solely in cultural memory or also in form's material structure? Meter has come under the most scrutiny. Blyden Jackson advised black poets to avoid iambic pentameter in favor of "the percussive movement of the trochaic line" to evoke African drums, "for certainly the percussive movement of a trochaic line may fall upon the ear like the big and small booms of tom-toms in the African bush."[54] Anthony Easthope argues that iambic pentameter's "normative dominance" ratifies "the capitalist mode of production and the hegemony of the bourgeoisie as the ruling class" by regulating speech, particularly the vernacular speech of the lower classes.[55] Dialect, the speech of the rustic and uneducated, does not "fit" into iambic pentameter, although as we see in chapter 4, Dunbar sought to "balance" the two. Clarence Major argues that black voices give "a clarity, a freshness to English: a new turn: a vivid life. Our language is born of sound clusters, as opposed to Shakespeare's which derives from the nexus, *sight*."[56] In the early decades of the last century, modernist poets as unalike as Ezra Pound and Bertolt Brecht strove to dethrone iambic pentameter as old-fashioned, though both wrote sonnets.[57] The Trinidadian critic C. L. R. James argued that a great poet born in the 1930s could use traditional forms such as the sonnet "and write the most magnificent poetry without bothering himself about new forms of poetry and technical experiments and the other preoccupations of most modernist writers."[58] James apparently wrote a sonnet on cricket but it is sadly lost.[59]

Much of the sonnet's cultural prestige resides in its original evocation and privileging of the metaphysical realm. Roland Greene argues that the conventions of Petrarchan sonnets, involving the articulation and celebration of an ideal and unrequited love and an imagined relationship with the material world, were profoundly useful in registering "the complex outcomes of European imperialism," involving unequal desire and uneven distribution of power and voice.[60] The idea is that as the sonnet speaker claims his beloved in an abstract sense (but does not really possess her), imperial explorers claimed the New World as their own but sought not to be seen as rapacious. The sonnet is the voice of the master contending that he is not really the master, as African American sonnet masters observed. Francini particularly sees the African American sonnet as "the site of a refined poetical syncretism between Western tradition and ethnic heritage, a potentially revolutionary and highly innovative mechanism of resistance against cultural hegemony," still marking the sonnet itself as a conservative artifact.[61] For Keith Leonard, the sonnet form is a technique of the Anglo-American literary tradition to be mastered by black poets—arguing for an instrumentality in service of the classification. Leonard analyzes European forms through a postcolonial lens, seeing formalist black poetry, including the sonnet, as a kind of strategic hybrid poetics, the result of an intersection of cultural and ethnic discourses of difference. He seeks to "break down false boundaries of authenticity" but concludes that "rather than being entirely strangled, the African American self was constructed and subtly affirmed by traditional poetic artistry."[62]

Critical debates about "authenticity" in the representation of the African American poetic voice—particularly in dialect poetry but also in blues, jazz poetry, rap, and hip-hop—have shaped much of the opposition to African American formal poetry. The two big anthologizing movements in the 1920s and 1960s expressly promoted poetry written in black forms, such as the blues or slave songs, or poems evoking Africa, though generally including a small handful of sonnets (always McKay's "If We Must Die") in most collections. Leonard argues that critics have not dealt well with the complexities of traditional poetic form as practiced by African American poets, adding that formalist black poetry has been for too long characterized as a white envelope containing a black message—that forms such as the sonnet have been marginalized by race ideologues as "almost exclusively the cultural province of white people into which black writers can only insert black content."[63]

Burdens of authenticity for black artists emerged in the postbellum era. Paul Gilroy cites the Fisk Jubilee Singers after the 1870s to argue that "[b]lack people singing slave songs as mass entertainment set new public standards of authenticity for black cultural expression." Du Bois's *The Souls*, Gilroy points out, "is the place where slave music is signaled in its special position of privileged signifier of black authenticity." More importantly, for Gilroy, "[t]he double consciousness which *The Souls* argues is the founding experience of blacks in the West is itself expressed in the double value of these songs which are always both American and black." The doubleness is a problem for those thinkers whose position depends on "an image of the authentic folk as custodians of an essentially invariant, anti-historical notion of black particularity to which they alone somehow maintain privileged access."[64] Slave songs carry the history in the form; the past is present to confer the lineage of suffering on the singer.

Keith Leonard is right to reject the idea of "explicitly affirming black folk culture as the only true source of African American identity," targeting critics such as Harvey Curtis Webster and Houston Baker, who dismiss white poetic forms as simply "mastered 'masks' with which black people cover their true selves."[65] Critical opposition to the sonnet and assumptions about its presumed "gentility" have always diverged from poetic practice.

The weight and baggage of the sonnet tradition is the very point of Hayes's sublime "Sonnet" (2002):

> We sliced the watermelon into smiles.
> We sliced the watermelon into smiles.
> We sliced the watermelon into smiles.
> We sliced the watermelon into smiles.
>
> We sliced the watermelon into smiles.
> We sliced the watermelon into smiles.
> We sliced the watermelon into smiles.
> We sliced the watermelon into smiles.

We sliced the watermelon into smiles.
We sliced the watermelon into smiles.
We sliced the watermelon into smiles.
We sliced the watermelon into smiles.

We sliced the watermelon into smiles.
We sliced the watermelon into smiles.

Hayes both embraces and critiques the sonnet as a matter of form. As a matter of literary history, Hayes's "Sonnet" is at once both a response to Rod Padgett's sonnet "Nothing in That Drawer" (on the bureaucratic nature of the sonnet) and to the particularly literary critical burdens of the sonnet for African American poets. With its brazen non-iambic ten syllables, its first-person plural speaker, the chilling image of sliced smiles, and the image of watermelon front and center, "We sliced the watermelon into smiles" might work equally well as the first line or the last line of a sonnet. Repeated thirteen times the line becomes far more than the sum of its parts; it becomes part of—and contends with—a tradition.

For all poets, including African American poets, sonnet writing begins as a matter of participation in this tradition, defined broadly as the set of forms and conventions that govern the sonnet, valuing its practitioners, its variations, and its evolution. In the late nineteenth century the sonnet increasingly appealed not only to African American poets but also to immigrants and radicals outside of mainstream American culture. (Emma Lazarus's "The New Colossus" of 1883, inscribed on the Statue of Liberty in 1903, is a sonnet.) But the African American experience is not the European immigrant experience, with its assumption of absorption and assimilation; the double consciousness of the sonnet was to Dunbar, and those who came after, differently attractive. And while Du Bois's idea of beauty included a southern spiritual as well as the cathedral at Cologne and the Venus de Milo, he, like most cultural critics, did not see black poetic formality as influential. If the mastery of European poetic forms has been an essential element of African American poetics, the influence of one formal poet on another has not been seen as essential.

The formal turn in poetry and poetic criticism has encouraged a closer look at the sizable catalog of African American sonnets. Nelson embraces traditional form on principle. "I'm convinced our inclination to create race-, gender- and ethnic-specific literary enclaves is dangerous; that it disinvites us from community," she writes. "The Anglo-american tradition belongs to all of us, or should. As does the community into which the tradition invites us. That means the metrical tradition, too." Wheatley's poems, Nelson observes, "have outlived their frail, unhappy creator by some two hundred years. This, I think, is what it means to own the masters. The Wheatleys *owned* Phillis, but the Wheatley name lives now only because Phillis owned it."[66] Kimberly Benston agrees that the role of "tradition" in black literature "has been difficult to perceive behind the masks of iconoclasm and apocalypse."[67] If tradition is a matter of interrelationship, African American sonnets are surely an influential black poetic tradition.

How does a work matter to its time and place as well as to the transhistorical phenomenon of literary history? The broader stakes of *Forms of Contention* are, simply, answering this and other fundamental questions of our field: What is the nature of the relationship of a work of art—a work of literature—to its author; its immediate cultural, historical, and political context; and the work it influences? How does convention—including the conventions of anthologizing, of tremendous importance to poets in particular—bind, free, starve, provoke, or nourish an artist and a tradition? How do forms and conventions serve history, and how does history serve conventions and form? And fundamentally, does form have an inherent cultural bond, and can extensive use by a different culture utterly transform that bond? Is neutral form the springboard for cultural literary difference?

Focusing on the sonnet form allows us to see how black poets use, exploit, or defy form both to speak to the past and to accomplish specific poetic goals in the present. While I focus primarily on the African American sonnet tradition, the black sonnet tradition is global. Consider the African poet Sarudzai's sonnet "Pan Africa" published in the September 1969 issue of Hoyt Fuller's *Negro Digest* (subsequently *Black World*), at the height of the Black Arts movement and two months after the first Pan-African Cultural Festival in Algiers:

> This is the edifice, the lovely dream,
> the castle in the clouds that none can build
> for who can captivate some bright star's gleam
> or grow the lily that a man could gild?
> For mighty Africa stands still, apart,
> to watch men scratch the surface of her plain,
> well knowing that they cannot touch her heart.
> Long after they are dead, she will remain;
> and what cares she, if men are merry fools,

> that Nature taught to break what they had made
> who try to play the game outside the rules
> and trample those foundations that were laid?
> Dream turned to nightmare, Africa is strange,
> solid, phlegmatic, and opposed to change.[68]

The sonnet form is key to emphasizing the sonnet's argument about the physical and metaphysical place of Africa in world politics. The octave addresses man's dreams about Africa in the context of Africa's impassiveness; the sestet elaborates on Africa's physical indifference to man and to any culture's attempt to dominate it. The images (castle in the clouds, gilded lily) and diction (merry, phlegmatic) are not organically African; the sonnet writer uses them to evoke a Western poetic tradition for which Africa is foundational and to which Africa is indifferent. The fact that this isn't a very "good" sonnet as a matter of its lumbering English diction is part of the point. "Pan Africa" reminds us that all sonnets are in some way about the sonnet form—about the form's permanence and indifference to the use a poet puts it to—and this poet insists on kinship between the sonnet form, a surface level understanding of English, and Africa. The sonnet form is permanent: solid, phlegmatic, and opposed to change, but also flexible, composed, workmanlike, and enduring.

Why are African American sonnet influences important? Because the fact of black sonnet writers influencing each other raises new questions about the relationship of form, authorship, and tradition. Is poetic form an unchanging or transfiguring cultural artifact? Do all forms carry cultural significance, or is it only that particular forms—sonnet, Spenserian stanza, ballad, haiku—are more freighted by cultural associations than others? Does form carry more or less cultural significance than words or phrases? If the sonnet signifies a certain kind of interaction between the present and the past, whose past are we talking about? Is the influence of a black sonnet always compromised? Is that part of the point?

❀ ❀ ❀

A note about terminology and method. Throughout this book, I will be using the terms "African American" and "black" interchangeably, even when these terms are anachronistic, as they are before the 1960s, when terms including "Negro" and "Afro-American" were in wider use.

When quoting writers who use the term "Negro," I will not change the term. After first introducing a writer, I will simply refer to that writer by his or her last name, unless the full name needs to be repeated for clarity. If quoting a reviewer who refers to Brooks as "Miss Brooks" (a tradition that lasted longer into the twentieth century than I would have expected), however, I will maintain the honorific.

My use of the term "tradition" apprehends its Latin roots (*traditio*) to mean the delivery and transmission of a practice or custom over time. Accordingly, the African American sonnet tradition, as I define it, means not simply the long-standing and widespread practice of African American poets writing sonnets, but rather the way that black sonnet writers over time grappled with a tradition of sonnet writing that increasingly included each other's works. In reading criticism of the use of the sonnet form by a black poet, I am continually surprised by the claim that the poet must have been reaching back to Shakespeare, as if she couldn't also have been reaching back to an intermediary sonnet writer such as Brooks. My goal is to foreground the influence of black sonnets over time.

Finally, since this is a study of influence, I spend little time and space on the biographies of poets: their personalities, personal histories, and social relationships. My reasons are twofold. First, good histories of eras and movements and biographies of the key personalities central to the history development of black poetry are available and continue to be written, and I have little to add. Second, my focus is on the sonnets themselves, how they speak thematically and formally over centuries; my interest narrowly is on the texts primarily. So, for example, while I note that Alice Dunbar-Nelson was married briefly and unhappily to Paul Dunbar, that she favored formal poetry (including sonnets), that he wrote to her about his sonnet-writing habits, that both poets are foundational to the African American sonnet tradition, and that she may have influenced how he is anthologized, I do not focus on their marriage or propose that any of his sonnets may be to or about her.

When I note educational background, it is to indicate formalized exposure to canonical Anglophone literature. I do not focus on the sexuality or complicated relationships of any of the writers or scholars I treat here. I do not focus on the famous gatherings or factions that are part of Harlem Renaissance or Black Arts lore. It may be interesting that McKay briefly wrote for Marcus Garvey's *Negro World* in the late 1910s and then distanced himself from Garveyism, but the effect of these politics on the circulation of McKay's sonnets in poetry anthologies is insignificant. McKay himself articulated the distinction that I make when he writes of the difference between Du Bois and his writing:

> The book shook me like an earthquake. Dr. Du Bois stands on a pedestal illuminated in my mind. And the light that shines there comes from my first reading of *The Souls of Black Folk* and also from *The Crisis* editorial, "Returning Soldiers," which he published when he returned from Europe in the spring of 1919. Yet meeting Du Bois was something of a personal disappointment. He seemed possessed of a cold, acid hauteur of spirit, which is not lessened even when he vouchsafes a smile....I did not feel any magnetism in his personality. But I do in his writings, which is more important.[69]

Texts speak to writers across years and centuries. While undoubtedly people influence people, my concern here is textual (sonnet) influence and the overlooked existence of a broad river of sonnets by African American poets that spoke to other sonnet-writing poets.

The history of African American sonnets can be divided into four periods, three of which saw a change in gatekeepers to publication. The first was the era before the dramatic rise of black periodicals after the Civil War, before the postbellum demand for poetry existed. The second era, the periodical era from about the 1880s until 1922, saw a tremendous increase in opportunities for large numbers of African American writers to publish poetry in the black press. While there were several important antebellum black newspapers, notably Frederick Douglass's newspapers, and many new journals after 1922, during the periodical era newspaper editors were the key gatekeepers for emerging poets. The anthologizing era began in 1922 with Johnson's *Book of American Negro Poetry*, followed by a half dozen influential anthologies in the next ten years and a dozen more over the next several decades. The editors of these anthologies— the new gatekeepers—tended to be writers and scholars; poetry selected for inclusion tended to hew to specific ideas about the definition and contours of African American poetry. The university era began with the Second Fisk University Writers' Conference in 1967 and the subsequent establishment of black studies programs in universities across the United States. While poetry continued to be published in journals and anthologies, the new gatekeepers of inclusion tended to be scholars and academics who influenced what was taught in the classroom. Chapters 3–6 of *Forms of Contention* will be organized roughly around these eras.

Chapter 2, "Suffering, Love, Bondage, and Protest," focuses on sonnet poetics, beginning with a brief history of the sonnet since twelfth-century Italy—its formal elasticity, variations, popularity, and development in Europe and America—as points of engagement for African American sonnet writers. Chapter 2 emphasizes the sonnet's affiliation with the Platonic philosophical tradition that privileges soul over body; the use of bondage metaphors in the Renaissance courtly love tradition; the Shakespearean legacy of the sonnet as memorial; the seventeenth-century development of the protest sonnet tradition; nineteenth-century attention to the sonnet's imprisoning form; the sonnet's continued self-evaluation about its nature, laws, and conventionality in its American incarnation in the context of both modernism and black aesthetics; and the politics of anthologizing, curriculum, and literary history that have marginalized black contributions to American poetic (and sonnet) history. Interspersed are examples of sonnets by black poets that are demonstrably in conversation with the sonnet tradition. While McKay engages most notably in the Miltonic protest tradition as well as with political sonnets by World War I poets and labor activists, the chapter notes Dunbar's and Cullen's engagement with Keats and Shelley, Brooks's with Wordsworth, and other poets' with Elizabeth Barrett Browning and Edna St. Vincent Millay in the twentieth century.[70] Chapter 2 lays the foundation for readings that are historically contextualized in subsequent chapters, where sonnets by African American poets can be seen as influencing other African American sonnet writers.

Chapter 3, "Antecedents (1768–1889)," details the prehistory of an African American sonnet tradition beginning with a single fourteen-line poem by Phillis Wheatley, "To the King's Most Excellent Majesty," written in 1768. While sonnet writing by black poets did not begin in earnest until after the Civil War, this chapter engages with the privileged place of the sonnet within the growing abolitionist movement in America from the 1780s until Emancipation, which is crucial to understanding the importance of the sonnet in the African American literary tradition and the American sonnet tradition. Dozens of literary societies, debating clubs, lecture series, and recitation venues were established in northern cities to oppose slavery and to promote learning and literacy among African Americans. The work of abolitionist writers such as Thomas Clarkson and William Wilberforce as well as poetry by William Wordsworth and Robert Southey circulated widely among northern readers in antebellum

America, fostering a literary abolitionist community that nurtured the writing of sonnets.

After the war, thousands of African Americans enrolled in colleges and universities and received an education that included courses in British literature and poetry. Scores of black-owned newspapers published stories and poetry by new African American writers desirous of making a literary name for themselves. In the late nineteenth century the nation as a whole was experiencing growth and industrialization: cycles of booms and busts—but mostly booms—that brought southern blacks northward even before the Great Migration. Influential works by Bret Harte, Mark Twain, and Joel Chandler Harris appeared featuring regional and "Negro" dialects. African American writers such as Frances Harper and Charles Chesnutt also published novels featuring dialect. While Joan Sherman notes that nineteenth-century black poetry "had scarcely any audience and no critical theorists," the poems produced—including a small group of sonnets—provide the foundation for a century-long concern with the authentic black poetic voice.[71]

Chapter 4, "Periodical Sonnets from Dunbar to McKay, 1890 to 1922," focuses on Dunbar's sonnets as the wellspring of the African American sonnet tradition that began in the pages of periodicals, primarily but not limited to African American newspapers and literary journals. Hundreds and perhaps thousands of sonnets by black poets were written and published. The rise of periodical studies over the past decade has allowed the gathering of these sonnets together, to compare them, to note trends and innovations, to identify authors, and to try to make sense of what was clearly a valued form for black poets. Gathered together for the first time, Dunbar's sonnets can be shown to have had a lasting influence on subsequent sonnet writers, who not only modeled sonnets on Dunbar's but also responded to his early death with sonnet tributes. Other key sonnet writers who emerge from the newspaper archives include H. Cordelia Ray, James Corrothers, Charles Bertram Johnson, Leslie Pinckney Hill, and Lucian Watkins. Finally, McKay emerges as the most accomplished sonnet writer of the era, publishing almost all of his early sonnets in the pages of periodicals.

The notion of an African American literary tradition of poetry did not exist until Johnson's *Book of American Negro Poetry* in 1922, with its influential preface, taking stock of and giving shape to the black literary canon, cited by Kenneth Warren as key to creating the idea of a literature self-consciously engaged in race promotion. Accordingly, chapter

5, "Anthologies and the African American Sonnet, 1923–1967," examines the surprisingly robust place of the sonnet in the era's anthologies that followed Johnson's. The new sonnet writers of this era, notably Marcus Christian, Sterling Brown, Margaret Walker, Gwendolyn Brooks, Melvin Tolson, Robert Hayden, and others, used the sonnet form to engage with local concerns as well as with the sonnet tradition, in increasingly modern diction. Brooks and Hayden particularly began shaping the sonnet form to accommodate their subject matter.

Chapter 6, "Power Lines: The Black Aesthetic and the Black Sonnet," examines how advocates for the Black Aesthetic in the late 1960s sought to define—and circumscribe—African American art and literature as radically distinct from a white American aesthetic even as leading proponents of the movement themselves wrote sonnets. The Black Arts movement called for new and innovative forms, an embrace of vernacular expression, and use of both experimental and traditional African rhythms and metrical patterns. Yet Baraka wrote sonnets even as he pressured Brooks to stop. And with the study of black literature institutionalized and professionalized in the academy, new anthologies and teaching texts were needed that tended to institutionalize contemporary views of black poetry and marginalize formal poetry, particularly the sonnet.

CHAPTER 2

Suffering, Love, Bondage, and Protest

All sonnets are a matter of influence. Poets who take sonnet writing seriously embrace the long history and conventions of the sonnet form, eager to join the long tradition of debate, desire, protest, cage-breaking, and self-questioning. Paul Dunbar took not a single undergraduate course in literary history yet recognized that the sonnet form, as David Caplan describes, is "attuned to the problem that has obsessed poetry for the last four centuries: how self-consciousness operates, especially when it faces the sharpest and most painful dilemmas."[1] Every black sonnet writer understands that to write a sonnet is to situate oneself in Western literary history. If, as Claudia Tate argues, black literary works are expected to "contest racist perspectives" and "foreground the injustice of black protagonists' persistent and contested encounters" with white culture, then Dunbar—and all subsequent black sonnet masters—situated that contestation at the very heart of the literary work: its structure.[2] The sonnet is a form of contestation that has made sonnets increasingly central to African American literary history, a changemaker of Western literary history.

Some foundational knowledge of sonnet history is necessary for demonstrating how African American poets drew on and transformed the sonnet in the twentieth and twenty-first centuries, particularly for apprehending an inventiveness that is neither mimicking nor mocking. This chapter provides a brief history of the sonnet form—its meter, rhyme scheme, and structural concerns—as well as key tropes that later poets borrowed, subverted, signified on, or contended with. The sonnet conventions that spoke to African American poets include battering and bondage metaphors (e.g., terms such as "yoked" or "fettered"); preoccupation with prisons and freedom; unrequited love of "fair" maidens; doubleness and double-voicedness; memorialization; and political protest. Subsequent chapters will address the development of the African American sonnet tradition historically and demonstrate the influence of black sonnet writers on each other's work. This chapter will offer a history of the sonnet and demonstrate African American sonnet writers' familiarity with this history, engaging with it even during the ascendance of modernist poetry "unshackled" by meter and rhyme.

The sonnet, or "little song," is fourteen lines of iambic pentameter with an organized rhyme scheme.[3] The rhyme scheme of Italian (also referred to as Petrarchan) sonnets is generally two quatrains with an ABBA rhyme scheme (an octave) followed by six lines (a sestet) with a rhyme scheme of CDECDE or CDCDCD or some variation. Sonnets are structurally dynamic: a volta, or shift, in tone, perspective, emotion, or thought appears between the first eight lines and the final six.

The sonnet first appeared in thirteenth-century Italy in the work of the Sicilian poet Giacomo da Lentini. Early practitioners included the Tuscan poet Guittone d'Arezzo and the Florentine poet Guido Cavalcanti. Cavalcanti's close friend and fellow poet Dante Alighieri wrote love sonnets to his beloved Beatrice. Francis Petrarch wrote more than three hundred sonnets, many to or about his beloved Laura, which circulated widely and were published in his *Canzoniere* (1358).[4] Petrarch's friend, the poet and writer Giovanni Boccaccio, wrote scores of sonnets on love, as did Michelangelo, more than a century later. The popularity and influence of Petrarch's sonnets established the stanza as particularly suited for performed deliberations on love and desire in a worldview that saw fleshly enslavement as the condition of all men.[5]

Petrarch sought to express the soul rising "pure and unfettered" from the passions of the flesh. Thus the figure of the slave signifies all suffering men on earth. Consider Petrarch's Sonnet 76, "Amor con sue promesse lusingando" (often translated as "Love Chains are still dear to him"):

> By promise fair and artful flattery
> Me Love contrived in prison old to snare,
> And gave the keys to her my foe in care,
> Who in self-exile dooms me still to lie.
> Alas! his wiles I knew not until I
> Was in their power, so sharp yet sweet to bear,
> (Man scarce will credit it although I swear)

> That I regain my freedom with a sigh,
> And, as true suffering captives ever do,
> Carry of my sore chains the greater part,
> And on my brow and eyes so writ my heart
> That when she witnesseth my cheek's wan hue
> A sigh shall own: if right I read his face,
> Between him and his tomb but small the space.[6]

The rhyme scheme is easily perceived: ABBAABBA CDCDEE. The volta is clear at line 9. In the octave, love attracts the speaker with promises and then imprisons him, giving the key to his enemy and keeping him in exile from himself. Prison is sharp but sweet; freedom is not wholly welcome. The sestet suggests that while there are chain marks on his face, while he is pale and close to death, the speaker is not wholly unhappy about the time spent in love's prison. Taking pleasure in chains—not a perverse pleasure but *pleasure*—is central to the sonnet tradition. We will see this influence played out in different ways over the centuries.

Petrarch's sonnet performs an argument with itself. The volta makes clear the sides of the argument. There may be a "sense pause" between the two quatrains in the octave, as Michael R. J. Spiller notes, but the more pronounced turn occurs after the second quatrain.[7] Paul Fussell suggests that "[i]t is perhaps more accurate to say that the turn occurs somewhere in the white space that separates line 8 from line 9, and that line 9 simply reflects or records it." In other words, the sonnet seems to enact a transition in real time. Petrarch's poetic speaker turns from questioning to meditation, from asking to attempting to answer. Readers, Fussell continues, "are presented with a logical or emotional shift by which the speaker enables himself to take a new or altered or enlarged view of his subject."[8] This dynamic is an essential part of every sonnet's structure and is perhaps central to its appeal. Petrarch's sonnet offers a glimpse of a private, internal quarrel while also performing the dispute openly.

A sonnet's argument cannot go on forever: the sonnet is one of the few poetic forms that are limited in length, like the haiku. The *terza rima* may have a rigid stanza structure, but a poem employing the stanza has no limitations. Thus a sonnet, as Barbara Herrnstein Smith argues, is not only obliged to end its internal debate in a fixed manner and at a fixed point; it also "must convince the reader of its conclusiveness" even when the conclusion is irresolution.[9]

Petrarch, like Dante, admired what he was able to read of Plato in the works of Augustine and the few available Latin translations of Plato's work. Although Petrarch had only an indirect knowledge of key Platonic texts such as the *Symposium*, with its articulation of the ascent from love of corporeal beauty to ideal love, Petrarch's sonnets express an attitude about spiritual love that reflects his readings of ancient, patristic, and scholastic authors who were steeped in Platonic thought.[10] Petrarch writes in the *Secretum*: "For what else does the sublime doctrine of Plato argue but that the soul must protect itself from the passions of the flesh and eradicate its fantasies so it may rise pure and unfettered to the contemplation of the mysteries of the divine, combining meditation on one's own mortality with that contemplation?"[11] Petrarch's sonnets transpose and enact praise of ideal beauty in the lyric voice of Renaissance humanism. His poetic speakers argue with themselves about spiritual love, discoursing on its mysteries.[12] They also ask themselves: Am I suffering? Should I be? Why is it that I am? These questions are of obvious interest to African American poetry.

Dante's sonnets, like Petrarch's, are similarly concerned with the relationship of the suffering individual, his beloved, and God. Even when the turn of the dialogue is subtle, almost imperceptible, as it is in Dante Gabriel Rosetti's 1861 translation of Dante Alighiere's sonnet "Tanto gentile e tanto onesta pare" (1290) from the *Vita Nuovo*, the sense of conversation is always present:

> My lady looks so gentle and so pure
> When yielding salutation by the way,
> That the tongue trembles and has naught to say,
> And the eyes, which fain would see, may not endure.
> And still, amid the praise she hears secure
> She walks with humbleness for her array;
> Seeming a creature sent from Heaven to stay
> On earth, and show a miracle made sure.
> She is so pleasant in the eyes of men
> That through the sight the inmost heart doth gain
> A sweetness which needs proof to know it by:
> And from between her lips there seems to move
> A soothing essence that is full of love,
> Saying for ever to the spirit, "Sigh!"[13]

In the first quatrain, the speaker praises the looks and demeanor of his lady, so gentle and pure that men cannot look on her or speak to her. She is a creature from heaven. In the second, the speaker notes that she remains miraculously humble despite the praise of her. Then, in the last six lines, the speaker turns to consider what sweetness he gains from the sight and sound of her; her loving, soothing essence provokes a sigh. The subject of the octave is the lady's beauty; the response is the sweetness that emanates.

Seven centuries after Dante (and one century after Rossetti's translation), the Jamaican poet Edward Baugh toys with the Petrarchan sonnet tradition of privileging abstract over corporeal beauty in "There's a Brown Girl in the Ring" (1965):

> When I speak of this woman I do not mean
> To indicate the Muse or abstract queen
> But to record the brown fact of her being,
> The undiluted blackness of her hair
> And that I lightly kissed her knee
> And how her feet were shy before my stare.
> It may be that I praise her memory here
> Because she is indeed but allegory
> Of meanings greater than herself or me
> Of which I am instinctively aware;
> But may such meanings never be a care
> For that fine head, and may my glory be
> That blood and brain responded well to slim
> Shy feet and smoothest knees and most black hair.[14]

"There's a Brown Girl in the Ring" begins with a couplet leading the sestet and ends with an octave, literally turning the form on its head. For Baugh's sonnet speaker, the ideal beloved is—or was—brown and present rather than fair and out of reach. Baugh's sonnet reaches into the past rather than to the future to praise her black hair and "the brown fact of her being."[15] He kisses the knee of an allegory. Baugh's sonnet offers an example of a black sonnet both influenced by and contending with the sonnet tradition—he is *signifying* on it—and making it relevant to his own circumstances and culture. Taking the view that a sonnet has a kind of agency, the form offers Baugh the opportunity to contend with Petrarch and Dante, to argue for the inclusion of the shy feet and black hair of a beloved who may not have wanted to be the subject of a sonnet.

The sonnet has always adapted itself to new cultures, languages, and influences. The Italian sonnet arrived in England in the late fourteenth century after Geoffrey Chaucer translated Petrarch's Sonnet 132 into vernacular English in the twenty-one-line "Canticus Troili" in *Troilus and Criseyde* (ca. 1380s). Chaucer's translation maintains a more regular rhyme scheme but in three seven-line stanzas of ABABBCC:

If no love is, O God, what fele I so?
And if love is, what thing and which is he?
If love be good, from whennes cometh my woo?
If it be wikke, a wonder thynketh me,
When every torment and adversite
That cometh of hym may to me savory thinke,
For ay thurst I, the more that ich it drynke. (I. 400–407)

A century and a half later, Sir Thomas Wyatt and Henry Howard, the Earl of Surrey, together translated Petrarch's sonnet into English, but with a transformed rhyme scheme: four quatrains of alternating rhyme—ABAB, CDCD, EFEF—followed by a closing couplet, GG. Given the comparative scarcity of English language rhymes, the Wyatt-Howard structure allows four rhymes for the octave and three for the sestet. This new rhyme scheme became the general rule for English sonnets, although writers continued to experiment with rhyme varieties.[16] In the 1580s Philip Sidney's sonnet sequence *Astrophil and Stella* (privately printed in 1591, published in 1598) featured English and Petrarchan rhyme schemes as well as sonnets in hexameter. In 1595 Edmund Spenser published a sequence of ninety love sonnets, *Amoretti*, to his wife, featuring a slightly different rhyme scheme: ABAB BCBC CDCD EE.[17]

William Shakespeare published his collection of 154 love sonnets in 1609; their popularity forever attached his name to the English form (as Petrarch's is attached to the Italian). The distinctive characteristic of English sonnets is the final couplet, which offers a sense of finality. The English rhyme scheme offers the opportunity for two voltas: the first at the ninth line and the second after the twelfth line. Shakespeare's sonnets take advantage of the final couplet to make a resounding pronouncement. Consider Shakespeare's Sonnet 18, disputing the idea of transient beauty in poetry. The first two quatrains propose a comparison of a beloved to a lovely summer day; the final six lines suggest that unlike the summer day, the beloved's beauty—his fair and gold complexion—is eternal and will not fade because of the speaker's poetic power:

Shall I compare thee to a Summer's day?
Thou art more lovely and more temperate:
Rough winds do shake the darling buds of May,
And Summer's lease hath all too short a date:
Sometime too hot the eye of heaven shines,
And oft' is his gold complexion dimm'd;
And every fair from fair sometime declines,
By chance or nature's changing course untrimm'd:

> But thy eternal Summer shall not fade
> Nor lose possession of that fair thou owest;
> Nor shall Death brag thou wanderest in his shade,
> When in eternal lines to time thou growest:
> So long as men can breathe, or eyes can see,
> So long lives this, and this gives life to thee.

The first turn, at the ninth line, is signaled by a "But": the beloved's beauty, unlike the summer day, is eternal and will evade death. The second, at the thirteenth line ("So"), reinforces the third couplet by shifting focus to the sonnet as the giver of eternal life (the "this" in the last line). Thus the speaker will immortalize the beloved's beauty because literature is eternal. Like Dante's "My lady looks so gentle and so pure," Shakespeare's sonnet begins with praise of a beloved's appearance, but in contrast with Dante's sonnet, which ends with contemplation of how his lady's beauty has power to spread spiritual bliss, Shakespeare's appropriates the power of life-giving to himself. For Shakespeare, the sonneteer has authorial power to give eternal life; the point of the final couplet generally is to restate this power.

Shakespeare also established a tradition of departure from established sonnet structure. Among his sonnets, Sonnet 99 has fifteen lines; Sonnet 145 is written in iambic tetrameter rather than pentameter; Sonnet 126 is composed of six couplets (only twelve lines) and yet Shakespeare calls it a sonnet. The sonnet tradition has always adapted itself, including occasionally shifting focus from the ideal to worldly or everyday subjects. Michael Drayton (1563–1631), for example, in his sonnet "Since there's no help, come let us kiss and part," uses the English rhyme scheme to make fun of "the patient resignation of the Petrarchan erotic sonnet," as Paula Feldman argues.[18]

Just as Baugh signifies on the Italian sonnet form to center the beauty of the dark female form, Claude McKay combines elements of both Petrarchan and Shakespearean sonnets to address the black female subject "upon a picnic day" in "The Harlem Dancer" (1917). More than any black poet before him, McKay uses the sonnet form as a technique for saying something new and particular to the black experience in America. Here, McKay gives the ideal or "perfect" woman at the center of his sonnet a public audience:

> Applauding youths laughed with young prostitutes
> And watched her perfect, half-clothed body sway;

Her voice was like the sound of blended flutes
Blown by black players upon a picnic day.
She sang and danced on gracefully and calm,
The light gauze hanging loose about her form;
To me she seemed a proudly-swaying palm
Grown lovelier for passing through a storm.
Upon her swarthy neck black shiny curls
Luxuriant fell; and tossing coins in praise,
The wine-flushed, bold-eyed boys, and even the girls,
Devoured her shape with eager, passionate gaze;
But looking at her falsely-smiling face,
I knew her self was not in that strange place.[19]

In the first three quatrains, the dancer is material and present, not abstract and ideal; with the terms "flutes," "players," "lovelier," and "false," McKay evokes Shakespeare even as the final couplet gestures toward the Petrarchan metaphysical ideal rather than the authorial hand: he observes from the face of the lovely dancer that her "self" is not really present. She cannot be idealized. Like "There's a Brown Girl in the Ring," "Harlem Dancer" signifies on the tradition to speak to the concerns of lovers and loving in the material world.

Eugenia Collier offers a Marxist reading of "Harlem Dancer," seeing the sonnet form's constraints as appropriately replicating the subject's limited opportunities: "Iambic pentameter is a slow, dignified meter, contemplative and often sad; and the theme of the poem is not lascivious dancing, but human dignity, not midnight gaiety but unobtrusive tragedy. The rhyme scheme of the sonnet is demanding and restrictive; so also are the social and economic forces that have shaped the life of the Harlem dancer. There is, then, no conflict between form and theme."[20] While Collier's reading of constraint seems right, she overlooks the very productive conflict between form and theme, or rather McKay's use of the form to showcase the sublime gulf between the form's history and the contemporary subject. Harlem is worlds away from Renaissance Italy, yet the sonnet form stretches to bridge the chasm. McKay's "but" in the final couplet offers up to the reader the central social and political conflict of the sonnet.

McKay appreciated the history and derivations of the courtly love tradition of unrequited love far better than his critics did, one of whom was too quick to see "the bugaboo of sex" in his sonnets. "Why should a Negro's love poetry be offensive to the white man, who prides himself on being modern and civilized?" McKay retorted.[21] Unrequited love means nobody is actually having sex. With its courtly love origins, the sonnet *should* be the safest form for a black poet, McKay's remark suggests, aware, however, that a black man writing a sonnet at all could be construed as an act of critique. And in fact McKay also wrote erotic sonnets, as we see in his not-often-anthologized "Honeymoon" (1934):

> Sweet, be your body a rare figured rug
> Upon which I may lay myself full length,
> And drink your warm breath as a potent drug,
> To make me amorous and increase my strength.
> Let me be drunken with your passion's wine,
> Our days are foodless, yet I know no pains;
> Your subtle presence is an anodyne
> That deadens native hungers in my veins.
> My heart beats in wanton mood to move
> With the strange rhythm of your spirit's motion.
> My soul's a laden boat propelled by love,
> And these uplifted days a heaving ocean
> Whereon we drift foam-sprinkled, shot with zest,
> Desiring not to reach a port of rest.

In a Shakespearean rhyme scheme, McKay's sonnet is simultaneously erotic and strangely humorous, with its well-worn terms ("passion's wine") and none-too-subtle images of climactic lovemaking. The diction in the sestet is particularly clumsy and unconvincing, as if he were in a rush to finish. The sonnet is unracialized.

Even without a British education like McKay's, most American poets would have been aware of courtly love traditions. Most survey courses of English literature taught in American colleges in the nineteenth and twentieth centuries would have at least touched on Renaissance poetry traditions, which had become newly fashionable. The male lover is always abject, obedient, silent in the face of injustice.

Paul Dunbar's fourteen-line "Passion and Love" (1896), in blank verse rather than a standard sonnet rhyme, reconsiders the courtly love tradition to consider women's agency:

> A maiden wept and, as a comforter,
> Came one who cried, "I love thee," and he seized
> Her in his arms and kissed her with hot breath,
> That dried the tears upon her flaming cheeks.

> While evermore his boldly blazing eye
> Burned into hers; but she uncomforted
> Shrank from his arms and only wept the more.
> Then one came and gazed mutely in her face
> With wide and wistful eyes; but still aloof
> He held himself; as with a reverent fear,
> As one who knows some sacred presence nigh.
> And as she wept he mingled tear with tear,
> That cheered her soul like dew a dusty flower,—
> Until she smiled, approached, and touched his hand![22]

The first seven lines (a complete sentence) tell of a suitor who ungallantly seizes a weeping maiden and kisses her. The second seven tell of a more chivalrous suitor who is physically aloof but sympathetic, whom she approaches. The maiden makes the first move. The turn in the poem is a matter of change in circumstance (the arrival of a new suitor) rather than a transformation of perspective or moment of rethinking, contending with the tradition of Platonic love in the age of independent womanhood.

Making the case for Dunbar's influence on the African American sonnet tradition is difficult because Dunbar is so closely associated with the minstrel tradition in African American poetry. Even more difficult is making the case that Dunbar's dialect poetry also engages with the courtly love tradition, but it does. "I am going to try my hand at a bit of a sonnet this afternoon," Dunbar wrote to his fiancée, Alice Moore, in 1898. "I wrote a darkey dialect love-poem yesterday called 'Dely,' so I want to balance the effect."[23] The first stanza of "Dely" shows the influence of Shakespearean summer sonnet conventions:

> Jes' lak toddy wahms you thoo'
> Sets yo' haid a reelin',
> Meks you ovah good and new,
> Dat's de way I's feelin'.
> Seems to me hit's summah time,
> Dough hit's wintah reely,
> I's a feelin' jes' dat prime—
> An' huh name is Dely.[24]

Dunbar's facility with dialect orthography is quickly apparent to readers who attempt to speak the verse aloud. Certain words are clipped ("Jes'," "yo'") while others are spelled correctly ("good," "you"); only on close scrutiny do you see that the orthography is a performance. Eugene Redmond argues that black poets are "almost always apt to select a word for its typographical, phonological and political dimensions," while European and American poets choose words "for allusory and intellectual reasons."[25] I would argue that allusion is not yet examined enough in black poetry, either in dialect poetry or African American sonnets.

Gwendolyn Brooks contends with Shakespeare's summer sonnet tradition directly by giving us the women's voice and perspective in "XIII / intermission: I / deep summer" from *Annie Allen* (1949):

> By all things planetary, sweet, I swear
> Those hands may not possess these hands again
> Until I get me gloves of ice to wear.
> Because you are the headiest of men!
> Your speech is whiskey, and your grin is gin.
> I am well drunken. Is there water near?
> I've need of wintry air to crisp me in.
> —But come here—let me put this in your ear:
> I would not want them now! You gave me this
> Wildness to gulp. Now water is too pale.
> And now I know deep summer is a bliss
> I have no wish for weathering the gale.
> So when I beg for gloves of ice to wear,
> Laugh at me. I am lying, sweet, I swear!

Evoking all the standard heavenly bodies that circulate in sonnet history—the sun, the moon, Venus—the speaker uses a Shakespearean rhyme scheme and diction that could be heard as Shakespearean or black vernacular ("until I get me") to speak to a male lover who is more Dionysian than Apollonian. Comparing him to a blissful summer's day, Brooks's speaker situates herself in the role of the suffering lover abjecting herself to her beloved. She wants wildness now.

In approaching poetry by black poets, the standard position taken by readers, critics, and scholars has been to ask: how does this poem speak to the African American experience? Does this poem speak to the circumstances or culture of black America? Accordingly, there are few canonical poems by African American poets that are categorized as love poems without clear racial markers. And yet the sonnet form allows traditions such as courtly love to be made relevant to the present, as Dunbar, McKay, Brooks, and Baugh do. Apprehending the relevance, however, requires understanding sonnet traditions. A key problem in most scholarship of African American poetry is the unfamiliarity of sonnet tropes at play.

Clearly the sonnet's power emerges from the entirety of its formal attributes and history. Black sonnets engage with the sonnet's historical metaphysical concerns, its metaphors, its meter, its formal double-voicedness, and its nature as simultaneously fixed and flexible. The sonnet is a kind of play structure to which the sonnet writer can evoke and argue with bondage even while insisting on freedom. Walker's sonnet "The Struggle Staggers Us" (1942), for example, is structured by binaries:

> Our birth and death are easy hours, like sleep
> and food and drink. The struggle staggers us
> for bread, for pride, for simple dignity.
> And this is more than fighting to exist;
> more than revolt and war and human odds.
> There is a journey from the me to you.
> There is a journey from the you to me.
> A union of the two strange worlds must be.
> Ours is a struggle from a too-warm bed;
> too cluttered with a patience full of sleep.
> Out of this blackness we must struggle forth;
> from want of bread, of pride, of dignity.
> Struggle between the morning and the night.
> This marks our years; this settles, too, our plight.

Walker's sonnet hews neither to Petrarchan nor to Shakespearean rhyme scheme; it is not overtly racialized, but as the closing poem of her volume *For My People*, the "our" throughout speaks to a particular community. Both the octave and the sestet resolve in couplets. The struggle, like the sonnet, is both settled and perpetual. James Smethurst notes "a sort of lyric didacticism with echoes of Walt Whitman's 'Song of Myself,'" but here, there are two selves.[26] If the speaker and the form are the "union of two strange worlds," the form invites Walker to use its seemingly alien nature to create this particular sonnet.

One could argue that all poetry involves doubleness, that all poems are a matter of the tension between structure (meter, line) and actualization, particularly when recitation is involved. Seymour Chatman and Samuel Levin argue for recognition of "*two* systems in any performance of a poem, the metrical system (with its events and prominences), and the suprasegmental system of English (with its stresses, intonations and junctures…). These co-existent systems are given different names: meter *vs* performance, traditional meter *vs* 'rhythm.'" Spoken performance of pentameter, Anthony Easthope argues, is open to variation, as pentameter is neither the pattern nor the voice but both, and "actual performance will vary widely according to whether the voice tends toward the abstract pattern (through never losing hold on the intonation) or toward the intonation (though it could only become non-metric speech by defying entirely the abstract pattern)."[27] Voice matters. And actualization work with a voice that may have its own distinct timbre and idiom matters too. Black sonnet writers have made the sonnet structure work for a distinctly black voice, as Baugh's sonnet above and John Murillo's in the previous chapter demonstrate.

Certainly the most fraught sonnet convention for African American poets is the trope of expressing the pain and joy of metaphorical enslavement to love. Consider Philip Sidney's Sonnet 47:

> What, have I thus betrayed my liberty?
> Can those black beams such burning marks engrave
> In my free side? or am I born a slave,
> Whose neck becomes such yoke of tyranny?
> Or want I sense to feel my misery?
> Or sprite, disdain of such disdain to have,
> Who for long faith, though daily help I crave,
> May get no alms but scorn of beggary?
> Virtue awake, beauty but beauty is;
> I may, I must, I can, I will, I do
> Leave following that, which it is gain to miss.
> Let her go! Soft, but here she comes. Go to,
> Unkind, I love you not. Oh me, that eye
> Doth make my heart give to my tongue the lie.

In the Petrarchan octave, Sidney's speaker asks if physical enslavement to love and beauty is his choice, his lot, or his nature. In the English sestet, the speaker is unable to break the spell of her beauty. The power of terms and phrases such as "burning marks," "slave," and "yoke of tyranny" depend on the notion that there are real slaves with branded flesh.

For African American sonnet writers, the dependency of these metaphors on real pain and real fetters offers opportunities to contend with these metaphors by foregrounding real pain, physical confinement, material encounters. Brooks's "A Lovely Love" (1960) engages with the suffering tradition as well as the courtly love tradition, pondering the sonnet's suitability for her love story:

Let it be alleys. Let it be a hall
Whose janitor javelins epithet and thought
To cheapen hyacinth darkness that we sought
And played we found, rot, make the petals fall.
Let it be stairways, and splintery box
Where you have thrown me, scraped me with your kiss,
Have honed me, have released me after this
Cavern kindness, smiled away our shocks.
This is the birthright of our lovely love.
In swaddling clothes. Not like that Other one.
Nor lit by any fondling star above.
Nor found by any wise men, either. Run.
People are coming. They must not catch us here
Definitionless in this strict atmosphere.[28]

The octave of Brooks's sonnet is Italian, or Petrarchan, while the sestet
is Shakespearean. The sonnet begins "Let it be," a plea that is repeated
twice more. "A Lovely Love" is concerned not with abstract love but with
the concrete place of love, and whether the sonnet is too confining and
"splintery" a box for these homeless lovers. In the first four lines she
evokes low places and high, alley and hall. The root of *janitor* is Janus, the
two-faced god of portals; *javelin* too evokes twoness, from the *ghabholo*
(fork, or branch of a tree). She evokes Hyakinthos, the prince loved by
Apollo, and killed for their love. In the sestet she evokes the holy family
but without anyone to watch over them.

Brooks's final couplet suggests that perhaps her lovers' furtive love is
trespassing on sonnet history. Mary Helen Washington reads this poem
as giving "the trappings of poetic form" to the poor: "[By] its repeated references to those public, dark, and indecent locales, the poem, like the
couple, violates the *lovelier* love traditionally associated with the sonnet."[29] Washington discounts the "battering" tradition here, but Brooks
seems to be gesturing toward Donne's holy sonnets (below) as much as to
Petrarchan and Shakespearean love sonnets. Brooks's sonnet is aware of
these traditions, and we see Brooks contending with them once again to
craft a love sonnet particular to her own concerns.

John Donne's "Sonnet XIV" (one of his "holy sonnets," written in 1609
or 1610) describes God's love as a physical assault:

Batter my heart, three-person'd God; for you
As yet but knock, breathe, shine, and seek to mend;
That I may rise, and stand, o'erthrow me and bend

Your force, to break, blow, burn and make me new.
I, like an usurpt town, to another due,
Labour to admit you, but Oh, to no end,
Reason your viceroy in me, me should defend,
But is captiv'd, and proves weak or untrue.
Yet dearly I love you, and would be loved fain,
But am betroth'd unto your enemy:
Divorce me, untie, or break that knot again,
Take me to you, imprison me, for I
Except you enthrall me, never shall be free,
Nor ever chaste, except you ravish me.[30]

The poetic speaker describes in the octave a kind of divine boot camp of knocking, beating, and burning to make him new. The speaker suggests he needs the beatings; in the sestet he confesses his marriage to the devil and asks to be imprisoned and ravished to break his ties and be free and chaste. The poem situates itself within the contemporary religious views that scourging and bodily suffering offer a merciful path to spiritual redemption.

James A. Emanuel's "Freedom Rider: Washout" (1968) updates the tradition to speak to the physical and spiritual battles of the civil rights movement:

The first blow hurt.
(God is love, is love.)
My blood spit into the dirt.
(Sustain my love, oh, Lord above!)
Curses circled one another.
(They were angry with their brother.)

I was too weak
For this holy game.
A single freckled fist
Knocked out the memory of His name.
Bloody, I heard a long, black moan,
Like waves from slave ships long ago.
With Gabriel Prosser's dogged knuckles
I struck an ancient blow.[31]

The title signals how the speaker's attempt at nonviolence—holy suffering—will end. Emanuel's speaker is so battered he cannot speak the full ten syllables of the standard iambic pentameter sonnet line. Emanuel's sonnet begins with a Shakespearean sestet, the "problem" part of the sonnet including the memorializing couplet. Two warring voices are speaking. "I was too weak," the octave begins, its five syllables matching "the first blow hurt." The enjambment emphasizes the "holy game" that Donne's sonnet plays. Emanuel exploits the raggedness of the Shakespearean rhyme scheme to leave the terms "weak," "fist," and "knuckles" exposed and unrhymed. The last six rhymes racialize the sonnet: the devil's freckled fist, slave ships. Gabriel Prosser, hanged for planning a slave uprising in 1800 Virginia, inspires the speaker's "ancient blow." The eleventh line, naming Prosser, is the only line reaching the full ten syllables, emphasizing its importance.

Reviewing Emanuel's poetry in *Negro World*, James Cunningham notes that Emanuel "leans in the very unfashionable direction of not-so-very long ago traditional devices such as rhymed quatrains and regularity of line and stanza length. Yet, for all of this, we are faced with a formidable, deadly serious and technically assured, and even mischievous, talent...[with] a verbal dexterity and tightness not unworthy of a Brooks."[32] Cunningham's "yet" does the usual work situating formality outside the black tradition even while Brooks herself was known for formal poetry. As vexed as his comment is, this is one of the few moments in black literary criticism where the work of an African American sonnet writer is alluded to as an influence on a later sonnet writer. Indeed, Emanuel clearly contends with "regularity of line and stanza length" to shape the sonnet into a form that enables his engagement with both "ancient" sonnet traditions and innovation in the tradition of Brooks.

The sonnet form invites innovation. In 1655 John Milton updated the Petrarchan form in his sonnet protesting the killing of innocents, "On the Late Massacre in Piedmont":

> Avenge, O Lord, thy slaughtered Saints, whose bones
> Lie scattered on the Alpine mountains cold;
> Even them who kept thy truth so pure of old,
> When all our fathers worshiped stocks and stones,
> Forget not: in thy book record their groans
> Who were thy sheep, and in their ancient fold
> Slain by the bloody Piemontese, that rolled
> Mother with infant down the rocks. Their moans
> The vales redoubled to the hills, and they
> To heaven. Their martyred blood and ashes sow
> O'er all the Italian fields, where still doth sway
> The triple Tyrant; that from these may grow

> A hundredfold, who, having learnt thy way,
> Early may fly the Babylonian woe.

The slaughter of a community of Waldensians in the Italian mountains by the Duke of Savoy outraged Protestants throughout Europe. The poetic speaker's fury will not permit an opposing view: where, according to the Petrarchan structure, there should be a turn, there is none. The single sentence of the octave ends before the close of the eighth line. The reader expects the poem to offer a response, but the deliberate avoidance of a turn signifies that there is no logical response. The octave asks God to avenge and forget not the massacre of murdered saints, mothers, and infants. The sestet observes that their moans and blood will nourish other opponents to the pope (the "triple Tyrant"), the court of whom Petrarch (Sonnet 108) called Babylon and "fountain of woe."[33]

McKay's editor, Frank Harris, cited "On the Late Massacre" in his first meeting with McKay. Harris was critical of McKay's sonnet "The Lynching," written in response to race riots in East Saint Louis, Missouri, in 1917, where white attackers burned thousands of homes and murdered more than a hundred African American residents:

> His spirit in smoke ascended to high heaven.
> His father, by the crudest way of pain,
> Had bidden him to his bosom once again;
> The awful sin remained still unforgiven.
> All night a bright and solitary star
> (Perchance the one that ever guided him,
> Yet gave him up at last to Fate's wild whim)
> Hung pitifully o'er the swinging char.
> Day dawned, and soon the mixed crowds came to view
> The ghastly body swaying in the sun
> The women thronged to look, but never a one
> Showed sorrow in her eyes of steely blue;
> And little lads, lynchers that were to be,
> Danced round the dreadful thing in fiendish glee.[34]

Harris thought McKay could strive to be more Miltonic:

> A sonnet like this, after reading the report of the St. Louis Massacre, which I published in *Pearson's*, sounds like an anticlimax. You should have risen to the heights and stormed heaven like Milton when he wrote 'On the Late Massacre in Piedmont': "*Avenge, O Lord! thy slaughtered Saints whose bones Lie scattered on the Alpine mountains cold....*"

There you have the sublime human cry of anguish and hate against man's inhumanity to man. Some day you will rip it out of your guts.[35]

Harris has a point: McKay's sonnet is perhaps not outraged enough. It opens with an octave describing a man who has just been burnt to death, the smoke rising to heaven while "a bright and solitary star" "hung" in the night air. The sestet describes the dawn, a gathering crowd, and future lynchers dancing. The sonnet contains no racial markers beyond the blue eyes of the pitiless women. The octave evokes a crucifixion; the little lads evoke the "white fiends" of McKay's "To the White Fiends" (discussed in chapter 4). If Milton's intervention was to ignore the dialectical form to preclude antithesis—to refuse to acknowledge there were two sides to the story—McKay ought to have been similarly single-minded in his indictment of lynching, Harris suggested. Instead, McKay was fatalistic. "Day dawned" and more massacres would occur.

And yet in using the sonnet form, McKay is also reaching back to Petrarchan traditions grappling with Platonic and Christian metaphysics. Lynching was becoming regularly characterized by black poets as a kind of crucifixion. But resurrection is not part of the lynching victim's story. Jon Woodson argues that there is "a deep intertextuality" between McKay's "The Lynching" and the lynching poems that followed into the 1930s as poets "struggled to overcome the conceptual problems (the divide between realistic and metaphysical treatments of the lynched body/soul)" that McKay struggled with.[36] The end of the story of a lynching cannot be heaven; the speaker must turn back to earthly life and sinful humankind. If there is a flaw in "The Lynching," it may be that it ends with a Shakespearean couplet suggesting a resolution rather than with a Petrarchan delayed rhyme, enabling ambivalence. Or it may be that McKay found that a sonnet cannot solve or resolve "the white man's moral and religious crisis," as Eugene Redmond observes, arguing that the sonnet's failure to resolve is deliberate. "Clearly this is not how Petrarch, Shakespeare, Spenser, Milton, Wordsworth, Arnold, or Santayana would have wanted the problem 'solved' or 'restated.'"[37] For Nilay Gandhi, McKay's innovations in combining the Shakespearean couplet and the slower-paced Petrarchan form with its "lengthened pauses" ask the reader to "pensively consider the descriptions. The couplet is a way of saying nothing that preceded it makes sense."[38] There is no answer to a lynching except for "fighting back."

❀ ❀ ❀

The sonnet examples by McKay, Dunbar, Brooks, and Baugh offered above demonstrate that African American sonnet writers knew
well and contended with the Renaissance and early modern metaphysical
and protest sonnet traditions. They understood these antecedents thor-
oughly. The late eighteenth- and early nineteenth-century romantic sonnet tradition, with its emphasis on individuality and freedom, offered
new models and invitations to respond. Drawing on Milton's innovations,
the sonnets of Robert Southey, Percy Bysshe Shelley, William Wordsworth, and John Keats influenced nineteenth-century black poets (particularly in the abolitionist community) and twentieth-century sonnet
writers.[39] African American sonnet writers were familiar with Wordsworth's sonnet to Toussaint L'Ouverture (discussed in chapter 3) and
Shelley's sonnet "England in 1819," written in response to the massacre of
that year, during which the cavalry, with sabers drawn, charged a throng
of starving protesters in Manchester. Shelley's target is the ruling class:

> An old, mad, blind, despised, and dying king,
> Princes, the dregs of their dull race, who flow
> Through public scorn, mud from a muddy spring,
> Rulers who neither see, nor feel, nor know,
> But leech-like to their fainting country cling,
> Till they drop, blind in blood, without a blow,
> A people starved and stabbed in the untilled field,
> An army, which liberticide and prey
> Makes as a two-edged sword to all who wield
> Golden and sanguine laws which tempt and slay;
> Religion Christless, Godless a book sealed;
> A Senate, Time's worst statute unrepealed,
> Are graves, from which a glorious Phantom may
> Burst, to illumine our tempestuous day.[40]

Shelley's sonnet is a single sentence with an unorthodox rhyme scheme
designed to avoid the idea of a volta. Like Milton's sonnet, it is single-
minded. An abrupt change in rhyme at the seventh line startles the
reader; expectations of rhyme and turn are disrupted. The army marches
through where the turn should be. The last couplet emphasizes the
speaker's hope that out of the grievous conditions of England, a new
spirit might emerge. Shelley's visionary and revolutionary politics can be

seen in the resistance to closure—the image of a bursting phantom that may change everything contradicts the formal completion of the rhymed couplet. External expectations and conventions are essential to Shelley's challenge to tradition, law, and power.

In "There is a bondage" (1802) and "Nuns fret not" (1807), Wordsworth transformed the sonnet tradition of physical confinement to suggest that the constraints of the prison allow transcendental freedom. "There is a bondage" indicts self-imposed bondage of the spirit as ultimately more damaging than political bondage:

> There is a bondage worse, far worse, to bear
> Than his who breathes, by roof, and floor, and wall,
> Pent in, a Tyrant's solitary Thrall:
> 'Tis his who walks about in the open air,
> One of a Nation who, henceforth, must wear
> Their fetters in their souls. For who could be,
> Who, even the best, in such condition, free
> From self-reproach, reproach that he must share
> With Human-nature? Never be it ours
> To see the sun how brightly it will shine,
> And know that noble feelings, manly powers,
> Instead of gathering strength, must droop and pine;
> And earth with all her pleasant fruits and flowers
> Fade, and participate in man's decline.[41]

Written in 1802, during a brief hiatus in the European wars, the poetic speaker warns against complacency in the war against tyranny. Those with fetters on their souls—who do not love liberty even when liberty is not threatened—are, for Wordsworth, the truly miserable. The sonnet circulated widely after the war among those endeavoring to create new citizens.

Countee Cullen's "From the Dark Tower" (1924) responds to Wordsworth's version of the "bondage" tradition in speaking for a "we," not an "I," whose artistic yearnings will not always be thwarted by social injustice:

> We shall not always plant while others reap
> The golden increment of bursting fruit,
> Not always countenance, abject and mute
> That lesser men should hold their brothers cheap;
> Not everlastingly while others sleep
> Shall we beguile their limbs with mellow flute,

Not always bend to some more subtle brute;
We were not made eternally to weep.
The night whose sable breast relieves the stark
White stars is no less lovely being dark,
And there are buds that cannot bloom at all
In light, but crumple, piteous, and fall;
So in the dark we hide the heart that bleeds,
And wait, and tend our agonizing seeds.[42]

While Collier calls this "a restrained, dignified, poignant work, influenced in form by Keats and Shelley rather than by the moderns,"[43] Cullen's sonnet evokes Wordsworth, though using a Shakespearean octave and hybrid sestet (three couplets) to indict the physical and emotional suffering of Jim Crow that prevents him from flowering as a poet. Cullen had studied and admired both Millay and Keats in college (and Lowell's widely praised biography of Keats had just come out), but Cullen's poem contends with the sonnet tradition generally rather than being influenced by one poet specifically. Cullen's first quatrain opens with a biblical allusion, as well as the long history of slavery; the second quatrain focuses on suffering under slavery.[44] The first couplet in the sestet praises blackness; the second alludes to Thomas Gray's "Elegy Written in a Country Churchyard" (1751), notably the line "Full many a flower is born to blush unseen," near lines about darkness and a mute Milton. Allusions to Gray's "Elegy" appear regularly in African American poetry. Cullen will make the point about the agony and futility of black artistry more strongly in his more famous sonnet, "Yet Do I Marvel" (see chapter 5). Here, he is contending with sonnet traditions that promote suffering to achieve spiritual awakening to argue that abjection can also destroy the drive to create.

Remarking on the inclusion of "From the Dark Tower" in the protest manifesto/magazine *FIRE!!*, Paul Peppis observes curiously that Cullen "rewrites the traditional sonneteer's posture of unrequited love in racial terms." Peppis's description of Cullen's "evident radicalism in making the quintessential love poetry genre a medium for racial protest—that Cullen's poem is a sonnet, and as such declines the pyrotechnic experimentalism of most canonical modernist poems"[45]—misses the importance of the sonnet tradition's influence on Cullen, who knew well the history of sonnet innovations.

Wordsworth's "Nuns fret not" more overtly and more provocatively

suggests that captivity allows creativity. For Wordsworth, cells are metaphorical; Joseph Phelan notes that the rule-governed form "becomes
an iconic representation of the poet's own freely chosen confinement;
both his acquiescence in the rules of the form and his minor creative in-
fractions of them acquire an almost immediate moral and political resonance, reinforcing…the poem's explicit discussion of the relative merits
of liberty and submission to authority":

> Nuns fret not at their convent's narrow room;
> And hermits are contented with their cells;
> And students with their pensive citadels;
> Maids at the wheel, the weaver at his loom,
> Sit blithe and happy; bees that soar for bloom,
> High as the highest Peak of Furness-fells,
> Will murmur by the hour in foxglove bells:
> In truth the prison, unto which we doom
> Ourselves, no prison is: and hence for me,
> In sundry moods, 'twas pastime to be bound
> Within the Sonnet's scanty plot of ground;
> Pleased if some Souls (for such there needs must be)
> Who have felt the weight of too much liberty,
> Should find brief solace there, as I have found.[46]

Wordsworth likens the limitations of the sonnet to a prison that "in
truth…no prison is." Like nuns in convents and hermits in cells, sonnet
writers do not mind being bound in a "scanty plot of ground."[47] Demonstrating Wordsworth's influence a century and a half later, Brooks challenged confinement metaphors as merely metaphors in "To a Winter
Squirrel" (1965), using the narrow-room tradition to rage against sub-
standard Chicago housing:

> That is the way God made you.
> And what is wrong with it? Why, Nothing.
> Except that you are cold and cannot cook.
> Merdice can cook. Merdice
> Of Murdered heart and docked sarcastic soul.
> Merdice
> The bolted Nomad, on a winter noon
> Cook guts; and sits in gas. (She has no shawl, her landlord has no coal.)
> You out beyond the shellac of her look
> And of her sill!

>She envies you your fury
>Buffoonery
>That enfolds your silver skill
>She thinks you are a mountain and a star, unbaffleable;
>With sentient twitch and scurry.[48]

"To a Winter Squirrel" is a quasi sonnet, with fifteen lines that "dismantle the sonnet form even as its complexities of address unravel the sonnet's traditions," as the editors of *The Art of the Sonnet* (2010) describe it.[49]
"Merdice" is well beyond fretting in her narrow kitchen: she is cold and
poor and envies the squirrel's freedom. The editors suggest somewhat
anachronistically that Brooks was responding to Black Aesthetic contro-
versies about the sonnet form "by inventing a jagged, self-complicating,
and sometimes self-accusing style," breaking apart the form and using
"the syncopations of Black English," though these pressures would not
manifest themselves until 1967. Elizabeth Alexander agrees that the sonnet "is a 'little room'" to Brooks, who uses the form to dramatize "specific structures and their inhabitants." Alexander (also a sonnet writer)
laments that her own work is "overpraised by narrow-minded white critics who seem relieved that some of my references and formal choices are
familiar to their own cultural milieu."[50] Yet "To a Winter Squirrel" is an
example of Brooks both drawing on and defamiliarizing the form to refer
to her own neighborhood, not Wordsworth's. They also seem to have influenced Alexander.

Brooks is both influenced by and contending with Wordsworth's
praise of the sonnet's imprisoning nature to complicate his notion of
imaginative freedom, and Brooks is doing so in her own idiom. Merdice is diverted by seeing the squirrel through the window of her cold
kitchen, but her "docked" soul is not necessarily nourished. Brooks herself describes Merdice as "a bolted nomad" and the squirrel she sees out
her window as a gypsy: "I see in it a poor young woman of color who can
find no way out of her slum misery. But she still has some imagination,
some ability to enjoy life if only she was free."[51] The poem appeared in a
Chicago Daily News feature on the Pulitzer Prize winner Brooks and her
family, under the headline "Gwendolyn Brooks Is at Least Two Women,"
poet and wife, noting that "the two halves meld in her poetry."[52] Brooks is
right that black poets are "twice-tried." "If one can speak of the African-
American sonnet tradition," Smethurst observes, "it is one that can be
generally seen as both self-consciously 'deformative' in content and con-

servative in its execution of formal 'mastery.'"[53] I argue that black sonnet writers transform rather than deform the sonnet to address particularly African American concerns.

The "caged bird" trope, for example, is one that is notably transformed from sonnets such as Wordsworth's "The Dunolly Eagle" (1833), provoked by the sight of an eagle temporarily imprisoned in a ruined castle:

> Not to the clouds, not to the cliff, he flew;
> But when a storm, on sea or mountain bred,
> Came and delivered him, alone he sped
> Into the castle-dungeon's darkest mew.
> Now, near his master's house in open view
> He dwells, and hears indignant tempests howl,
> Kennelled and chained. Ye tame domestic fowl,
> Beware of him! Thou, saucy cockatoo,
> Look to thy plumage and thy life!—The roe,
> Fleet as the west wind, is for 'him' no quarry;
> Balanced in ether he will never tarry,
> Eyeing the sea's blue depths. Poor Bird! even so
> Doth man of brother man a creature make
> That clings to slavery for its own sad sake.

Eva Dykes reads the poem as a "thrust at slavery," noting that Wordsworth "was an ardent lover of freedom and the words 'free,' 'freed,' 'freedom,' and 'liberty,' occur about three hundred eighty times in his poems."[54] But the trope of the caged bird—or freedom in any of Wordsworth's sonnets beyond "To Toussaint L'Ouverture"—did not pique the American imagination in the mid-century, even among abolitionists. In 1852 the *National Era* published a review of the American poet George H. Boker's collection of poems, "The Podesta's Daughter," which included sustained observation of the sonnet form as preferably avoiding politics: "The sonnet should be fountain-like, throwing up a slender column of thought—not, as too often it is made, a stream of continuous waves, of which we can see neither source nor end.…Any terrible or tragic conception seems strangely out of place in a form so artistic, and a grand thought seems to want room in such narrow limits. It is the nest of a singing-bird, not a perch for an eagle."[55]

By the late nineteenth century, however, African American poets saw new meaning in the caged-bird trope; Dunbar famously used the image in his poem "Sympathy" (not a sonnet), as did Leslie Pinckney Hill in "To a Caged Canary in a Negro Restaurant" (1921), which engages overtly with Wordsworth, Dunbar, and sonnet-prison conventions:

> Thou little golden bird of happy song!
> A cage cannot restrain the rapturous joy
> Which thou dost shed abroad. Thou dost employ
> Thy bondage for high uses. Grievous wrong
> Is thine; yet in thy heart glows full and strong
> The tropic sun, though far beyond thy flight,
> And though thou flutterest there by day and night
> Above the clamor of a dusky throng.
> So let my will, albeit hedged about
> By creed and caste, feed on the light within;
> So let my song sing through the bars of doubt
> With light and healing where despair has been;
> So let my people bide their time and place,
> A hindered but a sunny-hearted race.[56]

Using an Italian rhyme scheme but with a final couplet, Hill's use of enjambment in the octave (five out of eight lines) suggests that the "golden bird" is not restrained. The bird cannot fly, but he can sing. The image of the caged bird clearly evokes Dunbar's "Sympathy," and Hill acknowledges that bird is grievously wronged even as he is above the clamor of the "dusky throng" and his heart is glowing. The sonnet's sestet turns to suggest that the speaker, whose "will" is hindered by doubts, should draw on inner light and sing. Moreover, "my people," the speaker says, should likewise bide their time. While the octave employs archaisms ("dost," "thine"), the sestet uses none, suggesting a move from poetry to prose, from metaphorical thought to literal. If this were a Wordsworth sonnet, the cage would merely be wholly metaphorical, but for Hill and for the "dusky throng" in the Negro restaurant, the "grievous wrong" suggests real segregation and real ambivalence about the freedom it might offer. While the final couplet seems like a call for caution, the cage of the sonnet begs the question of whether even metaphorical "bars of doubt" should be so easily suffered. Therese Steffen argues that sonnet writing was a "survival strategy" for black poets seeking to express loss or pain "contained in the fine cage of a sonnet."[57] The sonnet form allows Hill to contend with Wordsworth and ponder the particular problem of Jim Crow imprisonment.

At the turn of the nineteenth century, in the midst of race violence and Jim Crow, Edwin Arlington Robinson published a sonnet on sonnets that signals not only an amnesia about slavery's recent history in the United States but also a blindness to the present. Thirty-five years after Emancipation and twenty years after the end of Reconstruction, slavery metaphors in Robinson's "Sonnet" (1897) are simply metaphors:

> The master and the slave go hand in hand,
> Though touch be lost. The poet is a slave,
> And there be kings do sorrowfully crave
> The joyance that a scullion may command.
> But, ah, the sonnet-slave must understand
> The mission of his bondage, or the grave
> May clasp his bones, or ever he shall save
> The perfect word that is the poet's wand.
> The sonnet is a crown, whereof the rhymes
> Are for Thought's purest gold the jewel-stones;
> But shapes and echoes that are never done
> Will haunt the workship, as regret sometimes
> Will bring with human yearning to sad thrones
> The crash of battles that are never won.[58]

"Sonnet" is concerned with poetic melancholy, not political action: the sonnet-slave is bound to a dead form, and the risk of poetic failure is ever present.[59] Robinson's sonnet, written a year after *Plessy v. Ferguson* upheld race segregation, shortly after the death of Frederick Douglass and Harriet Beecher Stowe, in the midst of an upsurge in lynching, and while America was reading *Uncle Remus*, *Huckleberry Finn*, and *Pudd'nhead Wilson*,[60] is blind to associations with American slavery. It is an extraordinary experience to read it alongside sonnets by black poets, a reminder that black sonnet writers were contending with their contemporaries as well, using sonnet traditions in new ways.

Nobody criticized Robinson for political naivete. James Dickey's assessment of Robinson, that "[n]o poet ever understood loneliness or separateness better than Robinson or knew the self-consuming furnace that the brain can become in isolation...fated to this condition by the accident of human birth,"[61] emphasizes the racial segregation that operates in poetry criticism in Robinson's time, Dickey's, and the present. Dickey completely overlooks Dunbar, who published "We Wear the Mask" in 1896. For Robinson and for Dickey, it is all just metaphor: the sonnet is the master, the poet the slave. For African American poets, sonnet history has offered an opportunity to challenge these metaphors as not merely rhetoric but political reality.

A vast output of late nineteenth-century sonnets by American poets such as Robinson may have been due to the sonnet's role as a status symbol, conferring prestige on its practitioners, as the British sonnet scholar William Sharp suggests:

> I have recently waded through considerably over two hundred volumes of American minor verse, by living or recently deceased authors, and have been amazed at the almost universal adoption of the sonnet, though of proof of the actual culture of this species of verse there is comparatively little. My sonnet search has convinced me, however, that a finer body of sonnets on general themes could be selected from the writings of the secondary poets of America than from those of our own minor bards.[62]

Sharp suggests that American sonneteers do not apprehend the "true significance" of the sonnet, that the form is "too exigent for writers who have not yet learned the great lesson that poetic speech must be golden," and that "an extraordinary structural looseness prevails." Among British writers, only amateur poets are "unaware of the conditions which govern the mould of a sonnet," Sharp continues. "But in America the sonnet goes forth in holiday. Oftenest it is content with casual divergences, but too frequently it goes off on a rampage of its own, and sometimes it returns so disguised as hardly to be recognizable."[63] Sharp did not know of Dunbar, but he seems to have anticipated Brooks.

In the twentieth century the influence of Keats on African American poets, notably on Braithwaite, Cullen, and Brooks, was considered curious and inappropriate, although without stopping to ask what it is about Keats that black sonnet writers might admire. Keats's influential "On the Sonnet" (also known as "If by Dull Rhymes") focuses on the constraints of a rhyme scheme that is perhaps not suitable for modern English language:

> If by dull rhymes our English must be chained,
> And, like Andromeda, the Sonnet sweet
> Fettered, in spite of painéd loveliness;
> Let us find out, if we must be constrained,
> Sandals more interwoven and complete
> To fit the naked foot of poesy;
> Let us inspect the lyre, and weigh the stress
> Of every chord, and see what may be gained
> By ear industrious, and attention meet;
> Misers of sound and syllable, no less

Than Midas of his coinage, let us be
Jealous of dead leaves in the bay-wreath crown;
So, if we may not let the Muse be free,
She will be bound with garlands of her own.[64]

Keats's interest in writing a sonnet on sonnets, as he wrote in a letter to his brother, was to find a better sonnet stanza, more loosely fettered by a rigid rhyme scheme, less imprisoned by the "dead leaves" of sonnets past.[65] The rhyme scheme is neither Italian nor English.[66] There are no couplets, no line resolutions. There is a volta at the tenth line. The speaker asks that if the sonnet must be chained to English rhymes, "let us" find different sandals, hear different sounds. After a semicolon, the speaker calls for a turning away from old texts (dead leaves) in order to be bound by new conventions. How could this not appeal to black sonnet writers?

Dunbar's "Sonnet: On an Old Book with Uncut Leaves" (1899), most likely the sonnet he was writing when he penned "Dely," laments the possibility of leaves not dead from overuse but from never being read at all:

Emblem of blasted hope and lost desire,
No finger ever traced thy yellow page
Save Time's. Thou hast not wrought to noble rage
The hearts thou wouldst have stirred. Not any fire
Save sad flames set to light a funeral pyre
Dost thou suggest. Nay,—impotent in age,
Unsought, thou holdst a corner of the stage
And ceasest even dumbly to aspire.
How different was the thought of him that writ.
What promised he to love of ease and wealth,
When men should read and kindle at his wit.
But here decay eats up the book by stealth,
While it, like some old maiden, solemnly,
Hugs its incongruous virginity![67]

"Sonnet" is an exercise in enjambment as a formal counterpart of uncut leaves: the lines fold in on themselves. The octave is made of four sentences, the first three of which end midline. There is an unmistakable turn after which the sestet degrades, each line shorter than the last. The volta offers a change of mood, turning the poem's attention from the book to the writer of the book. Dunbar's dialect craft was almost literally a matter of writing, as Keats describes, "By ear industrious, and attention meet; / Misers of sound and syllable, no less / Than Midas of his coinage, let us be / Jealous of dead leaves in the bay-wreath crown." The dialect love poem "Dely" features rhymes not dull at all. Anticipating Charles Chesnutt's story "Baxter's Procrustes" (1904), the idea of writing a book that will never be read even while he is crafting new ways of speaking is utterly painful to Dunbar's sonnet speaker.

Marcus B. Christian's sonnet "The Craftsman" (1948) is demonstrably influenced by the tradition of sonnets on sonnet writing and by Shakespearean immortality:

> I ply with all the cunning of my art
> This little thing, and with consummate care
> I fashion it—so that when I depart,
> Those who come after me shall find it fair
> And beautiful. It must be free of flaws—
> Pointing no laborings of weary hands;
> And there must be no flouting of the laws
> Of beauty—as the artist understands.
> Through passion, yearnings infinite—yet dumb—
> I lift you from the depths of my own mind
> And gild you with my soul's white heat to plumb
> The souls of future men. I leave behind
> This thing that in return this solace gives:
> "He who creates true beauty ever lives."[68]

In a Shakespearean rhyme scheme, Christian's sonnet evokes Wordsworth's "Nuns fret not" (souls, solace) and Shakespeare with his evocation of immortality in the couplet. (The source of the quote is unknown.) And while the sonnet is not racialized, phrases such as "laborings of weary hands" and "yearnings infinite—yet dumb" gesture to sonnets such as Cullen's "From the Dark Tower." Christian's sonnet is optimistic, while Dunbar's is not.

African American sonnet writers were influenced by the English sonnet tradition and contended with the tradition in return. Bondage metaphors are fundamental to this history, as Robert Hillyer observes: "[T]he sonnet is not a tyrant, but a benevolent despot elected, after hundreds of experiments, by the unanimous vote of the poets. If you do not mean to keep its laws, do not enter its territory."[69] Cullen studied with Hillyer at Harvard, and Brooks read Hillyer's *First Principles of Verse* regularly. Susan Stewart argues in *The Poet's Freedom* that "we speak of being the 'master of' the sonnet, the nocturne, the long poem. Praising, we are servants of the phenomena; making, we are masters of our forms."[70] While Hillyer and Stewart write from the perspective of the ahistorical, politically "free" poet, sonnets by African American poets make clear that "mastery" of the sonnet form involves contending with its multiple traditions and histories, including what it means to "master." Even the addition of a fifteenth line is a statement of freedom. The sonnet is resilient enough to be battered, knocked about, o'erthrown, broken, untied, ravished, and made new.

Marcellus Blount argues that for black poets, "the sonnet has served as a zone of entrapment and liberation, mediation and self-possession."[71] Some black poets saw in the sonnet a space for performance, others an opportunity to display poetic craft. And the sonnet's high status appealed to black poets and editors who valued its democratic availability and cultural prestige. As Baugh, McKay, Brooks, and other black sonnet writers demonstrate, valuing cultural prestige might mean drawing on that prestige for political critique. When Howarth notes that "[t]he sonnet's role as the gold standard of civilized self-discipline made achieving it, for a late nineteenth-century African American writer like Paul Laurence Dunbar, effectively a claim for public equality," he does not see Dunbar's transformation of sonnet tradition as speaking to the crisis of race violence, which I show in chapter 4.[72]

At the turn of the century, the improving social, cultural, and economic conditions that made possible the literary careers of Du Bois, Braithwaite, Dunbar, and Johnson (and later, McKay, Cullen, and Hughes) were disturbing and unnerving to white poets worried about a fragmented and unpredictable future and, for some, nostalgic for the southern past. Both white and black intellectuals, in separate journals and halls, debated the question of what white and black authors "should" be writing about as a matter of both culture and aesthetics.

In the *Dial*, the modernist poet and editor Amy Lowell was urging poets away from old forms, old conventions, old structures by calling on the most radical of nineteenth-century poets, William Blake: "I considered a monotonous cadence like that used by Milton and Shakespeare, and all writers of English blank verse, derived from the modern bondage of rhyming, to be a necessary and indispensable part of verse. But I soon found that in the mouth of a true orator, such monotony was not only awkward, but as much a bondage as rhyme itself."[73] Lowell clips Blake's quote before the notable line, "Poetry fettered, fetters the human race." Lowell advocated that "the business of a poet is to record what he sees with his own eyes in the manner natural to him; and while admiring the great figures of the past, we may at least concede that their world, and in consequence their thought, was different from ours." There are moments where in tone and sense of urgency, the literary discussions of naturalism, realism, modernism, and formalism that appeared in the pages of the *Dial* are not very different from those in the pages of W. E. B. Du Bois's *Crisis*.

Modernism was arguably as influential for black poets as the sonnet tradition was. Michael North argues persuasively for the existence of "two different modernisms, tightly linked by their different stakes in the same language" that emerged in the mid-1920s.[74] While Houston Baker, Jr., and others have argued that Anglo-American modernism is coincident but irrelevant to the modernism of the Harlem Renaissance, North notes that both movements depended on "strategies of linguistic rebellion" involving the dialect rejected by James Weldon Johnson.[75] North argues that "it is impossible to understand either modernism without reference to the other, without reference to the language they so uncomfortably shared, and to the political and cultural forces that were constricting the language at the very moment modern writers of both races were attempting in dramatically different ways to free it."[76] Yet, as Michael Bibby observes, "formally conventional poems of Wallace Stevens, Robert Frost, and even Edwin Arlington Robinson are typically canonized as 'modernist,'" even while the use of conventional form by "New Negro" poets is considered evidence of antimodernism.[77]

Both North and Bibby are right: both white and black poets were experimenting with form and language in new ways, but white "modernists" were in control of the modernist brand. The relationship of modernism to the Harlem Renaissance has been hard to piece apart, George Hutchinson argues, not only because of "racism in the academy" but also because both realism and naturalism "have served as a straw man designating whatever modernism is not in Europe and the United States since the 1930s."[78] Modern poetry anthologies published before 1945 overwhelmingly feature white poetry (and few sonnets). No black poets appear in Lowell's *Tendencies in Modern American Poetry* (1917); Louis Untermeyer does not include any black poets in "our contemporary poets" in his *The New Era in American Poetry* (1919); Laura Riding and Robert Graves do not include any black poets in *A Survey of Modernist Poetry* (1927).[79] Even Langston Hughes was not easily welcomed.[80]

For the sake of this brief history of the sonnet, let us simply say that the twentieth century saw a rise in and privileging of formally experimental modernist verse.[81] It may be true that modernism had a damp-

ening effect on sonnet composition in America; certainly modernist criticism of the sonnet abounds. Ezra Pound called the sonnet "the devil,"
habitual, mass-produced, a mere blueprint.[82] Wallace Stevens cried,
"Perish all sonnets!" to his fiancée after reading Edmund Clarence Sted-
man's 1895 *A Victorian Anthology*; "Sonnets have their place...but they
can also be found tremendously out of place: in real life, where things
are quick, unaccountable, responsive." André Breton wrote in 1933 (about
Mallarmé's sonnet "Salut"): "All these 'sonnets' that still get written, this
senile horror of spontaneity, all this rationalistic refinement, these stiff-
lipped supervisors, all this incapacity for love, leave me convinced that
escape is impossible from this ancient house of correction."[83]

William Carlos Williams inveighed against the sonnet as "fascistic"
and "a form which does not admit of the slightest structural change in its
composition."[84] Yet he changed his mind about the sonnet in the 1950s, in
part because of changes in language; Williams claimed that the diversity
of American language—the fact that American speech varies widely—
helps poets manage language in new ways.[85] American poets "must *listen* to the language" to make discoveries. To the English, the English language "is serious—too serious—in a way no dialect could be. But dialect
is the mobile phase, the changing phase, the productive phase—as their
languages were to Chaucer, Shakespeare, Dante, Rabelais in their day."[86]
Listening to language, Williams argues, offers an "opportunity to expand
the structure, the basis, the actual making of the poem." Williams's point
allows a synthesis of dialect, various modernisms, and the sonnet form
and anticipates eventual dominance of the sonnet form by African American poets.

The examples of Dunbar and McKay, who demonstrated skill in de-
constructing and reconstructing language in their dialect poetry and
then proceeded to write superb sonnets, certainly support Williams's
theory. Dialect poetry involves the same exactitude of thought, intensi-
fication, condensation, invocation, and scrupulous care that any poetic
practice involves. Howarth's claim that sonnets of the era were "complicit
with production-line thinking...with the genteel unreality in which an
industrialized culture had wished to preserve its art" overlooks efforts
at innovation.[87] Timo Müller identifies a "synthetic vernacular" that
emerged with Hughes in the 1930s as opening new possibilities for the
sonnet in works such as "Seven Moments of Love." Hughes's "blues sonnets" seek to accommodate the craft of sonnet writing within vernacular
poetry. Unfortunately, Müller notes, these hybrid poems don't work: "The

concluding couplets are not always effective, and the lines are too varied in length and content to establish the metrical and semantic rhythmicity that characterizes the blues."[88] Still, influenced by McKay and Cullen, Hughes tried.

George Santayana thought the sonnet too old-fashioned generally, devoting an entire article in the *New Republic* to the idea of updating Shakespeare's Sonnet 29:

> When, in disgrace with fortune and men's eyes,
> I all alone beweep my outcast state
> And trouble deaf heaven with my bootless cries
> And look upon myself and curse my fate,
> Wishing me like to one more rich in hope,
> Featured like him, like him with friends possess'd,
> Desiring this man's art and that man's scope,
> With what I most enjoy contented least;
> Yet in these thoughts myself almost despising,
> Haply I think on thee, and then my state,
> Like to the lark at break of day arising
> From sullen earth, sings hymns at heaven's gate;
> For thy sweet love remember'd such wealth brings
> That then I scorn to change my state with kings.

"The word *outcast* is still current," Santayana writes, "but the background which gave poignancy to that metaphor belongs to a bygone age. No one can be easily excommunicated in our tolerant society."[89] Without reflecting on the writings of his now-famous former student, W. E. B. Du Bois, Santayana continues: "[T]he phrase *I look upon myself* expresses something different from our self-consciousness. It describes the shock of suddenly seeing yourself as others see you, as when you unexpectedly come upon yourself in a mirror. The poet is borrowing men's eyes in order to consider and pity himself; he is not retreating into a psychological observation of what is hidden from others in his consciousness." Like Dickey reading Robinson, Santayana reads solely as an educated American white male; he seems not to have learned otherwise from Du Bois.[90] Santayana's sole purpose is to critique the "old-fashioned" sonnet form: "Humbug or philosophy, this Platonic mysticism has long been a classic refuge for hopeless emotion, and Shakespeare's sonnets march conventionally in the devout procession."[91]

And yet outside the modern poetry anthologies, and despite the standard narrative of modern poetry ascendance, the sonnet thrived, notably in political protest poetry traditions, including labor union poetry and social protest poetry.[92] Volumes of poetry and small circulation periodicals published in the first half of the twentieth century by Left and Far Left writers and editors, many destroyed during the McCarthy era, featured sonnets targeting power and corruption. Consider, for example, Arturo Giovannitti's 1914 sonnet, "The Prisoner's Bench":

> Through here all wrecks of the tempestuous mains
> Of life have washed away the tides of time.
> Tatters of flesh and souls, furies and pains,
> Horrors and passions awful or sublime,
> All passed here to their doom. Nothing remains
> Of all the tasteless dregs of sin and crime
> But stains of tears, and stains of blood and stains
> Of the inn's vomit and brothel's grime.
> And now we, too, must sit here, Joe. Don't dust
> These boards on which our wretched brothers fell,
> They are clean, there's no reason for disgust.
> For the fat millionaire's revolting stench
> Is not here, nor the preacher's saintly smell,
> And the judge never sat upon this bench.[93]

Helen Keller writes that "Giovannitti is, like Shelley, a poet of revolt against the cruelty, the poverty, the ignorance which too many of us accept in blind content....Behind Arturo Giovannitti stand the poets, prophets, wise men and patriots of Italy."[94] Reviewing the volume in *Poetry* magazine, however, Harriet Monroe critiques Giovannitti as "fettered by ordinary verse forms" in presenting his vision, praising instead the works with more modern and experimental structures, "beaten into beautiful forms of power."[95]

Ralph Chaplin, famous for his 1915 labor anthem "Solidarity Forever," chose the sonnet form to protest the lynching of an IWW activist: "Wesley Everest (Mutilated and murdered at Centralia, Washington, November 11th, 1919, by a mob of 'respectable businessmen')":

> Torn and defiant as a wind-lashed reed,
> Wounded he faced you as he stood at bay;
> You dared not lynch him in the light of day,
> But on your dungeon stones you let him bleed;
> Night came...and you black vigilants of Greed...
> Like human wolves, seized hard upon your prey,
> Tortured and killed...and, silent slunk away

Without one qualm of horror at the deed.
Once...long ago...do you remember how
You hailed Him king for soldiers to deride—
You placed a scroll above His bleeding brow
And spat upon Him, scourged Him, crucified...?
A rebel unto Caesar—then as now
Alone, thorn-crowned, a spear wound in his side![96]

Chaplin's Petrarchan sonnet features an accusatory speaker who, in the octave, accuses those who "dared not" act in daylight but "seized" their victim, "tortured and killed" him, and "silently slunk away." After the volta, the sestet compares the "human wolves" to those responsible for the crucifixion, situating the scene in broader context. Chaplin's poem should be seen in the tradition of lynching sonnets that would reach back to Southey and could include contemporary works by McKay, Hill, and perhaps even the anarchist poet Lola Ridge, with her startling 1927 sonnet, "Electrocution":

He shudders—feeling on the shaven spot
The probing wind, that stabs him to a thought
Of storm-drenched fields in a white foam of light,
And roads of his hill-town that leap to sight
Like threads of tortured silver...while the guards—
Monstrous deft dolls that move as on a string,
In wonted haste to finish with this thing,
Turn faces blanker than asphalted yards.
They heard the shriek that tore out of its sheath
But as a feeble moan...yet dared not breathe,
Who stared there at him, arching—like a tree
When the winds wrench it and the earth holds tight—
Whose soul, expanding in white agony,
Had fused in flaming circuit with the night.

Written in protest of Nicola Sacco and Bartolomeo Vanzetti's execution, Ridge's sonnet is built on an unorthodox rhyme scheme and halting, difficult meter and diction. The speaker describes the electrocution in real time, comparing the victim to a tree in a storm. Ridge's sonnet circulated widely, along with scores of labor sonnets and antiwar sonnets by English poets Sigfried Sassoon and Wilfred Owen in America in the 1910s through the 1930s. They were certainly read by and influenced McKay and Hill. These poems were for obvious reasons not anthologized in volumes for school use and unfortunately have disappeared from the critical consciousness that has addressed African American poetic influences.

Anthologies of twentieth-century American poetry feature more family-friendly sonnets by Edna St. Vincent Millay, Robert Frost, and e. e. cummings, amid the modernist verse. While only occasionally anthologized, one of cummings's earliest published sonnets was in fact selected by McKay to be published in the *Liberator* (July 1921) as "Maison" (later known simply as "my love is building a building"):

> my love is building a building
> around you, a frail slippery
> house, a strong fragile house
> (beginning at the singular beginning
> of your smile), a skillful uncouth
> prison, a precise clumsy
> prison (building that and this into Thus.)
> Around the reckless magic of your mouth
> my love is building a magic, a discreet
> tower of magic and (as I guess)
> when Farmer Death (whom fairies hate) shall
> crumble the mouth-flower fleet
> He'll not my tower, laborious, casual
> where the surrounded smile hangs breathless[97]

McKay tells the story of cummings's visiting the *Liberator* offices and discussing the sonnet at length; later McKay proposed to the editors later that they do a feature on cummings's work.[98] McKay's early, crucial assistance to cummings is overlooked by cummings and his biographers. The American poetic canon, Cary Nelson reminds us, is "a network of aesthetic assumption and social biases—and implicit cultural and economic priorities—built into and reinvoked by the range of texts it includes."[99] Consider what McKay may have seen in cummings's sonnet—two mentions of prisons, the anxiety about immortality—and situating this sonnet in a study of African American sonnets increases the range of its resonance.

Seven years after Santayana's critique of Shakespeare's Sonnet 29, McKay offered his own rewriting, "Outcast" (1922):

> For the dim regions whence my fathers came
> My spirit, bondaged by the body, longs.
> Words felt, but never heard, my lips would frame;
> My soul would sing forgotten jungle songs.

I would go back to darkness and to peace,
But the great western world holds me in fee,
And I may never hope for full release
While to its alien gods I bend my knee.
Something in me is lost, forever lost,
Some vital thing has gone out of my heart,
And I must walk the way of life a ghost
Among the sons of earth, a thing apart;
For I was born, far from my native clime,
Under the white man's menace, out of time.[100]

McKay's sonnet evokes a wandering, mythic speaker who argues with himself in Shakespearean form and idiom. The literary gods to whom McKay's speaker bows are neither of his era nor his culture, but forms such as the imprisoning sonnet that endure while the songs of his fathers are unknown and forgotten. Francini focuses on McKay's portrayal of blackness "a ghost," "a thing apart," and "out of time": "The turning point is in the second quatrain, where the black's hybrid cultural identity is acknowledged....Among these 'alien gods' there are the makers of the Western tradition and its forms, which are, as we have seen, inextricably woven into the language of McKay's sonnets, just as he is inextricably rooted in the Western culture that holds him 'in fee.'"[101] The sonnet form is essential to the argument, which turns at line 6, in the midst of a sentence. McKay's speaker breaks out of the traditional form in a response to both Shakespeare and Santayana. McKay's sonnet refutes Santayana's claim that "no one can be easily excommunicated in our tolerant society." Santayana's claim, like Robinson's slavery metaphor, is staggeringly obtuse. McKay's sonnet insists that Shakespeare's sonnet and the sonnet form itself remain relevant.

To read sonnets by black poets alongside the sonnets they were influenced by and the sonnets they influenced in turn makes clear that the black sonnet genealogy is richly interwoven. McKay's "Outcast" shows the influence of Charles Bertram Johnson's sonnet "A Shell" (1905), for example, published in the *Colored American*:

Nay, once I have not seen the sea, nor know,
By long familiar ear, her varying mood,
And passionate well, but here upon this rood,
I found this gypsy bard of hers and, lo!
Close-fitted to my ear, in gratitude,

It murmurs of its far-off parent flow.
O, wander Sprite! what Viking fortitude
Left thee, stranded waif, achance wind's blow?
I am a Shell, far from my native shore;
Unlike thee, gypsy bard, my long exile
Has made my native speech remembered vain;
Here self-communing thou and conning o'er
With insane ecstasy thy ancient style,
The while another's tongue relates my pain.[102]

Here, Johnson's speaker uses a hybrid Italian-Shakespearean octave (but only using two rhymes) and a complicated hybrid tense, part past, part present, evoking a nonnative English speaker, to tell the story of finding a shell, holding it to his ear, and hearing a parent's language. After the volta, the speaker, in present tense, compares himself to the shell, "far from my native shore," who has forgotten his native speech. The last three lines are curious: he seems to be lamenting that the shell is English, and his intense study of Shakespeare ("conning o'er / With insane ecstasy thy ancient style") means that he cannot express pain in his own language. The many echoes of "A Shell" in McKay's "Outcast" are provocative, particularly the lines "my native speech remembered vain" and "far from my native shore" from "A Shell" and "sing forgotten jungle songs" and "far from my native clime" from "Outcast." McKay's sonnet is stronger, but Johnson's is remarkable too for its expression of anguished ambivalence.

Further, Marcus Christian's "Southern Share-Cropper" (1937) draws on Shakespeare's sonnet (with its final couplet) to resist the influence of McKay's "Outcast," or rather, to contend openly with it:

He turns and tosses on his bed of moss;
The moon wheels high into the Southern sky;
He cannot sleep—production, gain, and loss
Harass him, while a question and a cry
Stir through the dim recesses of his soul—
This slave to one-fourth, one-third, and one-half;
His sow will litter soon; his mare win foal;
His woman is with child; his cow, with calf.
Earth screams at him—beats clenched, insistent hands
Upon his brains—his labor and his health
He gives unceasingly to her demands;
She yields to him, but others grow in wealth.

> What nailed his soul upon the wrack of things—
> That he must slave, while idlers live like kings?

The cry stirring the "dim recesses" of Christian's sonnet speaker's soul is harassed by work. He is in fee to his land, not the "great western world." "Earth screams at him," and he is slave to her. There is no ambivalence here, and no sentiment. Christian's narrator "is complexly single-voiced," Woodson argues even as he questions the state of things.[103]

African American sonnets have been claiming and transforming the sonnet tradition for well over a century. Yet David Bromwich's recent sonnet anthology exemplifies the sanitizing project in American sonnets, casting aside black sonnets that signify on and contend with the sonnet tradition—interventions that the sonnet tradition clearly welcomes. Bromwich's conservative biases are clear in his claim that "Frost is the author of the best sonnets in English written by anyone who was not Shakespeare."[104] Bromwich's first example is Frost's "The Silken Tent" (1942), whose debt to sonnet history is unmistakable:

> She is as in a field a silken tent
> At midday when a sunny summer breeze
> Has dried the dew and all its ropes relent,
> So that in guys it gently sways at ease,
> And its supporting central cedar pole,
> That is its pinnacle to heavenward
> And signifies the sureness of the soul,
> Seems to owe naught to any single cord,
> But strictly held by none, is loosely bound
> By countless silken ties of love and thought
> To everything on earth the compass round,
> And only by one's going slightly taut
> In the capriciousness of summer air
> Is of the slightest bondage made aware.

Frost's sonnet uses Petrarchan tropes and a Shakespearean rhyme scheme to engage with traditional themes of an unnamed woman, the freedom of the soul, the nature of poetic and earthly constraint. While Frost's use of the words "bound" and "bondage" may not carry specific contemporary political resonances, the appearance of this analogy in an anthology that includes only two sonnets by an African American poet (both by McKay; one is "Outcast") offers opportunities to engage with the question of how slavery and Jim Crow cast a shadow over poetical chains and fetters. Bromwich declines to observe the shadow. What kind of sonnet history might be written for bondage metaphors to be seen as not wholly free from political implications if the political implications were sensed, as I argue here, by black sonnet writers for more than a century?

CHAPTER 3

Antecedents (1768–1889)

To understand the influence of the sonnet on African American poetry, it is important to understand the formal roots of African American poetry and the influence of eighteenth-century British abolitionist poets—notably Robert Southey, Wordsworth, and Thomas Campbell—whose antislavery sonnets circulated in eighteenth- and nineteenth-century America. African American poetry from the beginning was caught up in questions of slavery, oppression, and freedom and was equally caught up in formal meter.

The founding poet of the African American literary tradition is Phillis Wheatley (1753–1784), whose first volume of formal verse, published when she was barely out of her teens, attracted the notice of George Washington, Thomas Jefferson, Benjamin Franklin, John Hancock, Samuel Adams, Voltaire, and other notables on both sides of the Atlantic. Wheatley's influence on nineteenth-century black poetry cannot be overstated. Her story is well known: she arrived in Boston Harbor on a slave ship in 1760 at about age seven, where she was bought by a local merchant named John Wheatley as a servant for his wife, Susanna. Most likely from Gambia, the "slender female child" was named Phillis, after the ship that had brought her across the ocean. The Wheatleys' fifteen-year-old daughter Mary taught Phillis to read, and soon the younger girl was reading and writing enthusiastically, translating Greek and Latin between her tasks as a house servant. Phillis Wheatley's first published poem, "On Messers. Hussey and Coffin," about two friends of her master who had almost been lost at sea in a storm, appeared in the *Rhode Island Mercury* on December 21, 1767. Four years later, Wheatley achieved international notice with a poem on the death of Rev. George Whitefield, printed in a memorial pamphlet. Subsequently Phillis was sent to London by the Wheatleys to publish a volume of her work, *Poems on Various Subjects, Religious and Moral*, in 1773.[1] One poem, "To the King's Most Excellent Majesty" (1768), is a sonnet. It begins, "Your subjects hope, dread Sire—" and continues:

> The crown upon your brows may flourish long,
> And that your arm may in your God be strong!
> O may your sceptre num'rous nations sway,
> And all with love and readiness obey!
> But how shall we the *British* king reward!
> Rule thou in peace, our father, and our lord!
> Midst the remembrance of thy favours past,
> The meanest peasants most admire the last.
> May *George*, beloved by all the nations round,
> Live with heav'n's choicest constant blessings crown'd!
> Great God, direct, and guard him from on high,
> And from his head let ev'ry evil fly!
> And may each clime with equal gladness see
> A monarch's smile can set his subjects free!

"To the King's Most Excellent Majesty" is a political sonnet of praise in the tradition of John Milton's "To the Lord General Cromwell" (1694). The poem is composed of seven iambic pentameter couplets in which the speaker praises the British king for repealing the 1767 Stamp Act and expresses hope that he will rule long.[2] Her fidelity to meter requires syncope (removal of a sound from the interior of a word: "num'rous," "heav'n's," "crown'd," "ev'ry"). The speaker reminds the king that recent favors are most admired by "the meanest peasants," that evil ideas should fly out of his head, and that he should smile on freedom. The poetic speaker, representing a "we" who is not British, raises the specter of peasant revolts and the need for God's protection, which may have appealed to her readers back in Boston. Wheatley may have been thinking of American freedom from taxation or her own freedom from slavery; it is difficult to tell, although modern scholars like to see rebelliousness. As Kathrynn Seidler Engberg argues, "While sounding like a blessing to royalists, for a patriot reader, the sonnet elicits a dry, sarcastic commentary on how the king has poorly conducted himself....Her lines make the king look less godly in his power, since he is in need of prayers."[3] Indeed, Wheatley's speaker suggests that the relationship between the Crown and the people is changeable; more importantly, the speaker speaks to and about the king as an equal.

Wheatley's fourteen-line poem is in rhymed couplets rather than following a Petrarchan or Shakespearean rhyme scheme, although one can discern four quatrains and a final couplet, hinting at a Shakespearean form. The volta at line 9, beginning with "May *George*," indicates a change in audience from speaking *to* the king to speaking *about* the king.

Wheatley's use of the sonnet form seems neither entirely purposeful nor conscious of sonnet history, however. Wheatley wrote formal poetry modeled on an eighteenth-century tradition that included Alexander Pope, Thomas Gray, and Milton, all of whom she acknowledged as literary influences. Wheatley did not signify on or contend with the neoclassical mode of these poets as much as strive to emulate it. Accordingly, in an era not known for sonnet writers (except for Milton), it is not surprising to find perhaps only this single fourteen-liner in all of Wheatley's writings. Pope famously criticized the sonnet form in his "Essay on Criticism" as hackneyed, and Samuel Johnson dismissed a "sonneteer" as "a small poet."[4] The neoclassical tradition was far more civic minded and intellectual than the Renaissance and courtly love traditions that had preceded it and the romantic movement that followed. The poetic voice of the seventeenth and eighteenth centuries looked outward rather than inward. Nobody reveled in shackles. Personification was far more dominant than abstraction, reflecting Enlightenment, rather than Platonic, ideals. Wheatley, in the tradition of that era, employed heroic couplets—pairs of rhyming iambic pentameter verse—or blank verse of unrhymed iambic pentameter, to write poems for occasions, elegies on recent deaths, meditations, and lengthy odes that frequently allude to biblical, Roman, or mythological figures. Wheatley was single-voiced, not double-voiced. In short, Wheatley's poetic choices, including an apparent lack of interest in the sonnet, are wholly of her time.[5] Nevertheless, Wheatley gave birth to the use of the sonnet form in the African American literary tradition.

Phillis Wheatley's prominence and formality set the poetic standard for nineteenth-century black poets, even if it is a stretch to claim her as the founder of a black sonnet tradition. Wheatley's robust embrace of her European literary ancestry over her African roots has been difficult for the African American literary tradition, as it developed in the twentieth century, to accommodate. "No later black poet has been able to point back to her and say, for example, 'I got my sense of rhythm from her,'" Blyden Jackson tartly observes.[6] Wheatley acknowledges her African literary heritage in her poem "To Maecanas," alluding to Terence, the acclaimed Roman poet/playwright of African descent; like Terence, she sought to be both black and part of a literary tradition. Moreover, while later sonnet writers depart deliberately from the strict sonnet form, this does not seem to be the case with "To the King's Most Excellent Majesty." Wheatley's poem is a foundational antecedent for an African American sonnet tradition, though not an influence.

More influential to the African American sonnet tradition is the circulation of abolitionist sonnets within what Joseph Rezek calls "the print Atlantic," a term for the "single, though internally various, culture" of readers and writers in England and America.[7] This literature included works by prominent British antislavery poets such as William Cowper ("The Task" [1785], "The Negro's Complaint" [1788]), Hannah More ("The Black Slave Trade" [1788]), William Blake ("The Little Black Boy" [1789]), Wordsworth, and Southey, as well as pamphlets by Thomas Clarkson and William Wilberforce, which were read widely in America, outside of the South.[8] While most abolitionist poetry took the form of sentimental ballads, a remarkable exception was Southey's six-sonnet sequence, "Poems Concerning the Slave Trade," first published in 1797 and revised significantly in 1809 to emphasize slave violence. Both the original and revised versions appear in collected editions of Southey's poems that circulated widely in America.[9] The revised versions are foundational to the tradition of sonnets about lynching and may well have influenced Owen Dodson's 1936 four-sonnet "Negro History: A Sonnet Sequence," which appeared in *New Masses*.[10]

Southey's "Slave Trade" sonnet sequence begins in Africa, exhorting the Africans to repel slave traders with violence. Consider Sonnet I:

> Hold your mad hands! for ever on your plain
> Must the gorged vulture clog his beak with blood?
> For ever must your Niger's tainted flood,
> Roll to the ravenous shark his banquet slain?
> Hold your mad hands! and learn at length to know,
> And turn your vengeance on the common foe,
> Yon treacherous vessel and her godless crew!
> Let never traders with false pretext fair
> Set on your shores again their wicked feet:
> With interdict and indignation meet

Repel them, and with fire and sword pursue!
Avarice, the white cadaverous fiend, is there,
Who spreads his toils accursed wide and far,
And for his purveyor calls the demon War.

The sonnet, split neatly into two septets rather than an octave and sestet, features a volta after the word "crew" in the seventh line, which goes un-rhymed until "pursue" at the eleventh. The sonnet features an unorth-odox rhyme scheme, neither Petrarchan nor Shakespearean, with the end rhyme of unexpected couplets emphasizing the sonnet's key points: blood/flood, know/foe, feet/meet, far/War. Written in an extreme mode "worthy of John Donne's best satires," the sonnet "offers an almost apoc-alyptic presentation of the coast of Africa, wracked by the wars occa-sioned by the demand for slaves, and drenched with human blood," ar-gues Peter Kitson.[11] Avarice is figured as white. In elevated poetic diction the speaker exhorts those left behind in Africa to rise up against the bloody slave trade, to band together to repel traders on their shores with fire and sword. The slave trade is wicked, greedy, and accursed; Africans must rise up to resist.

The speaker of the next three sonnets in the sequence describes the suffering of slaves while the unthinking public drinks sugar in their cof-fee ("sip the blood-sweetened beverage"). For Kitson, the sonnets "pres-ent the full tableau of slavery, moving from a war-torn Africa, via the middle passage, to the plantation, with its cycle of backbreaking work, sorrow, resentment, revolt, punishment, and execution."[12] The speaker of Sonnet V bluntly suggests that the murder of a slave master is justified:

Did then the Negro rear at last the sword
Of vengeance? Did he plunge its thirsty blade
In the hard heart of his inhuman lord?
Oh! who shall blame him? in the midnight shade
There came on him the intolerable thought
Of every past delight; his native grove,
Friendship's best joys, and liberty and love
For ever lost. Such recollections wrought
His brain to madness. Wherefore should he live
Longer with abject patience to endure
His wrongs and wretchedness, when hope can give
No consolation, time can bring no cure?
But justice for himself he yet could take.
And life is then well given for vengeance' sake.

Again the sonnet is a matter of two septets; the first, like the second, ends in the couplet and a full stop, suggesting a volta. The rhyme scheme here is roughly Shakespearean and opens with a series of questions. Again, there is no clear volta beyond the "Oh!" in the fourth line. The speaker asks: who shall blame a slave who stabs his master to death? Consider the loss of freedom, friendship, loss of home. Vengeance is understandable if not justified. The sonnet pushes the limits of British abolitionist thought, as Kitson observes, demonstrating "a full-blooded and realistic acceptance of slave violence as the inevitable consequence of the brutality of the slave system."[13]

The surprisingly blunt, revolutionary violence in Sonnet V is perhaps the key reason that Southey's 1809 revised version is almost never anthologized and is rarely the subject of critical scrutiny.[14] Elizabeth Bohls, a scholar of the earlier version, argues that poetry depicting slave vengeance is "less common" in abolitionist poetry generally and describes the "bold slave" in Sonnet V rearing his "sword / Of vengeance" in order "to skewer his owner."[15] Bohls sees the sonnet as "stale" and "strangely abstract." Marcus Wood similarly reads the earlier version as failing politically "because the diction, simultaneously emotionally effusive and aesthetically burned out, destroyed the clarity of the social analysis."[16] The problem, for Wood, is that the "histrionic" poetic speaker positions himself "as suffering witness to the enormities of slavery" in ways that crowd out the slave subject. Southey's later versions feature an angry speaker who sees that the slave is legitimately wronged and justified in seeking blood.

Southey's Sonnet VI most clearly prefigures twentieth-century sonnets on lynching, most notably Claude McKay's "The Lynching" (chapter 4). Southey's sonnet grows in outrage from the octave to the sestet:

High in the air exposed the Slave is hung
To all the birds of heaven, their living food!
He groans not, though awaked by that fierce sun,
New torturers live to drink their parent blood!
He groans not, though the gorging vulture tear
The quivering fiber. Hither look, O ye
Who tore this man from peace and liberty!
Look hither, ye who weigh with politic care
The gain against the guilt! Beyond the grave
There is another world!…bear ye in mind,
Ere your decree proclaims to all mankind

> The gain is worth the guilt, that there the Slave
> Before the Eternal, "thunder-tongued shall plead
> Against the deep damnation of your deed."

The focus in this 1809 version is on the consumers (who "tore this man from peace and liberty"); the sonnet suggests that blame and guilt for slavery rest on everyone who gains from the current economic system. "Look," the sonnet repeats, addressing the reader: you are part of this crime.

Southey's use of the sonnet form for his blast at the slave trade and his struggle to show the sonnet's appropriateness for such a violent subject are foundational to the African American sonnet tradition. Southey, like Wordsworth, was influenced by Milton's protest sonnets; unlike Milton or Wordsworth, Southey's use of the sonnet form to justify slave violence would influence twentieth-century black sonnet writers such as McKay. Southey's sonnets depart from most antislavery poems circulating in America, written in ballad form or rhymed couplets and telling pathos-filled stories in heartbreaking detail. To discuss slave violence was a literary taboo. "[T]here is a constant desire to sheer away from the notion that the slave can attain his or her freedom through violent rebellion," Wood notes. "There are no British poems celebrating slave rebellion in the British colonies.... [T]here are no ballads or Spenserian cantos celebrating Nat Turner's bloody revolt in Virginia in 1831."[17]

Thomas Campbell's sentimental sonnet excerpt, "The Pleasures of Hope," circulated far more widely than Southey's sonnets:

> Eternal Nature! when thy giant hand
> Had heav'd the floods, and fix'd the trembling land,
> When life sprung startling at thy plastic call,
> Endless her forms, and man the lord of all!
> Say, was that lordly form inspir'd by thee
> To wear eternal chains and bow the knee?
> Was man ordain'd the slave of man to toil,
> Yok'd with the brutes, and fetter'd to the soil;
> Weigh'd in a tyrant's balance with his gold?
> No!—Nature stamp'd us in a heav'nly mould!
> She bade no wretch his thankless labour urge,
> Nor, trembling, take the pittance and the scourge!
> No homeless Libyan, on the stormy deep,
> To call upon his country's name, and weep!—[18]

Campbell's sonnet is, like Wheatley's, composed of seven rhymed couplets, and it features syncope in nearly every line. The speaker asks the
Creator, "Eternal Nature," what inspired slavery? Before giving Nature
the chance to answer, the speaker responds "No!"—slavery is unnatural.
No political action is described or advocated beyond weeping. Campbell's
sonnet demands a focus on the literal meaning of the conventional metaphors, "chains," "yok'd," and "fetter'd," but does not belabor the political
importance of this demand as a matter of sonnet history. There is little
change of perspective or doubt—the first nine lines ask who "formed"
the slaves, but the final five don't address the question directly. In the
context of the African American sonnet tradition, it is a missed opportunity.

The most widely anthologized antislavery sonnet of the period is
Wordsworth's "To Toussaint L'Ouverture" (1802), which comes close to
praising slave insurrection but turns rather to praising its subject for
providing the author with a heroic subject for a memorial sonnet:

> Toussaint, the most unhappy man of men!
> Whether the whistling Rustic tend his plough
> Within thy hearing, or thy head be now
> Pillowed in some deep dungeon's earless den;—
> O miserable Chieftain! where and when
> Wilt thou find patience? Yet die not; do thou
> Wear rather in thy bonds a cheerful brow:
> Though fallen thyself, never to rise again,
> Live, and take comfort. Thou hast left behind
> Powers that will work for thee; air, earth, and skies;
> There's not a breathing of the common wind
> That will forget thee; thou hast great allies;
> Thy friends are exultations, agonies,
> And love, and man's unconquerable mind.[19]

Wordsworth, like Shakespeare, uses the sonnet to ensure immortality
for the leader of the rebellion and for all who remember him (including
the poetic speaker). Wordsworth wrote and published the sonnet while
Toussaint was an imprisoned romantic hero to abolitionists. The sonnet's
rhyme scheme is Petrarchan, but the volta is elusive, beginning half-
way through the ninth line with "Thou hast left behind / Powers that will
work for thee." What the speaker seems hesitant to say is that the power
left behind to work for Toussaint is the poet himself. Toussaint should

"[w]ear rather in thy bonds a cheerful brow," because of his legacy. The final rhyme is an eye rhyme (wind/mind), precluding a sense of satisfactory resolution. Liberation is coming, the "common wind" will not forget the insurrection, and never will readers will forget Wordsworth's sonnet (which nearly always appears in biographies of Toussaint).

Wordsworth's closing phrase, "man's unconquerable mind," was echoed in 1830 by the prominent American abolitionist and newspaper editor William Lloyd Garrison, whose sonnet "Freedom of Mind" (variously titled "The Free Mind" and "Freedom for the Mind") circulated widely in the antislavery press and in poetry anthologies before and after the Civil War. Garrison, then editor of *Genius of Universal Emancipation*, wrote the sonnet while serving six months in a Baltimore prison during 1826–1827 for libel after claiming that the ship *Francis* was engaging in "domestic piracy" for carrying slaves from Baltimore to New Orleans:

> High walls and huge the body may confine,
> And iron grates obstruct the prisoner's gaze,
> And massive bolts may baffle his design,
> And vigilant keepers watch his devious ways:
> Yet scorns the immortal mind this base control!
> No chains can bind it, and no cell enclose:
> Swifter than light, it flies from pole to pole,
> And, in a flash, from earth to heaven it goes!
> It leaps from mount to mount—from vale to vale
> It wanders, plucking honeyed fruits and flowers;
> It visits home, to hear the fireside tale,
> Or in sweet converse pass the joyous hours.
> 'Tis up before the sun, roaming afar,
> And, in its watches, wearies every star![20]

A Shakespearean sonnet, Garrison's poem scornfully resists the confining iambic pentameter. In phrases such as "devious ways," "swifter than light," "And, in a flash," and "roaming afar," an extra syllable leaps and wanders, even while the end rhymes are conforming and closed. "It," the immoral mind as named in the fifth line, cannot be chained, cannot be bound: "it" flies, leaps, wanders, returns home, and roams again. "Freedom of Mind" also recalls Wordsworth's "Nuns Fret Not," although it is less overtly concerned with the sonnet form per se than with the freedom that can be demonstrated by playful syllables. "Freedom of Mind" is not self-questioning; there is no change in perspective. Garrison included

"Freedom of Mind" and another popular abolitionist sonnet, "The Kneeling Slave," in a collected volume, *Sonnets and Other Poems*, in 1843, which was reviewed positively by Emerson.[21]

The influence of sonnets by Southey, Wordsworth, Campbell, and Garrison can be inferred in part by their circulation by antislavery advocates in the pages of American abolitionist newspapers that emerged in the 1820s. The opportunity to publish and republish protest literature is a critical development in the evolution of the African American poetry tradition and the slowly emerging sonnet tradition. *Freedom's Journal*, the first and oldest African American newspaper, was published from 1827 to 1829 in New York and enjoyed a wide readership in nearly a dozen states as well as Canada, Haiti, and England. The editors, Samuel Cornish and John Russwurm, were both educated free black men, active in both literary and political circles that included poets, novelists, and journalists such as John Greenleaf Whittier, Lydia Maria Child, and William Wells Brown. Cornish had attended the Free African School in Philadelphia and trained to become a Presbyterian minister; he moved to New York to found the city's first black Presbyterian church and became a leader of a growing free black community there. Russwurm was born in Jamaica of mixed-race parentage (his mother was enslaved) and grew up in Maine, where he attended Hebron Academy and later became the first African American graduate of Bowdoin College. Cornish and Russwurm wrote, worked, and socialized in an educated, literary New York abolitionist community that freely exchanged written work across the color line.

Freedom's Journal published several sonnets in its first year. The May 25, 1827, edition features a translation of the seventeenth-century Italian poet Vincenzo da Filicaja's famous "Sonnet":

> See a fond mother, and her young ones round,
> Her soul soft melting with maternal love,
> Some to her breast she clasps, and others prove
> By kisses her affection: on the ground
> Her ready foot affords a rest for one,
> Another smiling sits upon her knee;
> By their desiring eyes, and actions free,
> And lisping words their little wants are known:
> To those she gives a look, a frown to these,
> But all is love. Thus awful Providence
> Watches and helps us:—oft denies our sense
> But to invite more earnest prayer and praise;

> Or seeming to deny what we implore,
> In that refusal gives a blessing more.

Filicaja's "Sonnet" was republished in journals and Christian publications in America frequently in the eighteenth and early nineteenth centuries.[22] With its clear octave celebrating the fond mother and its sestet comparing her to "awful Providence" who often denies prayers, this ode resonated with abolitionist concerns for the brutal treatment of slave mothers, central to provoking moral outrage in white female readers. Filicaja's sonnet can be seen as an antecedent to the work of Frances Ellen Watkins Harper, who drew on the image of the slave mother torn from her children in her poetry but did not write sonnets.

The September 5, 1828, edition of *Freedom's Journal* features a sonnet written by "Arion," the pen name of an African American writer who was another frequent contributor, titled "Sonnet—To the Housatonic":

> Dear native river, I am on thy shore—
> When 'erst I wander'd in youth's joyous days,
> And with what rapture, he, who gaz'd before,
> In after years reviews again thy ways,
> Thy sweeping elms, each lofty sycamore
> In whose broad shade he stole from Phoebus' rays.
> Ah! might he live the dear scenes sweetly o'er
> Press'd to the heart of one, the lip of praise—
> But no, he may not. Memory no more
> Pierce the dim vista with thy glim'ring rays
> He sees, but still each scene he must deplore;
> They're gone forever from the heart they mov'd;
> Aye, all that could the tone of bliss restore
> The theme of his bright dreams, his soul's belov'd.

This sonnet to the Housatonic—a river in western Massachusetts and Connecticut, near Great Barrington, the birthplace of W. E. B. Du Bois—sits within a tradition of sonnets to rivers such as Sir Philip Sidney's "Oh Happy Thames" (1580) and Michael Drayton's Sonnet 32, "Our Flood's-Queen Thames" (1753). Arion's sonnet is well crafted, featuring a tight, if unorthodox, rhyme scheme: eleven lines of alternating rhyme followed by a new rhyme separated by the B rhyme. Syncope is required in a handful of lines. There is a clear change in perspective at line 9: the speaker recalls for the first eight lines the sweet beauty of his native river but for the last six lines laments he can no longer enjoy (and "must deplore") these scenes. The race of the poetic speaker is not apparent. The poem might be grouped with American verses about the Hudson River, the Ohio River, and the Mississippi; Du Bois praised his childhood river by name in "Reflections upon the Housatonic River."[23] The reason Arion chose the sonnet form is not readily apparent, but its appearance in an African American newspaper is worth noting, perhaps simply as the first African American poem to speak of rivers.

Freedom's Journal's editors were prominent supporters of literacy as well as abolition. In 1833 Cornish cofounded the Anti-Slavery Society with Arthur and Lewis Tappan, Garrison, and Theodore Weld. Leaders soon included literary figures such as Child and Lucretia Mott, educator, feminist, and one of the founders of Swarthmore College. In 1836 the Anti-Slavery Society began publishing an annual antislavery *Almanac* that featured poetry, stories, and illustrations designed to promote opposition to slavery. The abolitionist community in America over the next two decades would include some of the country's best-known literary figures: Emerson (who was both the author and subject of numerous sonnets), Thoreau (who attempted sonnets), Harriet Beecher Stowe, and Frederick Douglass. Garrison founded the antislavery newspaper the *Liberator* (1831–1865); Douglass founded the *North Star* (1847–1851, later *Frederick Douglass's Paper*, 1851–1855), and Gamaliel Bailey founded the *National Era* (1847–1860). These publications published and encouraged black poets and, in providing a writing community that engaged with a transatlantic literary tradition, were crucial to a growing sonnet consciousness among black authors.

In 1833 Cornish helped found the Phoenix Society of New York, dedicated to the theory "that the 'condition' of African Americans could 'only be meliorated by their being improved in morals, literature, and mechanic arts.'"[24] The goal of the Phoenix Society was to educate New York City's black population and instill habits of reading and reflection. The Phoenix Society was short lived, but several others, including the Phoenixonian Society, emerged to continue the project of education through reading, lectures, and debates. The Minor's Exhibition Society in Boston was specifically founded "for the laudable purpose of improving [young black people's] minds by committing to memory and reciting select articles of prose and poetry."[25] These efforts too were key to familiarizing a new generation of black poets with the sonnet form.

Freedom's Journal folded in 1829, but after establishing the Anti-Slavery Society, Cornish returned to journalism to found the *Colored*

American, a weekly newspaper that ran from 1836 to 1842. One of his co-editors was Charles Bennett Ray, an educated free black man from Connecticut who was admitted to Wesleyan University in 1832 but was told to leave two months later after white students protested. Charles Ray's daughter, Henrietta Cordelia Ray, would publish the first volume of sonnets by an African American poet. Cornish and Ray published poetry regularly in the pages of the *Colored American*. The November 28, 1840, edition featured a sonnet by "C.L.R.," the initials of Charles Lewis Reason, an African American abolitionist, educator, poet, and mathematician who was also known as C. L. Reason.[26] Little is known of his private life beyond the fact that he was married three times.[27] Reason's "Sonnet" may be the second of three sonnets (Wheatley's is the first) to be published by a named African American author before the Civil War:

> 'Tis not the flower which brightest hues adorn,
> That proves most cherish'd mid the gifts of spring;
> Or fondly prized, because in rich earth born
> And rarely shaped, that chariest perfumes bring.
> 'Tis not the bird who proudly mounts high air,
> That most is welcom'd when the warm days fell;
> Or deck'd in colors, glittering, soft, or rare,
> That sings most sweetly when the light winds call.
> E'en so, the cheek may glow with sunset light,
> And grace sit twined around each falling tress;
> "The eye may speak with glances sparkling bright,"
> The lip be form'd too pure for our caress;
> And yet, in such fair form, the soul may be
> Devoid of fragrance, or of melody.

Reason's "Sonnet" features a Shakespearean rhyme scheme requiring syncope and apheresis ("'Tis") and evokes Shakespeare's Sonnet 30, "My mistress' eyes are nothing like the sun," a parody of the Petrarchan sonnet's tribute to ideal beauty. Reason's speaker proposes that the most beautiful woman (the brightest flower, rarely shaped, decked in glittering colors) may not be the most cherished and may not sing the sweetest. However glowing her cheek and bright her eye, the most beautiful woman may contain a soul "devoid of fragrance, or of melody." While the poem is not racialized, the twelfth line, describing lips "form'd too pure for our caress," offers itself to a racial reading, given the first-person plural use of "our." The speaker implicitly prefers a woman who sings in warm weather, not a proud, well-dressed woman who is too pure. The speaker privileges smell and sound over sight, song and perfume over bright colors. It is a good sonnet.

The editors preface Reason's poem by praising both the author and the sonnet: "The following beautiful strains are the musings of an esteemed young friend and fellow laborer in the cause for the improvement of our people....We shall be glad to have our paper adorned with such thoughts, especially when they come in this condensed form." Reason may have published other sonnets, but none have yet been rediscovered; most of his poetic works are not collected or anthologized. Reason was an admirer of Wordsworth and Milton, as an article in the *Colored American*, covering a meeting of the Phoenixonian Society in July 1839, reports:

> The character which he gave of Wordsworth as a poet of the highest order, we believe was not overwrought, and the comparison which he instituted between Milton, the Homer of Britain, and the subject of his dissertation, was well sustained, and the judicious selections of the sublime and beautiful taken from each, and compared, showed clearly that Wordsworth was possessed of as creative a fancy, and of as sublime conceptions, as the illustrious author of *Paradise Lost*. We must readily say, that although we have always admired and loved Wordsworth, for the high-toned moral feeling, the impassioned sentiment and poetical eloquence which breathe throughout his poetry, yet after we heard the dissertation by our young friend and schoolmate, we must confess that we now love the bard more, and hereafter will read him more, and more attentively.[28]

Works by Milton and Wordsworth circulated widely even if poets were not yet drawing on the political possibilities of the sonnet form that they modeled.

The third antebellum sonnet published by a named African American poet is a single fourteen-line poem by George Moses Horton, "Eulogy," in 1845. Horton, born a slave in North Carolina in 1797, was a talented, self-taught poet who began his career writing verses for college students at the University of North Carolina who recognized his facility with poetical turns of phrase. Students would commission poems (often acrostics on the names of young women) in exchange for money or occasionally volumes or poetry by Shakespeare and Keats. Horton could not read until late in life; he recited poems aloud that he had composed at the plow, as a slave, and memorized. While many of these early poems were lost, with the help of novelist Caroline Lee Whiting Hentz (for whom Horton penned his sonnet), Horton began publishing his poems in newspapers.

The poem "Slavery and Liberty" appeared in the *Lancaster Gazette* (April 8, 1829); "Slavery" appeared in *Freedom's Journal* (July 18, 1828) and was republished by William Lloyd Garrison in the *Liberator* (March 19, 1834). In 1845 Horton published a collection of his works, *The Poetical Works of George M. Horton*, in which "Eulogy" appears, introduced as follows:

> To the much distinguished Mrs. Hentz of Boston, I owe much for the correction of many poetical errors. Being a professional poetess herself, and a lover of genius, she discovered my little uncultivated talent, and was moved by pity to uncover to me the beauties of correctness, together with the true importance of the object to which I aspired....In gratitude for all these favors, by which she attempted to supply and augment the stock of servile genius, I inscribe to her the following:
>
> > Deep on thy pillar, thou immortal dame,
> > Trace the inscription of eternal fame;
> > For bards unborn must yet thy works adore,
> > And bid thee live when others are no more.
> > When other names are lost among the dead,
> > Some genius yet may live thy fame to spread;
> > Memory's fair bush shall not decline to bloom,
> > But flourish fresh upon thy sacred tomb.
> > When nature's crown refuses to be gay,
> > And ceaseless streams have worn their rocks away;
> > When age's veil shall beauty's visage mask
> > And bid oblivion blot the poet's task,
> > Time's final shock shall elevate thy name,
> > And lift thee smiling to eternal fame.[29]

Horton's "Eulogy" is composed of seven couplets and offers a slight change of perspective with the ninth line, which begins with the word "When." The first eight lines suggest that the "immortal dame" will always be famous for the poetic geniuses she inspired; the last six reinforce that this fame will last until the end of time. The final couplet of "Eulogy" evokes Shakespeare's sonnets on the passage of time and the decay of physical beauty to be rendered immortal by the poet's pen.

Enslaved most of his life, Horton read as widely as he was able; in addition to his known favorites, Shakespeare and Keats, his library included works by Byron, Milton, and James Thompson ("Seasons"). He memorized and recited often Campbell's sentimental sonnet, "The Pleasures of Hope."[30] Horton might have hoped that Hentz's patronage indicated abolitionist leanings; unfortunately, Hentz's last novel, *The Planter's*

Northern Bride (1854), was a robust proslavery response to Stowe's *Uncle Tom's Cabin*.[31]

While Horton's poetry was not influential, the abolitionist literary community claimed Horton as an important slave poet, the first since Wheatley and the first to address slavery directly. In an 1848 essay on Horton for the *National Era*, "The Slave Poet of North Carolina," John Greenleaf Whittier (published under J. G. W.) emphasizes Horton's place in the poetic tradition of antislavery poets. Whittier strives to situate Horton in a poetic tradition that includes Milton and the Cuban sonnet writer Placido; for Whittier, Horton might have been capable of greatness if he had not had to labor as a slave:

> Something of that inspiration of genius which enabled Haydn to hear the choral harmonies of the Creation—the songs of the morning stars, and the rejoicing of the sons of God—seems to have struggled in the breast of the poor negro rhymer.…Who can say that the glorious natural gifts of Burns, or Milton, would have shone forth more brightly than that of poor George, if, like him, these world renowned masters of song had been born the chattel slave of a Carolina planter!

Whittier's measure of worth is emotional resonance, not technical skill, although the suggestion is that he might have written more sonnets. Perhaps some from Horton's early years are lost. None beyond "Eulogy" appear in his published work.[32]

More influential was the Cuban revolutionary Gabriel de la Concepción Valdes, known as Placido. Accused of inciting a slave revolt, Placido and his compatriots were executed in Cuba by firing squad on June 28, 1844. Placido's sonnets circulated widely in Cuba and among poets at the time, and his work gathered increasing acclaim after his death. The sonnet "Farewell to My Mother" was written in prison while Placido was awaiting his trial. In 1849 William Cullen Bryant published a translation of the sonnet in a long essay, "The Poetry of Spanish America":[33]

> The appointed lot has come upon me, mother,
> The mournful ending of my years of strife,
> This changing world I leave, and to another
> In blood and terror goes my spirit's life.
> But thou, grief-smitten, cease thy mortal weeping
> And let thy soul her wonted peace regain;
> I fall for right, and thoughts of thee are sweeping
> Across my lyre to wake its dying strains.

> A strain of joy and gladness, free, unfailing
> All glorious and holy, pure, divine,
> And innocent, unconscious as the wailing
> I uttered on my birth; and I resign
> Even now, my life, even now descending slowly,
> Faith's mantle folds me to my slumbers holy.
> Mother, farewell! God keep thee—and forever!

In dramatic detail, Bryant tells the story of the self-educated Placido, "born to humble parents," triumphing over obstacles and deficiencies "to assume the higher parts of a hero and martyr":

> He passed through the streets with the air of a conqueror, walking with a serene face and an unwavering step, and chanting his "Prayer" with a calm, clear, voice. When they reached the Plaza, he addressed his companions with words of brave and effectual consolation, and made all his preparations with undisturbed composure. He was to suffer first; and when the signal was given, he stepped into the square, and knelt with unbandaged eyes before the file of soldiers who were to execute the sentence. When the smoke of the first volley rolled away, it was seen that he had merely been wounded in the shoulder, and had fallen forward bleeding and agonized...but Placido, still self-possessed, slowly recovered his knees, and drawing up his form to its greatest height, exclaimed, in a broken voice, "Farewell, world, ever pitiless to me! Fire—here!" raising his hand to his temples. The last tones of his voice were lost in the report of the muskets, this time more mercifully aimed.[34]

Bryant's translation of Placido's sonnet and description of his death were popular in British and American abolitionist circles.[35] But for Bryant, Placido "erred" in participating in a violent insurrection rather than simply using his poetic voice: "[W]e rejoice that he was saved from the horrors of a sanguinary triumph [and] we most earnestly desire that his heroic spirit may animate other more far-seeing friends of liberty to use means as stainless as their ends with courage and constancy like his."[36]

Demonstrating the long-standing influence of Placido's sonnet, seventy years later James Weldon Johnson critiqued Bryant's translation in the preface to the *Book of American Negro Poetry* (1922):

> Placido's sonnet to his mother has been translated into every important language; William Cullen Bryant did it in English; but in spite of its wide popularity, it is, perhaps, outside of Cuba the least understood of all Placido's poems. It is curious to note how Bryant's translation totally misses the intimate sense of the delicate subtlety of the poem. The

American poet makes it a tender and loving farewell of a son who is about to die to a heart-broken mother; but that is not the kind of a farewell that Placido intended to write or did write.

The key to the poem is in the first word, and the first word is the Spanish conjunction *Si* (if). The central idea, then, of the sonnet is, "If the sad fate which now overwhelms me should bring a pang to your heart, do not weep, for I die a glorious death and sound the last note of my lyre to you." Bryant either failed to understand or ignored the opening word, "If," because he was not familiar with the poet's history.[37]

Placido's mother was a white woman who abandoned him, Johnson emphasizes. Placido's poem to her, under the circumstances, does not mean what Bryant suggests. The opening "If" creates a tension in the octave (composed of one sentence) that does not occur in Bryant's translation (composed of two sentences):

> (Written in the chapel of the Hospital de Santa
> Cristina on the night before his execution)

> If the unfortunate fate engulfing me,
> The ending of my history of grief,
> The closing of my span of years so brief,
> Mother, should wake a single pang in thee,
> Weep not. No saddening thought to me devote;
> I calmly go to a death that is glory-filled,
> My lyre before it is forever stilled
> Breathes out to thee its last and dying note.
> A note scarce more than a burden-easing sigh,
> Tender and sacred, innocent, sincere—
> Spontaneous and instinctive as the cry
> I gave at birth—And now the hour is here—
> O God, thy mantle of mercy o'er my sins!
> Mother, farewell! The pilgrimage begins.

The attention to Bryant's translation of Placido's sonnet in Johnson's foundational anthology signals the importance of the sonnet for black poetry in 1922. The example of Placido ensured that the sonnet's political potential would be carried through generations of African American poets.

But in the mid-nineteenth century, the scarcity of strong African American poetic voices in the antebellum era was lamented in contemporary newspaper accounts. In 1847, a year before Whittier's essay on Horton, the anonymous writer of "Alexander Pushkin" in the *National Era* complains:

With our feet on the neck of the black man, we have taunted him with his inferiority; shutting him out from school and college, we have denied his capacity for intellectual progress; spurning him from the meeting house and church communion, we have reproached him as vicious, and incapable of moral elevation....With such examples of the intellectual capacity of the colored man as are afforded by L'Overture and Petion, of Hayti; Dumas, of France; Pushkin, of Russia; and Placido, the slave poet and martyr of Cuba, to say nothing of such men as James McCune Smith, Frederick Douglass, Henry H. Garnett, and Henry Bibb, in our own country, it is scarcely in good taste for white mediocrity to taunt the colored man with natural inferiority.

Whittier overlooks the poet James Monroe Whitfield, born free in New Hampshire and well known in the abolitionist community. Whitfield wrote almost entirely in tetrameter and did not write any sonnets. However, his 160-line "America" (1853) features one 14-line sentence (lines 23–36) that evokes a sonnet within the poem.[38]

When black and white fought side by side,
    Upon the well-contested field,—
Turned back the fierce opposing tide,
    And made the proud invader yield—
When, wounded, side by side they lay,
    And heard with joy the proud hurrah
From their victorious comrades say
    That they had waged successful war,
The thought ne'er entered in their brains
    That they endured those toils and pains,
To forge fresh fetters, heavier chains
    For their own children, in whose veins
Should flow that patriotic blood,
    So freely shed on field and flood.

The fourteen-line sentence captures the rage of Whitfield's entire poem. His sense of a volta in the ninth line—the turning from two quatrains of alternating rhyme to three couplets—puts weight on the devastating second half of the sentence, the fury that the descendants of black Revolutionary War soldiers would become slaves. Whitfield's performance of two perspectives, the black ancestors who fought for freedom and the speaker who sees their children now in chains, demonstrates an understanding of the sonnet's potential. Whitfield's work is a precursor to the fiery sonnets of McKay in the first decades of the twentieth century.

Still, the scarcity of African American poetic voices was regularly lamented in the black press. A lawyer using the pseudonym "Dion" lamented in *Frederick Douglass's Paper* on September 23, 1853, that "the name of no colored American has as yet been blazoned upon its rolls of heraldry":

> Our Prescotts, and Bancrofts, our Coopers and Hawthorns, our Bryants and Whittiers, all belong, by birth and complexion, to that race which so arrogantly claims for itself an intellectual superiority, and assigns to its darker hued compatriots a lower rank in the scale of mental being....The lines of the poet, Gray, with a few slight alterations, are unfortunately but too applicable to colored men, who, by the dispensations of Providence, have found a place within the limits of this country. Our Miltons are all "mute and inglorious."...A Wheatley indeed, may have sung in brief, yet admirable snatches, while in her chains; a Horton may have caused the dark wall of his prison house to echo to notes so sublime as almost to persuade surrounding lordlings to grant him freedom.[39]

Sadly, the writer observes, "colored American literature exists only, to too great an extent, in the vast realm of probability." The allusion to Thomas Gray's 1751 "Elegy Written in a Country Churchyard" ("some mute, inglorious Milton") will become a trope in African American sonnets in the late nineteenth and early twentieth centuries, as evidenced by George McClellan's "A January Dandelion" (1895):

> All Nashville is a chill. And everywhere
> Like desert sand, when the winds blow,
> There is each moment sifted through the air,
> A powdered blast of January snow.
> O! thoughtless Dandelion, to be misled
> By a few warm days to leave thy natural bed,
> Was folly growth and blooming over soon.
> And yet, thou blasted yellow-coated gem,
> Full many a heart has but a common boon
> With thee, now freezing on thy slender stem.
> When the heart has bloomed by the touch of love's warm breath
> Then left and chilling snow is sifted in,
> It still may beat but there is blast and death
> To all that blooming life that might have been.[40]

McClellan's sonnet begins with a description of a winter day in the American South, with powdery January snow blowing like desert sand. The speaker turns to address a dandelion that bloomed too early and is now freezing; the flower should be comforted that others too have bloomed by the warmth of love but are chilled when love is gone. The ninth line alludes to Gray's "Elegy": "Full many a gem of purest ray serene, / The dark unfathomed caves of ocean bear: / Full many a flower is born to blush unseen, / And waste its sweetness on the desert air" (lines 53–56). McClellan's allusion suggests the universality of Grey's lament to include the chill of Nashville. The sonnet form allows an ambivalence about whether the poem's subject is a dandelion, a person, or a race.

Lamenting the silencing of black poetic voices will continue as a theme of black poetry into the twentieth century. African American sonnet writers will continue to be influenced by the Shakespearean sonnet's preoccupation with immortality. But black protest sonnets in the Petrarchan and Miltonic tradition did not appear until Dunbar, even with the new English translations of Dante and Michelangelo circulating in Boston in the second half of the nineteenth century, influencing writers such as Emerson, Garrison, James Russell Lowell, and Charles Eliot Norton. Few political protest sonnets in the manner of Milton or Shelley by white American poets are to be found.[41] In fact, few American sonnets on war appear in the nineteenth century. A comprehensive anthology of Civil War poetry published in 1896 includes only three sonnets out of nearly two hundred poems (all by white poets).[42] A more recent anthology of Civil War poetry includes only two sonnets, both by Dunbar, both written in the twentieth century.[43]

Frances Watkins Harper, one of the most prolific African American poets of the nineteenth century, did not publish any sonnets. Harper's fervent abolitionist poetry might be characterized as concerned with the suffering of slaves but not with suffering as a historical or universal phenomenon that would lend itself to the sonnet form. Little of Harper's verse can be characterized as "timeless." Harper's poetry is almost entirely sentimental verse in iambic tetrameter, rather than pentameter. Some of her postwar poetry involves dialect and unorthodox spelling ("Mistus" for "Mistress"), which also serves to locate her work in the particular geography of the South rather than in a universal tradition.

Meredith McGill offers an account of Harper's 1866 Philadelphia lecture by antislavery activist Grace Greenwood:

> The woe of two hundred years sighed through her tones. Every glance of her sad eyes was a mournful remonstrance against injustice and

wrong. Feeling on her soul, as she must have felt it, the chilling weight of caste she seemed to say: "I lift my heavy heart up solemnly, / As once Electra her sepulchral urn." As I listened to her, there swept over me, in a chill wave of horror, the realization that this noble woman had she not been rescued from her mother's condition, might have been sold on the auction-block, to the highest bidder.[44]

Greenwood quotes extemporaneously from Elizabeth Barrett Browning's Sonnet 5, "I lift my heavy heart up solemnly," from *Sonnets from the Portuguese* (1850), indicating her familiarity with the popular sonnets. Barrett Browning was raised among the enslaved on a sugar plantation in Jamaica, and at least one scholar has suggested that the poet was of mixed race.[45] Barrett Browning was known to be dark complexioned ("I am little and black")[46] and had published "The Runaway Slave at Pilgrim's Point" in the abolitionist collection *The Liberty Bell* (1848). Nearly eighty years later, Charles S. Johnson included "The Runaway Slave" in his collection *Ebony and Topaz* (1927), with an illustration by Charles Cullen, demonstrating Barrett Browning's continued influence on African American poetry. Reaching for Barrett Browning's sonnet about love and grief to capture "the woe of two hundred years" suggests that Greenwood apprehended the sonnet's appropriateness for what Harper "seemed to say" but never did.

During the first years of Reconstruction, some of the most prestigious of the new black colleges and universities, including Fisk University, Howard University, Morehouse College, Morgan State University, and Tougaloo College, were founded to educate newly emancipated slaves and their children, producing teachers and theologians. By the late 1870s and 1880s these colleges (as well as Wilberforce University, founded in 1856, and Hampton Institute, founded in 1868) were beginning to graduate a first and occasionally a second generation of African American writers.[47] Scores of new regional black newspapers were established across the country in the last quarter of the nineteenth century, dedicated to publishing the work of black writers and critics. Literacy and the increasing opportunity to read about black life across the country provoked new interest in literature and poetry by and about African Americans. Looking back at the era, John T. Morris writes in the *A.M.E. Church Review*, "The sphere of Negro literature rapidly broadens as the means for literary attainments become more accessible, and a greater opportunity is afforded for extending our literary researches. The Negro press is the bulwark of our success, a focus of race thought, ability and accomplishments; in it lies our history and rapid development, our power and position in the nation."[48] In 1870, Morris noted, there had been 16 journals in circulation; by 1880, there were 36; by 1890, 118. The average circulation was about three thousand. During the same era, women's groups in New York City and Chicago, such as the National Association of Colored Women, the Women's Era Club, and the Women's Loyal Union, were founded to promote literacy and literary race consciousness among new arrivals in the North.[49]

Brilliant literary success was not immediate, however. Despite the gains in education and opportunities for publication, the years from 1866 to 1877, during which "hopes for racial equality" were raised and dashed, were, as Sherman argues, "unfruitful for black poetry and black culture generally." And though, as Sherman adds, the African American poetry of the era was "American in subject, versification, and attitude," reflecting and responding to the political and cultural events of the day, a debate emerged about the nature of the African American poetic voice.[50] How should the black poet speak, and about what? Loggins calls the era "the determining period in the history of American Negro literature," and the goal was to show evidence of middle-class respectability.[51] Assessing the unprecedented burst of literary activity after the collapse of Reconstruction, Dickson Bruce sees traditions forming along two distinct lines of development through the 1910s.[52] The first main line includes the formal, conservative, and "genteel" works (novels, essays, poetry) promoting literary achievement and registering racial "improvement."[53] The second line is vernacular verse in "Negro dialect."

The decades after the Civil War, from Reconstruction to the Gilded Age, as Mark Twain and Charles Dudley Warner called it, were not particularly brilliant years for American literary achievement generally. The "genteel" literature and philosophy of the era is thin, pale, sterile, decorous, pious, and quaint.[54] A small number of influential works appeared, including Louisa May Alcott's *Little Women* (1868), Bret Harte's *The Luck of Roaring Camp and Other Sketches* (1870), Henry James's *The Europeans* and *Daisy Miller* (1878, 1879), Joel Chandler Harris's *Uncle Remus* (1881), Helen Hunt Jackson's *Ramona* (1884), Mark Twain's *Huckleberry Finn* (1884), William Dean Howells's *The Rise of Simon Lapham* (1885), and Emily Dickinson's *Poems* (1890). But with the great exception of Dickinson, some late Walt Whitman editions of *Leaves of Grass*, and perhaps Herman Melville's epic *Clarel*, the poetry of the era is not remarkable.

In the Boston literary marketplace, the "official custodian of the genteel in letters" was Thomas Bailey Aldrich, editor from 1881 to 1890 of the *Atlantic Monthly*, the most important literary magazine of the era. The *Atlantic's* embrace of gentility under Aldrich had wide-ranging political effects, Parrington notes: "[I]t had become the refuge of a stale mentality, emptied of all ideas save beauty, and that beauty became cold and anemic. Its taboos were no more than cushions for tired and lazy minds. The idea of morality—with its corollary of reticence…became empty conventions, cut off from reality…a refuge for respectability, a barricade against the intrusion of the unpleasant."[55] Ellery Sedgwick adds that in regard to poetry specifically, Aldrich's taste was conservative:

> He loathed all of dialect poetry becoming popular at the time as a degradation of the art. He held a mortal prejudice against the Shakespearean form of the sonnet, was unsparing in counting metrical cadences…his aesthetic values mirrored his conservative social values. He worked to maintain a literary style above what he considered debased popular usage and forms and felt a rather pessimistic anxiety about defending waning linguistic and literary traditions against the threatening tide of vulgar mass culture.[56]

It is difficult to determine what Aldrich was *for*; indeed, despite his dislike of dialect poetry (and strong views on racial inferiority), the *Atlantic* published Chesnutt's humorous "conjure stories" in the late 1880s, ignorant of the race of the author,[57] as well as sonnets such as Longfellow's "Wapentake, A poem for Alfred Tennyson" in 1877 and Harriet Monroe's early, genteel "To W.S.M, With a copy of Shelley" in 1889.

Yet remarkably, William Stanley Braithwaite paid tribute to Aldrich on his passing in 1907 with a double (Petrarchan) sonnet, "On the Death of Thomas Bailey Aldrich":

> What sudden bird will bring us any cheer
> Whose song in the chill dawn gives hope of Spring;
> Can we be glad to give it welcoming
> Though April in its music be so near?
> Not while the burden of our memories bear
> The weight of silence that we know will cling
> About the lips that nevermore will sing
> The heart of him with visions voiced so clear.
> There is a pause in meeting before speech
> Between men who have fed their souls with song;
> The strangeness of an echo beyond reach

Cleaves silence deep for speech to pass along.
There are no words to tell the loss, but each
Of our hearts feels the sorrow deep and strong.

The Wondersmith in vocables is dead!
The Builder of the palaces of rhyme
Shall build no more his music out of Time.
In the deep, breathless peace to which he fled
He sits with Landor's hands upon his head
Watching our suns and stars that sink and climb
Between him and our tears' continuous chime—
Sorrowing for his presence vanishèd.
Aldrich is dead! but the glory of his life
Is in his song, and this will keep his name
Safe above change and the assaults of strife.
Poet, whose artistry, his constant aim
Kept true above defections that were rife,
Death taking him, still leaves his deathless fame.[58]

Published in his second collection of poetry, *The House of Falling Leaves and Other Poems* (1908), Braithwaite's sonnet evinces no real politics and no apparent self-questioning. It simply memorializes. Braithwaite's poems are not overtly racial; James Weldon Johnson deemed them simply "lyrics of delicate and tenuous beauty."[59]

The African American middle class in the 1870s and 1880s was made up of ministers, teachers, doctors, lawyers, and businessmen interested in prosperity and upward mobility. As a matter of education and economics, a rising middle class is generally attended by an impulse to conform to dominant middle-class expectations. Widespread ideas of a deep connection to Africa would not emerge for decades; the era's literary output was almost entirely within the respectable American mainstream.[60] Much of the work of the era appeared in journals such as the *A.M.E. Church Review*, which began publishing in 1884.

The representative traditionalist African American poet of the era is Albery Allson Whitman, who was singled out by Johnson for poetry distinguished by "not only the greatest imagination but also...skillful workmanship"[61] but dismissed by George M. McClellan as "the William Cullen Bryant of the Negro Race."[62] Albery Whitman, who was born a slave, advocated the American model of self-reliance and success, concerned largely with psychological resistance to racism and in literature's role in providing opportunities to transcend racism, if only momentar-

ily. He attended Wilberforce University (but did not graduate), studied
with Bishop Daniel Payne, joined the AME church, dedicated his life to the
ministry, and published three important books of poetry: *Not a Man and
Yet a Man* (1877), *The Rape of Florida* (1884), and *An Idyl of the South* (1891),
as well as stories, essays, and dramas. Bruce observes that for Whitman, writing poetry provided "an opportunity to experience psychological freedom, even in the face of the worst racial oppression."[63] Whitman
sought to put slavery behind him, as he states in the preface to *The Rape of
Florida*:

> I am a colored man, and as such, I accept the situation, and enter the
> lists with poised lance. I disdain to whine over my "previous condition."
> I despise the doctrine of the slave's allowance. Petition and complaint
> are the language of imbecility and cowardice—the evidences of that
> puerile fear which distinguishes the Soul. The time has come when all
> "Uncle Toms" and "Topsies" ought to die.[64]

Whitman casts himself as a medieval knight jousting in the lists, or perhaps as a fictional portrayal from Walter Scott's *Ivanhoe*. Whitman's attention to literary form was a matter of both his conservatism and his
aesthetic sensibility: what better way to transcend slavery and per-
form cultural refinement than to craft poetry in sonnets and Spenserian stanzas, "as near reproducing the sonorousness of Byron's *Childe
Harolde* as anyone else has ever come."[65] His 251-stanza epic appropriates the form and elevated diction of Elizabethan verse to voice an African American response to contemporary white racism. Consider the
opening stanzas:

> The negro slave by Swanee river sang;
> Well-pleased he listened to his echoes ringing;
> For in his heart a secret comfort sprang,
> When Nature seemed to join his mournful singing.
> To mem'ry's cherished objects fondly clinging;
> His bosom felt the sunset's patient glow,
> And spirit whispers into weird life springing,
> Allured to worlds he trusted yet to know,
> And lightened for a while life's burdens here below.
>
> The drowsy dawn from many a low-built shed,
> Beheld his kindred driven to their task;
> Late evening saw them turn with weary tread
> And painful faces back: and dost thou ask

How sang these bondmen? how their suff'rings mask?
Song is the soul of sympathy divine,
And hath an inner ray where hope may bask;
Song turns the humblest waters into wine,
Illumines exile hearts and makes their faces shine.

Whitman understands the nature of the Spenserian stanza: eight lines of iambic pentameter with a strict rhyme scheme (ABABBCBC) with a ninth C rhyme in iambic hexameter meant to close every stanza definitively. Each stanza is its own complete thought. Whitman's subject is a standard romantic figure who happens to be depicted as a negro slave rather than a country laborer. The slave lives in a shed rather than a rustic cottage, but Whitman's subject could without difficulty trade places with Wordsworth's "Solitary Reaper" (1803), figured as bending over her sickle, binding the grain, and singing "of natural sorrow, loss, or pain." Stanza 19 articulates a characteristically Wordsworthian sentiment that bondage is not a matter of physical fetters:

Oh! sing it in the light of freedom's morn,
Tho' tyrant wars have made the earth a grave;
The good, the great, and true, are, if so, born,
And so with slaves, chains do not make the slave!
If high-souled birth be what the mother gave,—
If manly birth, and manly to the core,—
Whate'er the test, the man will he behave!
Crush him to earth and crush him o'er and o'er,
A man he'll rise at last and meet you as before.

The hexameter last line thunders to a close Whitman's dramatic statement of principle about inner worth. Whitman works deliberately within the conventions of romantic-era poetry, "looking back to legendary pastoral worlds,"[66] although his poem seems to have arrived about seventy years after such poetry was current. A century later the Black Aesthetic advocate Louis Rubin would see in Whitman's long poem, "written in cantos after the style of Byron and Scott, but with a meditative strain suggestive at time of Wordsworth...an Indian tale set in Florida as a metaphor for the plight of the black man in the United States."[67]

Whitman borrows Wordsworth's eagle and castle imagery for "Sonnet—The Montenegrin" (1877):

Undaunted watcher of the mountain track,
Tho' surging cohorts like a sea below,

Against thy cliff-walled homes their thunders throw;
Proud, whilst thy rocky fastness answers back
The fierce, long menace of the Turk's attack,
Thy eagle ken above the tumult flies,
The hostile plain spurns, and its prowess black,
And lights on strongholds terraced in the skies;
There thou wilt quicker than the roe-buck bound,
If bolder dangers mount to force thy pass;
But not till thou a signal brave hast wound,
That hears responses from each peak around,
And calls thy comrade clans-in-arms, to mass
In high defence, when battle stern begins—
Then who can conquer the Montenegrins?

Whitman's octave describes the eagle as a representation of a Serbian fighter in a battle with Turkey; the last seven lines describe how he does not fight without comrades. The eagle's prowess is "black." Together, the fighters will prevail. Whitman's sonnet is not particularly good as a sonnet—it has fifteen lines, no change of perspective or mood, no ambivalence or double-voicedness—and neither was it influential, but it is notable as an example of the breadth of African American sonnets.

Albery Whitman's earlier epic, *Not a Man and Yet a Man*, "a metrical extravaganza of over 5,000 lines," as Sherman puts it, is about a stalwart, handsome mixed-raced slave, Rodney, who saves his master's daughter from an Indian massacre and is sold south as a reward. Written in heroic couplets, the poem shows the marked influence of Longfellow, to whom Whitman sent a copy "as a tribute of respect."[68] Johnson notes "Whitman's capacity for dramatic narration":

A flash of steely lightning from his hand,
Strikes down the groaning leader of the band;
Divides his startled comrades, and again
Descending, leaves fair Dora's captors slain.
Her, seizing then within a strong embrace,
Out in the dark he wheels his flying pace;
He speaks not, but with stalwart tenderness
Her swelling bosom firm to his doth press;
Springs like a stag that flees the eager hound,
And like a whirlwind rustles o'er the ground.
Her locks swim in dishevelled wildness o'er
His shoulders, streaming to his waist and more;
While on and on, strong as a rolling flood,
His sweeping footsteps part the silent wood.

Whitman was clearly comfortable with iambic pentameter. And of all the black writers of the era producing genteel protest poetry, Bruce observes, "none was more self-conscious about his craft and its meaning than Whitman. And no one's work more clearly revealed gentility's key implications for black literature and thought."[69] In other words, while Whitman was influenced by the stewards of Boston gentility, he was never published by them. Still, Whitman's work was well regarded by a growing circle of African American writers and critics, including William Simmons, James Corrothers, and McClellan, writing in the 1890s.

"A Sonnet" by John Willis Menard, from a slight volume of poetry titled *Lays in Summer Lands* (1879), is also best described as "genteel":[70]

> The Sun, upon the western sky,
> Has painted ev'ry cloud with gold;
> And now he shuts his fiery eye
> To sleep in his hesperian fold!
> And twilight with presumptuous Night,
> Are battling on the plain for sway;
> While in the dell, in sweet delight,
> The nightingale pipes out his lay.
> The new-born Moon, with silver sheen,
> Now seeks the gloomy earth to woo;
> While from the Stars, glad tears are seen
> To fall in crystal drops of dew,
> Into the cups of gay-eyed flow'rs,
> That sparkle bright from woodland bow'rs!

Written in iambic tetrameter rather than pentameter, in rhymed couplets rather than a Shakespearean or Petrarchan rhyme scheme, and without any discernible self-questioning or change of perspective, Menard's poem is a sonnet in name only. It is nonracial, optimistic, and apolitical. Menard, elected to the U.S. House of Representatives from Louisiana in 1868, was barred from taking office and never served, although in pleading his case he became the first African American to speak in the chamber. Menard's work is typical of the era during which no black poets "denounce a President or an oppressive law by name," though they plead for civil rights.[71] Most of the poems in the volume are about love. While Menard's work was not influential and has been neglected by anthologizers of black poetry, it is notable as an example of black poetry on nature and imagination from Wheatley through the present.

In just a few years, everything will change with the arrival of Dunbar. While poets such as Whitman and Menard (and later H. Cordelia Ray) focused on writing formal verse, poets such as Dunbar, Johnson, and Corrothers began their careers writing dialect poetry and then turned to sonnets. The first wave of sonnets published by African American authors—and the first volume of sonnets by an African American poet—appeared in the 1890s, on the heels of the rise in lynching, with newspapers reporting upward of two hundred a year by the end of the decade. The ratification of Jim Crow laws with *Plessy v. Ferguson* (1896) and the surge of mob violence against blacks, notably the Wilmington, North Carolina, race riot of 1898, augured the nadir of the nadir.[72] Violence continued with the September 1906 race riot in Atlanta; the August 1908 race riot in Springfield, Illinois; and further riots in 1910.

During the years between Reconstruction and the founding of the NAACP, black intellectuals questioned and debated the nature of citizenship and the work of building and belonging to a literary culture. The growing circle of African American writers who corresponded with each other and read each others' work, from abolitionist-era writers such as Frances Harper to postwar activists and writers such as T. Thomas Fortune, Booker T. Washington, and W. E. B. Du Bois, wondered how to approach the relationship of history, slavery, and current conditions. What role should the past play in the writing about the present and educating for the future? How best to resist the "morbidity and degeneracy" of looking backward at slavery while yet acknowledging the past and its effects?[73] What role would poetry play? And while the Booker T. Washington–W. E. B. Du Bois debates over the utility of a liberal arts education would begin in this period and rage for decades, there was little stated concern that a canonical Western literary education—one that would include sonnets—was problematic for African American students until Carter Woodson published *The Mis-Education of the Negro* in 1933.

As a matter of sheer numbers published, the 1880s and 1890s were bountiful years for American sonnets generally. Every important poet, including Bronson Alcott, Aldrich, Bryant, Emerson, Holmes, Howells, Longfellow, James Russell Lowell, Whittier, and many others, were either writing sonnets or translating them from the Italian. Most of these sonnets were unremarkable. Not surprisingly, sonnets by African American poets who followed their model, such as Joseph Seamon Cotter, Sr.'s "Oliver Wendell Holmes" (1895), were equally unremarkable:

Who can hold up the intellect and say:
"From here to there scampers a vein of wit
With laughing humor by the side of it,
Assisting cold philosophy to play
The game of thinking?" Not a single ray
That boldly shines therefrom will e'er admit
Of close analysis. So, bit by bit
We fall to guessing out the mind's true way
Of forming wholes. O, astute analyst.
And royal merchant in the mart of song,
Because of this we see as through a mist
Thy charming whole. Yet know to thee belong,
Howe'er they be arranged, the God-like three—
Wit, humor, and sublime philosophy.[74]

Cotter's sonnet, like Braithwaite's, demonstrates that a robust practice of sonnet writing was taking hold among black poets as well as white. The sonnet form flourished because the poetic practices of reproduction with modification begun by Renaissance sonneteers appealed to communities of writers who could compete with each other to write sonnets on similar subjects.[75] Yet while hundreds and perhaps thousands of sonnets were being written in the 1880s and 1890s, few were political. Fewer still, by any poets white or black, rose to the standards of earlier practitioners such as Keats or Shelley. From these decades, only Emma Lazarus's "The New Colossus" and Longfellow's "Cross of Snow" are still regularly anthologized.[76]

While there was yet no call by modernists to "make it new," trying one's hand at conventional forms is part of poetic apprenticeship, as Paul Dunbar understood. Soon, Dunbar would begin using the sonnet form's traditions to situate the African American experience along a historical continuum. These years saw the development and flourishing of the African American sonnet not simply as an elevated form for serious poetry or a difficult poetic form to be mastered but rather as a form to decry race violence and Jim Crow.

CHAPTER 4

Periodical Sonnets from Dunbar to McKay, 1890–1922

If a high school and college education ensured the influence of Shakespeare, Milton, and Wordsworth on African American poets, the black press enabled the influence of black poets on each other. By the late nineteenth century, it was increasingly possible for African American poets to publish in mainstream journals such as *Lippincott's Magazine, Harper's, Century Magazine,* and the *Atlantic Monthly* as well as in scores of black periodicals, including the *Colored American Magazine,* the *Freeman, New York Age,* the *Independent,* the *Cleveland Gazette,* the *San Francisco Elevator,* the *Colored Patriot Topeka,* the *Weekly Pelican New Orleans, AME Church Review,* and many others.[1] Hundreds of sonnets appeared in these newspapers in the decades after 1890. Only in the past decade have these works become easily recoverable through the digitization of newspaper archives. Nearly every issue of every newspaper contains sonnets.

Of the four historical periods of African American poetry, the second period—the periodical era, from the late nineteenth century through the first decades of the twentieth—saw hundreds of African American sonnets published. Newspaper editors were the key gatekeepers for emerging poets until the anthologizing era began in 1922 and James Weldon Johnson's *Book of American Negro Poetry* appeared. In examining hundreds of sonnets by black poets that appear in newspapers during these decades, at least two separate and differently influential traditions emerge. The first is simply the general practice of African American poets writing and publishing sonnets in an era when everybody was writing sonnets. I refer to this as the background sonnet tradition, which encouraged sonnet writing generally. Literature courses in American middle schools, high schools, and colleges—including black liberal arts colleges—taught the sonnets of Dante, Shakespeare, Milton, Wordsworth, Keats, and Elizabeth Barrett Browning, as well as new sonnet translations by Emerson, Longfellow, and Howells. Students were often assigned to write formal verse.[2] Newspaper editors needed content, and sonnets were available and convenient. Many of these sonnets were not racialized; most were uplifting and even patriotic in their praise of famous artists, athletes, or historical figures. Many were probably schoolroom assignments.

H. Cordelia Ray was perhaps the best known of the many African American sonnet writers publishing at the time, and her work is emblematic of this first tradition. Her volume *Sonnets* (1893), the first book of sonnets published by an African American poet, featured poems that had been circulating for years in the black press. Ray's work, discussed in the second half of this chapter, does not grapple overtly or self-consciously with sonnet traditions or with the shadow of race violence that began to fall over the era. Her sonnets were highly praised in the black press, although they were usually not on black subjects. The diction of her sonnets is largely indistinguishable from sonnets written by white poets of the era.

Paul Laurence Dunbar established a second tradition of influential sonnet writing that overtly and self-consciously used the sonnet form to express the crisis of the black experience in America. Writing in the years after *Plessy v. Ferguson* and amid the growing horror of lynching, Dunbar offers a distinctly black voice in conversation with sonnet writers such as Shakespeare, Milton, and Wordsworth. Dunbar's sonnets increasingly break away from sonnets written by white poets of the era. Dunbar's sonnets influenced contemporary black poets such as James Corrothers, Lucian Watkins, and Leslie Pinckney Hill, who followed his models and paid tribute to him in sonnet form. Claude McKay can be seen as joining this influential tradition and ensuring the survival of the African American sonnet tradition after the background sonnet tradition faded at the end of the 1930s.

While I foreground the influence of a specific sonnet tradition and distinguish it from the general practice of African American poets publishing sonnets in the black press, I also argue for a relationship of mutual support and engagement between the two practices. The background practice of sonnet writing supported and encouraged Dunbar and McKay. The innovations of Dunbar and McKay supported and encouraged more sonnet writing by African American poets.

Dunbar has not yet been recognized as a sonnet innovator for two key reasons: first, he was categorized primarily as a dialect poet, and as the overwhelming popularity of dialect poetry faded and was finally condemned, Dunbar fell out of critical favor. Dunbar's poetic voice "has often been muffled rather than sharpened by the debate over his work," as Martin Griffin observes.[3] Second, in organizing his volumes of poetry, Dunbar included formal poetry and dialect poetry. His relatively small number of sonnets (perhaps a dozen) were never published or collected together. But reading his sonnets alongside each other, his poetic growth becomes apparent. Dunbar was the first African American poet to write sonnets on race violence, well ahead of any other poet of his time.

The 1890s were an era of bourgeois editorial respectability, particularly in the pages of literary magazines.[4] Despite the "contrary examples of Mark Twain and Howells," H. L. Mencken quipped, "all the more pretentious American authors try to write chastely and elegantly; the typical literary product of the country is still a refined essay in the *Atlantic Monthly*."[5] Boston editors particularly "missed pretty much everything vital and significant in American life."[6] During the growing epidemic of lynching and race attacks in the 1890s, white literary journals were largely silent. While former abolitionists in Boston retained "a well bred interest in negro schools," southern violence was not a pressing cause.[7] Howells, Jacqueline Goldsby argues, "could not conceive of lynching as a fictional subject" even as black poets—including Dunbar—were writing vital and significant poetry about the bloody, ongoing clashes.[8] Howells, who "discovered" Dunbar in 1896, had, a decade earlier, written passionately about the "longing for freedom" expressed by Italian sonnets, noting that "the Italian poets of the last hundred years constantly inspired the Italian people with ideas of liberty and independence."[9] Howells conceived of Dunbar as a poet who would "study," "analyze," and "represent" his race "humorously, yet tenderly, and above all…faithfully," but he did not see Dunbar's powerful sonnets as akin to the Italian specimens.[10]

Two sonnets by Dunbar, "Robert Gould Shaw" and "Douglass," indict the absence of strong leadership at a time of growing violence. "Robert Gould Shaw" was published in the *Atlantic Monthly* in 1900:

Why was it that the thunder voice of Fate
Should call thee, studious, from the classic groves,
Where calm-eyed Pallas with still footstep roves,
And charge thee seek the turmoil of the state?
What bade thee hear the voice and rise elate,
Leave home and kindred and thy spicy loaves,
To lead th' unlettered and despised droves
To manhood's home and thunder at the gate?
Far better the slow blaze of Learning's light,
The cool and quiet of her dearer fane,
Than this hot terror of a hopeless fight,
This cold endurance of the final pain,—
Since thou and those who with thee died for right
Have died, the Present teaches, but in vain![11]

Dunbar follows Milton in using the Italian sonnet rhyme scheme, which allows equivocating on the answer to the question posed: was the death of this Civil War hero in vain? Was Fate wrong to ask the young student to leave his books for the noble cause of freeing the enslaved? The sestet, with its singsong rhyme scheme, suggests that Fate played a cruel joke: turmoil and terror reign and Shaw's sacrifice was for nothing.[12] The "despised droves" are no less despised than they were before the war; "this hot terror" indicts the "Present" "hopeless fight," not that of the past. The speaker of Dunbar's sonnet is authoritative and comfortable with both rhetorical questions and the "thees" and "thous" of heightened diction. And in the middle of a sonnet on an educated white man leading an African American regiment, Dunbar offers a sly apocope, or elision, "th' unlettered," perhaps subtly alluding to his own dialect poetry.[13]

Dunbar's choice of the double-voiced sonnet form is crucial to the poem's meaning: the heroic rhetoric of the octave evokes the standard view of Shaw's noble service; the sestet roundly rejects the premise. The two "thunders" as Griffin argues—fate and the gate of Fort Wagner, South Carolina, where Shaw was killed in July 1863—heighten the question of what was at stake in Shaw's sacrifice for what would be a "hopeless" cause: would he simply be "an absurd marginal note in an American history defined by racial equality"?[14] Would Shaw have made the same decision had he foreseen *Plessy v. Ferguson*, continued racial injustice, and an epidemic of lynching? Benjamin Brawley calls "Robert Gould Shaw" "the expression of pessimism as to the Negro's future in America."[15] Allen Flint finds Dunbar's sonnet to Shaw startling: "No poems written before

1900 even hint that Colonel Shaw's sacrifice was in vain. Quite the contrary, all earlier poems have seen Shaw's mission as divine, his sacrifice successful, his martyrdom assured."[16] No later black poets questioned Shaw's death in this way. For example, Benjamin Brawley's 1915 hymn, "My Hero," sentimentally compares Shaw to Lancelot, Sir Bedivere, and Galahad. Cordelia Ray's sonnet to Shaw (below) is simply heroic.

Had Howells looked more closely, he might have seen "Robert Gould Shaw" as a sonnet "longing for freedom" in the manner of the Italian sonneteers or even the British protest tradition. Dunbar had studied Shelley as well as Wordsworth and Keats and knew this tradition well.[17] Dunbar is appropriating "the cultural memory of the English lyric tradition as his own," Griffin argues, "and deploys it to sketch a future in which he will be accepted as an original peot and his people will achieve their right of equal citizenship."[18] The sonnet form, with its cultural heft, is key here. "Rather than accept the easy association of Shaw with Christ, or exaggerate the importance of Shaw's personal sacrifice, Dunbar uses the sonnet form to raise questions about memorials to Shaw," Flint argues.[19] What was the point of tributes to Shaw's death in the context of lynching, legal segregation, and dashed hopes? Dunbar's sonnet asks. Dunbar's sonnet also assumes its own status as a memorial created by a black poet.

If "Robert Gould Shaw" is the most overtly political sonnet written by an African American poet since Placido's sonnet to his mother, it has seldom been recognized as such. Read alongside "Douglass," published three years later, one can even more easily see Dunbar's strategy in drawing on the sonnet form to protest race violence:

> Ah, Douglass, we have fall'n on evil days,
> Such days as thou, not even thou didst know,
> When thee, the eyes of that harsh long ago
> Saw, salient, at the cross of devious ways,
> And all the country heard thee with amaze.
> Not ended then, the passionate ebb and flow,
> The awful tide that battled to and fro;
> We ride amid a tempest of dispraise.
> Now, when the waves of swift dissension swarm,
> And Honor, the strong pilot, lieth stark,
> Oh, for thy voice high-sounding o'er the storm,
> For thy strong arm to guide the shivering bark,
> The blast-defying power of thy form,
> To give us comfort through the lonely dark.[20]

Dunbar's first line echoes the apostrophe to Milton in William Words-worth's sonnet "London 1802": "Milton! thou shouldst be living at this hour," calling on a commanding voice for help and moral inspiration.[21] "Fall'n on evil days" evokes Milton's *Paradise Lost*: "More safe I Sing with mortal voice, unchang'd / To hoarse or mute, though fall'n on evil days, / On evil days though fall'n, and evil tongues; / In darkness, and with dan-gers compast round" (7:24–27).[22] In lines 6–7, "the passionate ebb and flow, / The awful tide that battled to and fro" gestures toward Matthew Arnold's "Dover Beach" (1867), with its lines on writers past grappling with human misery.[23]

Marcellus Blount rightly sees "Douglass" as an influence on twentieth-century African American sonneteers, who "were able to draw upon the example of their black literary precursors, refining and extending their stops along the way."[24] In contrast to the unracialized speaker of "Rob-ert Gould Shaw," the speaker of "Douglass," with his "we" in the first line, declares he is black. The octave calls out in an apostrophe that storms are raging in Douglass's absence—storms that even he could not imag-ine would still be raging. The sestet yearns for his strong arm and com-forting voice. The volta signals a change in mood accompanying a turn to the present day, with the word "Now" and a repeated apostrophe to Douglass—"Oh, for thy voice"—reinforcing the fact of absence. The son-net exhibits self-consciousness about containment in the sestet, with the speaker's desire for guidance.

Dunbar drew on the memorial sonnet tradition to critique as well as lionize. Dunbar's sonnet "Booker T. Washington," which appeared in the *Outlook* (1900), is in its diction (no "thees" or "thys") more modern than "Robert Gould Shaw" and "Douglass":

> The word is writ that he who runs may read.
> What is the passing breath of earthly fame?
> But to snatch glory from the hands of blame—
> That is to be, to live, to strive indeed.
> A poor Virginia cabin gave the seed,
> And from its dark and lowly door there came
> A peer of princes in the world's acclaim,
> A master spirit for the nation's need.
> Strong, silent, purposeful beyond his kind,
> The mark of rugged force on brow and lip,
> Straight on he goes, nor turns to look behind
> Where hot the hounds come baying at his hip;

With one idea foremost in his mind,
Like the keen prow of some on-forging ship.[25]

In the octave of this sonnet, published five years after Washington's famous speech about hard work and economic success at the 1895 Cotton
States and International Exposition, Dunbar's speaker reprises Washington's philosophy of the glory of work over intellectual pursuits. The sestet describes a ruggedly purposeful man, going "straight on," with "one
idea" in his mind. The lack of a clear volta is cleverly deliberate in "Booker
T. Washington": the "flaw" in the sonnet is the flaw in the man who is "beyond his kind" and will not stop to look around him. Dunbar's speaker
does not speak in first-person singular or plural as he does in "Douglass,"
nor does he imply that his subject's actions affected him, as he does in
"Robert Gould Shaw." The speaker of "Booker T. Washington" is silent
on race; the sonnet's critique is focused instead on the inadequacy of a
race leader who seems not to look around and see conditions around him.
Dunbar's choice of "some" rather than "great" tartly reduces the metaphor of Washington as an "on-forging ship."

Appreciating Dunbar's remarkable ability and influence as a sonnet
writer requires looking at the sonnets gathered together rather than distributed among his other works. They were never published together.
"Harriet Beecher Stowe" first appeared in *Century* magazine in November
1898:

> She told the story, and the whole world wept
> At wrongs and cruelties it had not known
> But for this fearless woman's voice alone.
> She spoke to consciences that long had slept:
> Her message, Freedom's clear reveille, swept
> From heedless hovel to complacent throne.
> Command and prophecy were in the tone,
> And from its sheath the sword of justice leapt.
> Around two peoples swelled a fiery wave,
> But both came forth transfigured from the flame.
> Blest be the hand that dared be strong to save,
> And blest be she who in our weakness came—
> Prophet and priestess! At one stroke she gave
> A race to freedom and herself to fame.

Dunbar's sonnet is formally Italian in its rhyme scheme but opens with two
three-line sentences ending on the B rhyme, followed by a two-line sentence that ends on the A rhyme, creating two moments of tension before

a premature sense of completion at the end of the octave. The historian-speaker in the sestet speaks to the firestorm of controversy her book (not named) provoked and the transfiguration of people by the flame of war. The "But" at the beginning of the tenth line signals a change in circumstance as well as a change of mood. The moments of tension in the poem do not add up to a powerful argument, and yet something crucial occurs in this poem. The pronoun "our" in the twelfth line quietly indicates the poetic speaker's membership in the race liberated by Stowe's writings. The speaker is black. The last line emphasizes Stowe's fame as the consequence of her strength of hand, an engagement with the Shakespearean tradition of sonnets bestowing immortality on an author. The sonnet praises her as an author who "gave a race to freedom" with the stroke of a pen and also gave hope to writers who hoped to make a living writing about race in America.

"Harriet Beecher Stowe" contains no syncope or apheresis, no "thees" or "thous," and no conventional poeticisms beyond "blest be." Yet a growing sense of playfulness with the sonnet form is apparent from his unexpected emphasis on the B rhymes in the octave and from the trochee leading the thirteenth line ("prophet"), which also signals a Shakespearean finish, although without the resolution of a couplet. Dunbar's Stowe sonnet does not have the power of his sonnets to Shaw and Douglass, but his grasp of the form's potential for writing about the African American experience is emerging.

Even Dunbar's less overtly political early sonnets, such as "Nature and Art" from *Lyrics of Lowly Life*, engage key questions of art and authenticity that are central to African American poetry. "Nature and Art" is dedicated to Charles Booth Nettleton, a drawing instructor and superintendent of penmanship in Dayton, Ohio, with whom Dunbar remained close.[26] It is a curious poem; it ends provocatively, abruptly. The first sonnet, featuring a Petrarchan octave followed by a hybrid sestet with a couplet finish, introduces a storyteller-speaker who tells the tale of proud Queen Nature who longed to see an image of herself. She wanders in vain until an "inventive" elf, Art, makes a glass to show her. Dunbar revised the sonnet's second line, "fell upon evil days," for use in "Douglass." The line in "Nature and Art" is deliberately clumsy, disrupting the iambic pentameter. But the four pairs of couplets give the sonnet a sprightly air, and we root for Art's intervention. The sonnet's interest in nature wedded to art is meaningful in the context of Dunbar's relationship with dialect poetry and deserves closer scrutiny.

Dunbar's hard-won mastery over the sonnet form is evident in one of his final poems, "Slow Through the Dark" (1903), a key influence on later black sonnet writers:

> Slow moves the pageant of a climbing race;
> Their footsteps drag far, far below the height,
> And, unprevailing by their utmost might,
> Seem faltering downward from each hard won place.
> No strange, swift-sprung exception we; we trace
> A devious way thro' dim, uncertain light,—
> Our hope, through the long vistaed years, a sight
> Of that our Captain's soul sees face to face.
> Who, faithless, faltering that the road is steep,
> Now raiseth up his drear insistent cry?
> Who stoppeth here to spend a while in sleep
> Or curseth that the storm obscures the sky?
> Heed not the darkness round you, dull and deep;
> The clouds grow thickest when the summit's nigh.[27]

Using only four rhymes in the whole poem, "Slow Through the Dark" is both particular to the black "race" on an unevenly upward and dark climb and universal to any group striving uncertainly toward a goal. The first quatrain's speaker refers to the climbers in the third person; the speaker of the second quatrain joins the climbers. These two stanzas contain alliterations that hasten and repetitions that slow the pace. Returning to archaic diction ("raiseth," "curseth") in the sestet, the speaker questions: who would falter, cry out, stop, or curse? The speaker is aware that the climate is dark and stormy. "Heed not the darkness," he urges. Dunbar offers two turns in the sonnet—from they to we, from we to an implied "you"—mapping his own engagement with the sonnet form. The climbers trace "a devious way thro' dim, uncertain light," the devious way signaled by the sonnet's only apocope, "thro'." Dunbar's last published sonnet is preoccupied with achieving poetic greatness. In declining health, Dunbar died in 1906, at age thirty-three.

Grouped together, Dunbar's sonnets can been seen as a determined effort to use the sonnet form and draw on the sonnet's traditions and history to protest a violent and segregated America. It is unclear whether Dunbar would have wanted to be categorized as an African American poet or as a poet in the tradition of Milton and Shelley—most likely both. He saw himself as an insider to the poetic tradition. "I know all about English literature," he wrote to Alice in 1901 before a lecture on literature at

Tuskegee University, "because I make it."[28] He saw himself as changing the canon from within.

Yet because Dunbar was primarily known as a dialect poet, he was regularly sidelined by anthologizers and critics charged with creating a black poetry canon in the 1920s and 1930s. "The two chief qualities in Dunbar's work are humor and pathos," Braithwaite argued in 1924. "No agitated visions of prophesy burn and surge in his poems. His dreams were anchored to the minor whimsies."[29] Dunbar was merely "a rank sentimentalist," Wallace Thurman declared in 1928; "neither his aesthetic feeling nor his expression ever attained enough depth to be of permanent value."[30] "Dunbar shied away from direct protest," wrote Sterling Brown and Arthur P. Davis, "coming nearest to it in such poems as 'We Wear the Mask' and 'The Haunted Oak,' [although] some of his sonnets, such as those to Frederick Douglass, Harriet Beecher Stowe, and Robert Gould Shaw[,] show a really deep love and aspiration for his people."[31]

Dunbar famously lamented that his serious work wasn't appreciated. Even twenty-first-century critics and scholars who praise his standard verse overlook his sonnets as particularly good or constitutive of the tradition that would soon include McKay, Hill, and others. Griffin is one exception. Another is Keith Leonard, who argues that "Dunbar offers his most substantial affirmation of African American ethnic identity not in his dialect poems…but in the Standard English odes" that lionize valiant figures.[32] Yet certainly Dunbar's sonnet to Shaw is a departure from the sentimental memorials to Shaw by artists and writers such as Augustus Saint-Auden, Edmonia Lewis, Elizabeth Gaskell, and William James. Carol Loranger argues that Dunbar's sonnet "ends with the speaker noting that even the most heroic interventions do not necessarily shift the social institutions, in this case the structures of racial oppression, that constrain us," but this reading seems to misunderstand the very real horrors of lynching to which Dunbar was clearly referring.[33]

Yet while ignored by Howells at the time and by most scholars of black poetry even in the present, Dunbar's sonnets were valued by a small but influential and growing number of his contemporaries. A few years after Dunbar's death, the poet James David Corrothers wrote:

> I arose from my bed…and began to write of Dunbar, of my Dunbar, my poet, my friend. I had been thinking of him for days. I seemed almost to commune with his beautiful spirit. With wet cheeks and streaming eyes, I wrote, until far into the night, what I meant to be a *poet's* poem to a poet, as unto his very spirit. Twelve stanzas in sonnet form I wrote to

the memory of my friend. Then, for some days afterward, I rewrote and wrought lovingly upon it.[34]

Corrothers sent the twelve sonnets to *Harper's* magazine, which declined to publish them, although the editor, H. M. Alden, encouraged Corrothers, praising their "wonderful beauty and imaginative power."[35] Corrothers kept revising. Eventually, after requesting further changes, the new editor of the *Century* magazine, R. U. Johnson, accepted the first two sonnets of the sequence in 1912, publishing them under the title "Paul Laurence Dunbar":

> He came, a youth, singing in the dawn
> Of a new freedom, glowing o'er his lyre,
> Refining, as with great Apollo's fire,
> His people's gift of song. And thereupon,
> This Negro singer, come to Helicon,
> Constrained the masters, listening, to admire,
> And roused a race to wonder and aspire,
> Gazing which way their honest voice was gone,
> With ebon face uplit of glory's crest.
> Men marveled at the singer, strong and sweet,
> Who brought the cabin's mirth, the tuneful night,
> But faced the morning, beautiful with light,
> To die while shadows yet fell toward the west,
> And leave his laurels at his people's feet.
>
> Dunbar, no poet wears your laurels now;
> None rises, singing, from your race like you.
> Dark melodist, immortal, though the dew
> Fell early on the bays upon your brow,
> And tinged with pathos every halcyon vow
> And brave endeavor. Silence o'er you threw
> Flowerets of love. Or, if an envious few
> Of your own people brought no garlands, how
> Could Malice smite him whom the gods had crowned?
> If, like the meadow-lark, your flight was low,
> Your flooded lyrics half the hilltops drowned;
> A wide world heard you, and it loved you so
> It stilled its heart to list the strains you sang,
> And o'er your happy songs its plaudits rang.

The first sonnet-stanza follows the Italian rhyme scheme, with a delayed volta at the eleventh line. "He came," proclaim the first nine lines; "Men

marveled," proclaim the last five, but the poet died young. With its allusions to Greek mythology, Corrothers's sonnet figures Dunbar as an Or-
phic hero who, at the home of the Muses, constrained his masters who
sat still while admiring his poetry. The space before the second sonnet
indicates another turn. The first line of the second stanza, "Dunbar, no
poet wears your laurels now," also evokes the first line of Wordsworth's
"London 1802." Both "Dunbar" and "Milton" are trochees rather than
iambs, but the names are made to fit. Like Wordsworth's sonnet to Milton and Dunbar's to Douglass, Corrothers's sonnet to Dunbar extols the
poet as hero not as a matter of vision but as a matter of withstanding criticism: "how / Could Malice smite him whom the gods had crowned?" The
last five lines (the volta is again delayed) turn back to the poet. Dunbar is
compared to a meadowlark, a cheerful songbird, perhaps less heroic than
an eagle, but his verse soared and plaudits rang "o'er your happy songs,"
the speaker concludes. The syncope evokes Dunbar's dialect verse by gesturing toward the perceived difference between conventional poeticisms
('twas, o'er) and those used in dialect poetry.

Corrothers saw his intense efforts with these sonnets as a kind of labor of poetic uplift:

> For two years, at various times, I worked over these and another son-
> net, "The Negro Singer," writing, rewriting and interlining; changing
> and correcting this and that. I wrote one line in seventy-six different
> ways, and spent five weeks on three and one-half lines in the octave of
> "The Negro Singer." I considered that I was making a new start in litera-
> ture; and that I was working for my *race*, as well as for myself and fam-
> ily. In addition to this, I was doing a higher class of work than I had ever
> done before, my other published literary efforts having been almost ex-
> clusively in Negro dialect, while this was not. It was a complete chang-
> ing of styles for me, and therefore hard work. I felt that I had mastered
> Negro dialect; but I was far from having mastered the art of expressing
> worthy thoughts in literary English. Besides, I moved in an element of
> society which, for the most part, did not use good English.[36]

Like Dunbar, Corrothers had been initially known as a dialect poet. He
was born in Michigan in 1868, studied for a short time at Northwestern
University, worked a newspaper reporter in Chicago, and feted Frederick Douglass at the 1893 World's Columbian Exposition.[37] Corrothers had
helped put Dunbar in the public spotlight with positive reviews of his
books in the *Chicago Journal* and the *Chicago Times-Herald*. "With each
write-up there was a picture of Dunbar, who acknowledged the appear-

ance of the articles with a grateful note," Corrothers writes, taking some deserved credit for himself. "Perhaps a year after this, Howells graciously brought Dunbar to the attention of the English-speaking world."[38] Like Dunbar, Corrothers published poems in *Century*, including "The Snapping of the Bow" (1901), a political work in standard verse, and "Me 'n' Dunbar," a dialect work. He published a collection of humorous and dialect pieces in *The Black Cat Club* (1902), which he later regretted as not serious enough. "But I shall dig me deeper to the gold," Corrothers writes in "The Negro Singer" (1912).[39] Dunbar inspired him to better work.

Corrothers's sonnets to Dunbar are a key link in the chain of connection between Dunbar and later black sonnet writers.[40] Dunbar drew on the sonnet history to contend with the nation, to contend with expectations of what he should be writing about, and to contend with the genteel sonnets being published at the time. Dunbar's influence launched the black sonnet *tradition*. That is, Corrothers recognized Dunbar's poetic achievement and memorialized him in the form that he thought most appropriate. Corrothers was determined to build on Dunbar's sonnets to carry a sonnet-writing practice pertinent to African American culture and concerns into the twentieth century. In the coming decades, sonnets to Dunbar included Waldo H. Dunn's "To Paul Lawrence Dunbar [*sic*]" (1907), Angelina Weld Grimké's "To the Dunbar High School: A Sonnet" (1917), Carrie Clifford's "Paul Laurence Dunbar" (1922), and James Edward Andrews's "Dunbar" (1939).[41]

While Dunbar and Corrothers were writing and publishing distinctly black sonnets, the background practice of African American poets writing and publishing sonnets in newspapers continued to flourish. New journals were founded in the early years of the century, notably Monroe Trotter's Boston *Guardian* (1901), Robert S. Abbott's *Chicago Defender* (1905), W. E. B. Du Bois's *Crisis* (1910), and on the West Coast, John J. Neimore's *California Eagle* (1912).[42] In 1917 the socialist journal the *Messenger* was launched by A. Philip Randolph, the labor activist, and Chandler Owen, an economist.[43] The *Messenger* published poetry, including notable sonnets by McKay.[44] In 1918 the *Liberator*, a radical socialist journal, was founded by Max Eastman, which published poetry (including sonnets) of authors of all races, including McKay.[45] Hubert Harrison launched or edited a number of newspapers including the *Voice* (1917–1918) and *New Negro* (1919). He edited *Negro World* (1920) and *Voice of the Negro* (1927), the latter featuring "Poetry for the People," including sonnets.

Samuel Beadle, James Madison Bell, Benjamin Brawley, Braithwaite,

T. Thomas Fortune, Georgia Douglas Johnson, George Marion McClellan, and Ray were some of the more notable poets publishing sonnets regularly, the majority of which were indistinguishable from sonnets by white poets. The sheer number of newspaper sonnets—often in the schoolroom style—prolonged the idea that sonnets were simply genteel Victorian holdovers. Distinguishing between two sonnet traditions explains the critical opposition to and slow disappearance of the background sonnet form as practiced by Braithwaite, Ray, and other once-influential poets. The sonnets by Brawley (founding dean at Morehouse College and later chair of English at Howard University) and Braithwaite (poetry editor, onetime critic for the *Boston Evening Transcript*, and a professor of literature at Atlanta University) are characterized by erudition and literary allusions and are notably nonracial. Ray's sonnets too are representative of late nineteenth-century genteel and educated sonnet-writing practice. Dennis Looney notes that Ray's "Champions of Freedom" sonnets demonstrate a Dantean sense of law and freedom characteristic of the era.[46]

Braithwaite's sonnets particularly—technically proficient, derivative, and ponderous—perhaps gave sonnets a bad name and dampened the sonnet accomplishments of Dunbar and others. In 1917 McKay sent some of his own sonnets to Braithwaite, after learning that Braithwaite was "a colored man" but before reading Braithwaite's poetry. Braithwaite responded that McKay's poems "were good, but that, barring two, any reader could tell that the author was a Negro [and] would advise me to write and send to the magazines only such poems as did not betray my racial identity."[47] McKay promptly went in search of Braithwaite's work, finding "a thin volume containing some purely passionless lyrics, only one line of which I have ever remembered (I quote from memory): 'I kissed a kiss on a dead man's brow . . .'"[48] McKay adds acidly, "I did not entertain, not in the least, Mr. Braithwaite's excellent advice."[49]

Cordelia Ray's *Sonnets*—the first book of sonnets published by an African American poet—appeared in 1893, the same year Dunbar published his first book of poetry, *Oak and Ivy*. Ray's *Sonnets* feature poems on Shakespeare, Milton, Beethoven, Raphael, Niobe, and other noted figures of Western art and culture.[50] Ray expanded the collection in 1910 to include sonnets on William Lloyd Garrison, Wendell Phillips, Charles Sumner, Robert Gould Shaw, and Toussaint L'Ouverture (in a sequence called "Champions of Freedom"), most of which had been circulating for years in the black press. The *New York Age* had in 1890 praised Cordelia Ray's sonnet to Toussaint, and the *Cleveland Gazette* praised her in 1892 as "one of the best sonnet writers of her race."[51] Jesse Fauset reviewed Ray's 1910 volume of poetry in the August 1912 issue of the *Crisis*, noting that Ray used "almost every sort of poetic form" and wrote on "almost every imaginable subject." "The quality of the verse is uneven, perhaps, but much of it is very, very good.... [The ballads] have a distinct flavor of old far-off times and reveal much of the poetic atmosphere in which this author undoubtedly moves."[52]

Ray was publishing royalty. She was the daughter of Charles Bennett Ray, the editor and publisher (with Samuel Cornish) of the early nineteenth-century newspaper the *Colored American*.[53] Cordelia's mother, Henrietta Green Regulus Ray, cofounded the African Dorcas Association in 1828 to provide funds and clothes to children in the African Free Schools in New York City; she was also the first president of the New York Female Literary Society. Cordelia graduated from the University of the City of New York and the Sauvenor School of Languages. She worked briefly as a teacher before turning to writing full-time, supported by her sister Florence, also a teacher.[54] Their older sister, Charlotte, became in 1872 the first black woman to receive a law degree from Howard University. The younger Ray's poetic debut was a public reading of her ode "Lincoln" in 1876, at age twenty-four, at the unveiling of the Freedmen's Monument in Washington, D.C. President Ulysses S. Grant was present; Frederick Douglass gave an oration. When Ray died in 1916, the *Crisis* noted her passing, praising her as "an unusually gifted woman, being well-read in Greek, French, and German literature."[55]

Comparing Ray's sonnet to Robert Gould Shaw to Dunbar's is perhaps the best way to illustrate the difference between the background practice of sonnet writing and a growing genealogy of influential African American sonnets. Here is Ray's "Robert G. Shaw":

> When War's red banners trailed along the sky,
> And many a manly heart grew all aflame
> With patriotic love and purest aim,
> There rose a noble soul who dared to die,
> If only Right could win. He heard the cry
> Of struggling bondmen and he quickly came,
> Leaving the haunts where Learning tenders fame
> Unto her honored sons; for it was ay
> A loftier cause that lured him on to death.
> Brave men who saw their brothers held in chains,
> Beneath his standard battled ardently.

O friend! O hero! thou who yielded breath
That others might share Freedom's priceless gains,
In rev'rent love we guard thy memory.[56]

Ray uses an Italian rhyme scheme but without a clear change in perspective. Unlike Dunbar's Shaw, who, Dunbar suggests, died in vain, Shaw's sacrifice for a lofty cause is unquestioned in Ray's poem. Shaw is simply a hero. Shaw "yielded breath / That others might share Freedom's priceless gains" and is a memorialized friend. Ray evokes no present dangers. Ray's sonnet lacks a questioning sensibility or double-voicedness. Ray's poetic voice is not in an argument with anyone, including herself. Most importantly, Ray's sonnets have not been cited as an influence by any later sonnet writers.

By contrast, Dunbar and those he influenced were after something new and different: synthesizing the sonnet with an African American perspective, creating a distinct genre. It is certainly partly true, as Heidi Morse argues, that the "artificial critical division between African American literature and classicism" has kept Ray outside the canon.[57] The problem for Morse and other critics has been that Ray's subject matter, such as a sonnet to Beethoven, has seemed problematic to twentieth-century critics as not focused enough on race. And yet on the matter of subject I take Ray's side. Beethoven was praised regularly in the black press—in *Freedom's Journal*, the *North Star*, the *National Era*, and the *Christian Recorder*—as a sympathetic and liberal figure who composed for the masses; as a radical who broke the shackles of classical tradition; as a genius who died still misunderstood.[58] The centenary of Beethoven's birth, in 1870, was followed by the publication of an American edition of his piano sonatas that sold widely in New York and became the standard edition for music students across the country.[59] Ray's sonnet to Beethoven is in the tradition of T. Thomas Fortune's 1895 sonnet to the "dark-browed" Edgar Allan Poe. These figures were of deep interest to the African American community even if Ray's and Fortune's uses of the sonnet form were not inspired.

Georgia Douglas Johnson belongs to both the background and influential sonnet tradition. While her sonnets were not influential, they increasingly show the influence of other black sonnet writers. Her sonnets are more racialized than Ray's but much less attuned to sonnet traditions than Dunbar's. Her goal was to uplift, not to upset. The dominant image in Johnson's sonnets, Gloria T. Hull argues, "is that of the 'mantle,' meaning the cloak of 'darkness' surrounding the black race."[60] Johnson's poetry was designed to countermand race prejudice. "Sonnet to the Mantled" appeared in the *Crisis* in 1917 and was republished by Du Bois in *Phylon Quarterly* in 1942:

And they shall rise and cast their mantles by,
Erect and strong and visioned, in the day
That rings the knell of Curfew o'er the sway
Of prejudice—who reels with mortal cry
To lift no more her leprous, blinded eye,
Reft of the fetters, far more cursed than they
Which held dominion o'er human clay,
The spirit soars aloft where rainbows lie.
Like joyful exiles swift returning home—
The rhythmic chanson of their eager feet,
While voices strange to ecstasy, long dumb,
Break forth in major rhapsodies, full sweet.
Into the very star-shine, lo! they come
Wearing the bays of victory complete![61]

"Sonnet to the Mantled" is in Italian form, the third line evoking the first line of Gray's "Elegy Written in a Country Churchyard" with the sense of opportunity lost. It is unclear who exactly is "reft of the fetters," but "fetters" is clearly not a metaphor. The sonnet looks forward to the unfettered, long silent, "break[ing] forth in major rhapsodies."

Georgia Johnson was a well-known figure to editors; she was famous as a teacher and poet who published to put two sons through college (Bowdoin, Dartmouth) as well as Howard law school (for one) and medical school (for the other). Johnson's two volumes, *The Heart of a Woman* (1818) and *Bronze, a Book of Verse* (1922), were read and praised as "exquisite" and "sincere."[62] James Weldon Johnson writes in *The Book of Negro Poetry* that she was a poet "neither afraid nor ashamed of her emotions. She limits herself to the purely conventional forms, rhythms and rhymes, but through them she achieves striking effects. The principal theme of Mrs. Johnson's poems is the secret dread down in every woman's heart, the dread of the passing of youth and beauty, and with them love."[63] Alice Dunbar-Nelson, reviewing Johnson's *Bronze: A Book of Verse* in the *Messenger*, writes of "a certain overstrained eulogy" in Johnson's sonnets, although "Sonnet to the Mantled" offers "that delicate joy in the completeness of an exquisite thing."[64] Braithwaite in "The Negro in Literature" (1924) deems Johnson's poetry "adequate." Arnold Rampersad dismisses her as the "eccentric but lovable and maternal Georgia Douglas Johnson,"[65] offering little positive assessment of her poetry.

Leonard makes the curious claim that in Johnson, "[t]he sonnet—that icon of Western poetics—becomes a central pillar of African American antiracist poetic expression."[66] Jon Woodson argues that African American poets turned to the sonnet form in the 1930s as an "exceptional" site for "antilynching discourse." Both claims overlook the sonnets of Dunbar at the turn of the century and sonnets on race violence and labor violence circulating widely in the 1910s. Both also overlook the influential lynching sonnets published by Du Bois's *Crisis*.

The *Crisis* was perhaps the most influential journal of the era dedicated to addressing "the great problem of inter-racial relations."[67] Poems, short stories, book reviews, and essays appeared alongside reporting on Jim Crow segregation, lynching, and race riots.[68] As an undergraduate at Fisk University in 1888, Du Bois had edited the *Fisk Herald*, which, like the *Crisis*, featured poetry that tended to be learned and formal. The sonnet's cultural prestige was most likely helpful during years when the Justice Department was threatening to shut down black presses for inciting violence.[69] Vendors faced arrests and fines for selling the *Crisis* in areas of the South and Midwest experiencing riots and massacres in the 1910s. Du Bois was facing challenges as well for advocating for more black leadership of black colleges and universities, and it may be that the sonnet's venerability had a political appeal. That the black press regularly published sonnets speaks to the form's popularity, usefulness, cultural prestige, and conventionality.

The first poem published in the *Crisis* was a sonnet, Leslie Pinckney Hill's "Jim Crow" (1910):

> By what dread logic, by what grand neglect,
> Wide as our nation, doth this relic last—
> This relic of old sterile customs past
> Long since into deep shame without respect?
> Even I whom this contrivance fain would teach
> A low submission, pray within my soul
> That these my masters may not reap the dole
> Of finding remedy beyond their reach.
> In lofty mood I mount the reeking box,
> And travel through the land. So Terence once
> Moved in old Rome, so—wondrous paradox—
> Moved Esop in old Greece, the dwarf and dunce,

> Then I reflect how their immortal wit
> Makes the world laugh with mockery of it.[70]

With its hybrid Italian-Shakespearean rhyme scheme, its allusions to Greece and Rome, and its use of archaisms such as "doth" and "fain," "Jim Crow" banks on the perceived archaism of the sonnet form to critique outmodedness. In a lumbering idiom the poetic speaker asks why the "relic" of segregation exists and prays that a "remedy" is not out of reach. In the sestet, the sonnet speaker mounts the "reeking box"—a platform for speaking and also an overripe sonnet-cage—to note how Terence and Aesop (both had been slaves) traveled the land and wrote satirical works that are still relevant. From the sonnet perch "in lofty mood" (which re-calls Wordsworth's "in sundry mood"), the speaker mocks segregation as "sterile."

Next to Braithwaite, Hill was perhaps the most highly educated son-net writer of the era. Born and raised in Lynchburg, Virginia, Hill entered Harvard in 1899, graduated with both a bachelor's and master's degree in education, and taught at Tuskegee Institute while Booker T. Washington was president. His sonnet "Tuskegee" (1906) shows the influence of his literary education and keen sense of how a sonnet works:

> Wherefore this busy labor without rest?
> Is it an idle dream to which we cling,
> Here where a thousand dusky toilers sing
> Unto the world their hope? "Build we our best.
> By hand and thought," they cry, "although unblessed."
> So the great engines throb, and anvils ring,
> And so the thought is wedded to the thing;
> But what shall be the end, and what the test?
> Dear God, we dare not answer, we can see
> Not many steps ahead, but this we know—
> If all our toilsome building is in vain,
> Availing not to set our manhood free,
> If envious hate roots out the seed we sow,
> The South will wear eternally a stain.[71]

Like Dunbar's sonnet to Washington, "Tuskegee" is not exactly a sonnet of praise. Hill's speaker, in first-person plural, questions the end result of the physical work to which the "dusky toilers" attend. The sonnet fol-lows an Italian rhyme scheme and uses more modern diction. The single enjambment in the octave suggests a poetic voice breaking free from the cage of sonnet labor. The sestet responds that the answer to the question may be painful; there is a possibility that the work may be in vain. Here too we see Hill's deft use of enjambment ("see / not many steps ahead") to emphasize the painful vision of an empty harvest for laboring men in the South. Hill, like Dunbar, was skeptical of Washington's tactics to focus on practical education and economic gains rather than social and civic gains, supporting equality and "manhood." Hill's choice of the sonnet form is thoughtful and sly: the form itself evokes higher education and the possibility of "idle dreams" that are far from idle; Hill's speaker gestures toward the sonnet's emphasis on the metaphysical to suggest that physical labor is not enough. Dreams, songs, hope, and blessings matter too.

Hill's "Vision of a Lyncher" was written for the January 1912 issue of the *Crisis* and is accompanied by photographs of a lynching. It is "dedicated to His Excellency, the Governor of South Carolina":

> Once looked I into hell—'twas in a trance
> Throughout a horrid night of soul-wrought pain;
> Down through the pit I saw the burning plain,
> Where writhed the tortured swarm, without one glance
> Upward to earth or God. There in advance
> Of all the rest was one with lips profane
> And murderous, bloody hands, marked to be slain
> By peers that would not bear him countenance.
> "God," cried I in my dream, "what soul is he
> Doomed thus to drain the utmost cup of fate,
> That even the cursed of Tartarus expel?"
> And the great Voice replied: "The chastity
> Of dear, confiding Law he raped; now Hate,
> His own begotten, drives him forth from hell."

Here, in an Italian sonnet drawing on traditions including Odysseus's descent into Hades and Dante's *Inferno*, Hill's speaker looks into hell and sees the governor of South Carolina (Coleman Livingston Blease) being shunned even by the most cursed of Tartarus. Blease was not only racist and prolynching, even by the standards of South Carolina politics of the era, but also infamous for pardoning white criminals for whimsical reasons (such as bearing the same name as a boyhood friend). He was quoted regularly as saying, "To hell with the Constitution," which he denied in 1912, explaining that "the remark was misrepresented. No man would be more conscientious than I in keeping my oath to support the Constitution of South Carolina, or of the United States, but where black men commit crimes against white women and are lynched for it, I declare Constitutions do not apply. For that there is a higher law than the Constitution."[72] In Hill's sonnet, God explains that the leader with "murderous, bloody hands" had raped the chastity of law.

Hill's sonnets protesting race violence demonstrate the influence of Milton and Keats, but Hill learned from Dunbar the sonnet's appropriateness for the anguished reality of black life in America. Hill saw how Dunbar used the form's perceived "stateliness" to address the politically explosive topic of race violence. Hill drew on the form's familiarity with Greek and Roman tales of tyranny and carnage to indict politics of the present day. Hill's sonnets are key to the developing African American sonnet tradition in their efforts to combine a black voice with the sonnet's powerful heritage. Woodson, in his study on 1930s sonnets, does not mention either Dunbar or Hill.

Du Bois may or may not have apprehended Hill's poetic innovations; as magazine poetry, sonnets were convenient for Du Bois and other editors: concise, recognizable, international, cosmopolitan, tasteful, and easy to fit at the end of a column of text, given their regulated length and width. There is little uncertainty in publishing a sonnet. Accordingly, journals such as the *Crisis*, especially given Du Bois's conservative and internationalist literary sensibility, published sonnets regularly.[73] Not all were political.[74] Alice Moore Dunbar-Nelson's "Sonnet," first published in the *Crisis* (1917), is also a key early contribution to the African American sonnet tradition. "Sonnet" also appears in Johnson's *Book of American Negro Poetry* and remains widely anthologized:

> I had not thought of violets of late,
> The wild, shy kind that spring beneath your feet
> In wistful April days, when lovers mate
> And wander through the fields in raptures sweet.
> The thought of violets meant florists' shops,
> And bows and pins, and perfumed papers fine;
> And garish lights, and mincing little fops
> And cabarets and songs, and deadening wine.
> So far from sweet real things my thoughts had strayed,
> I had forgot wide fields, and clear brown streams;
> The perfect loveliness that God has made,—
> Wild violets shy and Heaven-mounting dreams.
> And now—unwittingly, you've made me dream
> Of violets, and my soul's forgotten gleam.

A romantic contemplation of nature's beauty as compared to "manmade" beauty, Dunbar-Nelson's sonnet calls to mind Wordsworth's sonnet "Surprised by Joy" in its sudden recollection of a memory (in this case a happy memory). Using a Shakespearean rhyme scheme, "Sonnet" situates itself in a pastoral tradition, comparing wild violets with flowers in a city florist's shop; with "clear brown streams," it quietly announces its resistance to what is white and fair in that tradition. Read historically, with the recent introduction of the hothouse African violet to American florist's shops, it can also be read as a political engagement with race. Married briefly (and unhappily) to Paul Dunbar, Alice Dunbar-Nelson pushed Dunbar intellectually and encouraged him in his writing of formal poetry. Her own poetry is entirely formal. Without overstating the case, it is evident that her influence on Dunbar's formal poetry and her own sonnet contributions are key to the growing influence of African American sonnets. Her sonnet belongs alongside other flower sonnets that engage with race, such as Samuel Beadle's "To a Flower on a Corpse" (1899), about beauty at a time of violence; George Marion McClellan's "A January Dandelion"; and Charles Reason's "Sonnet."

Lucian B. Watkins, a noted poet and veteran of World War I, was also a regular sonnet contributor to the *Crisis*; his sonnet "Go!" on the runner Howard P. Drew appeared in January 1916, and his memorial sonnet, "Ballade to Paul Laurence Dunbar," appeared in the December 1918 issue:

> We would not call you, Dunbar, from your rest,
> For you were weary when you softly sang
> The lullaby that soothed your love-sweet breast,
> And o'er the raptured world divinely rang,
> Amid the storms of Life's tumultuous clang,
> Of battle-thunders in the fateful Night
> That hide the smiles of Heaven from our sight;—
> Lo, while you sleep the sleep of Paradise,
> We seek the blessed morning and its light,
>   "Ere sleep comes down to soothe the weary eyes!"
> Ah Poet Paul! You sang and all is right!
> We feel our souls expanding for the fight—
> Lord help us breathe to Thee a prayer and rise
> And touch Thy Truth Eternal on the Height.
>   "Ere sleep comes down to soothe the weary eyes!"

Watkins takes slight liberties with the form (acknowledged by calling the poem a ballade), but this is clearly a sonnet that is familiar with Dunbar's

sonnets, notably "Slow Through the Dark" and "The Path," as well as Corrothers's sonnets to Dunbar. "We would not call you," the speaker says
and notes the unhappiness of Dunbar's life while climbing upward. But
Watkins's speaker feels his soul "expanding for the fight" ahead and upward. Watkins's sonnet is speaking to Dunbar's sonnet. While Watkins's
sonnets are rarely anthologized, the publication of "Ballade to Paul Laurence Dunbar" marks another public tribute to Dunbar in sonnet form.

The *Crisis* also championed Joseph Seamon Cotter, Jr., whose sonnets
were published regularly in the black press, notably in the *A.M.E. Zion
Quarterly Review*, and whose "Sonnet to Negro Soldiers" was regularly anthologized into the 1930s:[75]

> They shall go down unto Life's Borderland,
> Walk unafraid within that Living Hell,
> Nor heed the driving rain of shot and shell
> That 'round them falls; but with uplifted hand
> Be one with mighty hosts, an armed band
> Against man's wrong to man—for such full well
> They know. And from their trembling lips shall swell
> A song of hope the world can understand.
> All this to them shall be a glorious sign,
> A glimmer of that Resurrection Morn
> When age-long Faith, crowned with a grace benign,
> Shall rise and from their brows cast down the thorn
> Of Prejudice. E'en though through blood it be,
> There breaks this day their dawn of Liberty.[76]

Cotter's sonnet is wry, confident, and hopeful. The Italian octave describes the bravery of the soldiers who know "full well" the hell of man's
wrong to man. The Shakespearean sestet signals a change of mood from
fearlessness to faith that after a night of blood, dawn will bring the end of
prejudice. The sonnet's use of enjambment—half of the lines have no end
punctuation—emphasizes the freedom offered to black soldiers in World
War I. Cotter was optimistic that the freedom would bear fruit after the
war; he died young, of tuberculosis, and did not witness the full extent of
postwar race violence in America.[77] By the end of the 1910s, some of the
most influential African American sonnets had appeared in the pages of
the *Crisis* and other publications.

The publication of McKay's "If We Must Die" in the *Liberator* in July
1919 ought to have normalized the sonnet for African American poetics. Sonnets by McKay were appearing in the *Messenger, Pearsons, Work-*

ers' Dreadnought, and *Seven Arts.* McKay collected most of these in *Harlem Shadows* (1922), including "If We Must Die," "Harlem Dancer," "The Lynching," "Outcast," "Baptism," and "America," alongside new work. *Harlem Shadows,* which garnered more positive notices than any collection by a black poet until Countee Cullen's *Color* appeared in 1925, put the sonnet form squarely at the center of the emerging African American poetic canon.[78] More than a third of McKay's poetry written and published over the course of his lifetime is in sonnet form. But the influence of his sonnets has been as little discussed as who influenced McKay. McKay never seemed to have acknowledged Dunbar or Charles Bertram Johnson.

McKay was born in Clarendon, Jamaica, in 1889 and had a traditional British education—one that included literary works by Shakespeare and Tennyson—and also grew up hearing Jamaican patois. McKay was always double-voiced, at home in two languages and two literary heritages. His first book of poetry, *Songs of Jamaica* (1912), featured poems written in Jamaican-English dialect, inspired partly by the Scottish dialect poems of Robert Burns.[79] McKay moved to the United States to attend Tuskeegee Institute and was shocked by the racism and segregation in the American South.[80] McKay's sonnet "To the White Fiends" was written soon after McKay's arrival in the United States, in 1912:

> Think you I am not fiend and savage too?
> Think you I could not arm me with a gun
> And shoot down ten of you for every one
> Of my black brothers murdered, burnt by you?
> Be not deceived, for every deed you do
> I could match—out-match: am I not Afric's son,
> Black of that black land where black deeds are done?
> But the Almighty from the darkness drew
> My soul and said: Even thou shalt be a light
> Awhile to burn on the benighted earth,
> Thy dusky face I set among the white
> For thee to prove thyself of highest worth;
> Before the world is swallowed up in night,
> To show thy little lamp: go forth, go forth![81]

The performance of doubleness, competition, opposition, and repetition are all on view here. The speaker is fiend and savage, threatening repayment in multiples, repeating the terms "match," "deed," "black," or "forth." McKay divides the stanza into two septets rather than octave and sestet. The first half threatens violence, the second, with its Miltonic al-lusions and "thou's" and "thy's," puts the speaker forward as divinely and poetically chosen to show the truth of black worth. The self-questioning sonnet form allows "To the White Fiends" to turn a social relationship into a rhetorical situation involving the speaker, the reader, and the son-net itself. "Think you?" the speaker asks, twice. "Be not deceived…am I not Afric's son?" the speaker both warns and asks. "But," the speaker says, and then quotes "the Almighty," who has the last word. Du Bois re-jected McKay's "To the White Fiends" for the *Crisis*.[82] Wallace Thurman remarks, "This is propaganda poetry of the highest order although it is crude and inexpert."[83] More recently David Caplan argues that McKay's use of the sonnet form "asserted cultural superiority, recasting the white racist as the 'savage.'"[84]

William Maxwell characterizes McKay as "collaborating" with the sonnet form: the sonnet was "an old and prestigious template of white lit-erary authority" that with "a thousand preceding voices" welcomed "the vitality the black content could supply." McKay, Maxwell argues, saw the sonnet as "a fellow vagabond equipped with centuries of worldly advice on living through the century of the color line."[85] Melvin Tolson, a son-net writer himself, sees McKay drawing on the sonnet to universalize his particular outrage. Focusing on the "if" and the "must," Tolson argues: "McKay insures the catholicity of his theme in two ways: he does not re-veal the ethnic identity of his protagonist, nor does he hog-tie the free will of the attacked by the imposition of an affirmative decision."[86] In the "holocaustal year 1919," Tolson continues, "If We Must Die" "signalized Claude McKay as the symbol of the New Negro and the Harlem Renais-sance," even as the poem is "a pillar of fire by night in many lands." Mc-Kay's sonnet is both particular and universal. "If We Must Die" "is the most powerful fusion of art and outrage that it is possible to find any-where," Tony Martin argues.[87]

McKay's passion is far more double-voiced in his sonnet "America" (1922):

> Although she feeds me bread of bitterness,
> And sinks into my throat her tiger's tooth,
> Stealing my breath of life, I will confess
> I love this cultured hell that tests my youth!
> Her vigor flows like tides into my blood,
> Giving me strength erect against her hate.
> Her bigness sweeps my being like a flood.

> Yet as a rebel fronts a king in state,
> I stand within her walls with not a shred
> Of terror, malice, not a word of jeer.
> Darkly I gaze into the days ahead,
> And see her might and granite wonders there,
> Beneath the touch of Time's unerring hand,
> Like priceless treasures sinking in the sand.[88]

Using the Shakespearean form, the speaker in "America" is divided, being pulled in two directions; he knows he is being treated badly but loves the challenge. He confesses this fact, proposing an intimacy between speaker and reader. In terms passionate and sexual ("vigor," "erect," "bigness," "with not a shred") he stands ready to be ravished by this feline, female-gendered nation in a manner that evokes Donne's holy sonnets (chapter 2). The final couplet evokes Shelley's sonnet "Ozymandias" (1818), with its king whose stone likeness sinks into sand. "The elemental fierceness of the conflict endured by every Black man is pictured with simple strength," Emanuel notes; "America treacherously gives and cruelly takes away; but in so doing she increasingly draws forth Black masculine vigor."[89]

For Tolson, McKay's radicalism was a matter of content rather than form. McKay was able to "etch, with a Dantean simplicity terrifying in detail, a picture of himself as surgeon in the grotto of the self."[90] In "America," in the manner of Renaissance sonneteers, McKay's internal surgeries are on full display. While the poem is outward-facing, protesting political conditions, the speaker is inwardly brooding, arguing with himself about his emotional attachment to America and her physically abusive imprisonment "within her walls." The sonnet's limited enjambment—only lines about confession and emotion have no end punctuation—mark his acknowledgment of self-confinement. He is pondering, not protesting.

While McKay's sonnets are often unracialized and tending to the universal, his interest in the relationship of poet to place and particularity was long-standing:

> of all the poets I admire, major and minor, Byron, Shelley, Keats, Blake, Burns, Whitman, Heine, Baudelaire, Verlaine and Rimbaud and the rest—it seemed to me that when I read them—in their poetry I could feel their race, their class, their roots in the soil, growing into plants, spreading and forming the backgrounds against which they were silhouetted. I could not feel the reality of them without that.[91]

His own approach to literature was "eclectic," McKay added, and unorthodox. These traits would not endear him to canon makers in his time. McKay was easy to critique in part because he was not a central figure in Harlem, despite the centrality of his poetry.[92] McKay was thirty years old in 1922, and *Harlem Shadows* was his third collection of poetry, but Johnson in the preface to *The Book of American Negro Poetry* called McKay a young man who had not only demonstrated "power, breadth, and skill" but also "passed beyond" the danger that threatens many poets of allowing polemics to "choke their sense of artistry":

> He demonstrates mastery of the three when as a Negro poet he pours out the bitterness and rebellion in his heart in those two sonnet-tragedies, "If We Must Die" and "To the White Fiends," in a manner that strikes terror; and when as a cosmic poet he creates the atmosphere and mood of poetic beauty in the absolute, as he does in "Spring in New Hampshire" and "The Harlem Dancer."[93]

James Weldon Johnson characterizes the form of McKay's "sonnet-tragedies" as merely a vessel for his bitterness and rebellion rather than an agent for his argument. In a few short years Johnson would update this view. "Incongruous as it may seem," Johnson wrote of McKay's protest poetry in 1930, "he took the sonnet form as his medium."[94] Johnson ignores an entire generation of sonnets and sonnet writers. Yet it seems clear that McKay read and was influenced by sonnets written by his contemporaries, including Dunbar, Braithwaite, Hill, and Charles Bertram Johnson. McKay's sonnets would also influence later sonnet writers, notably Marcus Christian and Melvin Tolson (chapter 5).

Paul Dunbar and Claude McKay are complicated figures in the literary history of African American poetry. Both might be characterized as poets who put poetic craft before politics and who turned to prose, to the novel form, for more sustained and political engagement. Both were considered the "new best" poets of their era—Dunbar the "best since Wheatley," McKay the "best since Dunbar"—and both suffered the indignity of being introduced to the public by white editors whose tone of admiration is painfully mixed with racism. In the introduction to *Lyrics of Lowly Life*, Howells writes, "So far as I could remember, Paul Dunbar was the only man of pure African blood and of American civilization to feel the negro life aesthetically and express it lyrically."[95] In his introduction to *Harlem Shadows*, Max Eastman writes that McKay's poems "have a special interest for all the races of man because they are sung by a pure-blooded

Negro."[96] After 1922, with the push by black intellectuals to define, circumscribe, and *own* black poetry, such introductions would be less common—although Allen Tate's introduction to Melvin Tolson's *Libretto for the Republic of Liberia* (1953) is a throwback to the earlier era, with the statement: "For the first time, it seems to me, a Negro poet has assimilated completely the poetic language of his time and, by implication, the language of the Anglo-American tradition."[97] But for twentieth-century black poetry canon makers, "If We Must Die" too overtly dwelt in multiple literary histories, gathering unto itself the black protest tradition, the Shakespearean and Miltonic protest sonnet traditions, and contemporary labor poetry and sonnets by English war poets. McKay's sonnets are not seen as influential, even though they clearly were. Cary Nelson argues for the importance of McKay's work: "[H]is use of anger as both an aesthetic resource and a source of psychic integration anticipates the Black Arts movement of the 1960s."[98] The more accurate term is *influences*.

James Weldon Johnson's groundbreaking *Book of American Negro Poetry* features twelve important African American sonnets published by black poets in the previous decades—including five by McKay and one by Johnson himself. Johnson's preface, which initiated the practice of describing and circumscribing African American poetry, offered a new approach to assessing African American poetry. *BANP* was "both a cultural history and a cultural manifesto," as Gerald Early argues: "[T]he book that really kicked off the phase of the New Negro Movement known as the Harlem Renaissance—the phase that tried to produce a school or an identifiable discipline of black American letters."[99] But Johnson's project did not include a focus on influence.

The endeavor to define and circumscribe black poetry begun by Johnson would almost immediately enable twentieth-century criticism of the sonnet as wholly European in origin—or at least white, in the case of Edna St. Vincent Millay—and as problematic for black poetry, even if the notion had not occurred to Johnson. Black poets after 1922 certainly continued to write sonnets, even after Hughes remarked to a newspaper reporter in 1927 that the sonnet was not the right "mould" for poems about Harlem.[100] Black newspapers were filled with sonnets; a young Gwendolyn Brooks began publishing sonnets in the *Chicago Defender*. Of the poems published in *Opportunity* in the 1930s, Woodson notes, one-third were sonnets, including three by Hughes. But as Woodson's recovery work (and my own) makes clear, anthologies soon became the privileged dataset of African American poetry. If the sonnet form became ever so slightly less welcome and approved, it also became a form to be more muscularly innovated on, particularly by Gwendolyn Brooks, Robert Hayden, Tolson, and even LeRoi Jones.

CHAPTER 5

Anthologies and Canon
Formation, 1923–1967

After 1923, anthologies of African American poetry became the locus of influence on subsequent generations of black poets.
While scores of new sonnets on every subject were published in the black
press every year, the anthologizing movement limited posterity to a small
canon of African American "greatest hits" sonnets, the imprint of which
can be discerned in later sonnets. Key essays on African American literature that appeared in the decades after 1923 (including prefaces to anthologies) grappling with broad questions about the category, nature, and
subject matter of black poetry remained silent on the sonnet as a popular form for black poets and rarely noticed black poets influencing other
black poets. Rather, the central concern for black poetry canon makers
and scholars was that black poetry should reflect black culture. In short,
while sonnets were being published and anthologized regularly, little notice was taken of how the form was developing and being adopted by new
poets over time.

Not surprisingly, the sonnets regularly appearing in black poetry anthologies were the most influential: works by Claude McKay, Countee
Cullen, Gwendolyn Brooks, and Robert Hayden that are double-voiced,
synthesizing sonnet history and the African American experience. But
patterns of influence are difficult to detect with sonnets dispersed across
anthologies, over decades. Sonnets by lesser-known poets such as Marcus
Christian or James Corrothers that demonstrate McKay's or Dunbar's influence rarely appear in the same anthology as McKay or Dunbar and are
never triangulated with broader sonnet traditions (metaphorical slavery,

Shakespearean concern for immortality). African American sonnets on the same theme or subject (lynching, "New Negro" ideology, black soldiers after war) are not grouped together. In short, not only are influence and tradition almost impossible to see, but the forewords and prefaces to anthologies are uninterested in questions of influence and don't encourage readers to look.

This chapter examines the genealogy of sonnet influence by focusing on sonnets as they appeared to most readers after 1923, in the pages of eighteen black literature and poetry anthologies, including volumes designed primarily for classroom use. Roughly chronological, I note the significant sonnets included in each anthology and those that fall away over time. Reading this most vital and productive era of African American literature through the very narrow lens of black poetry anthologies brings the sonnets themselves into focus as they would been introduced to the majority of new readers. Both during the vibrant and culturally rich era still popularly known as the Harlem Renaissance and after, most Americans encounter poetry in school, in textbooks and anthologies, where their influence is often cited by poets.

The push to anthologize was a key part of the drive to define black literature as well as to celebrate it. Anthologizing is as much a sociological and political enterprise as a literary one, and early anthologies were responding in part to the exclusion of black poets in anthologies of American poetry.[1] As Henry Louis Gates, Jr., observes, the early anthology movement "defined as its goal the demonstration of the existence of the black tradition as a political defense of the racial self against racism."[2] As a secondary concern, the study of black literature in black colleges and universities required teaching anthologies. Accordingly, black poetry anthologies began to focus on what Gates, Kenneth Warren, and others call the instrumental and indexical aspects of black literature: how literature served to achieve racial goals and served as an index of progress. So many anthologies arrived so quickly that as Jeremy Braddock noted, the anthology "could reasonably be claimed as the preeminent black literary form of the twenties, enacting as it did a performance of collectivity and interpellation, political demand and representation, and also, in some cases, canon formation."[3] Rebecca L. Walkowitz notes the self-referential nature of African American literature and its anthologies, each of which serves "to construct and confirm the 'tradition' that justifies its publication."[4]

Anthologies, structured as they are by chronology and author, don't lend themselves to promoting the idea of influence even as they play a key role in the influential reception of African American poetry. General overviews of black poetry and foundational criticism, from Sterling Brown's *The Negro in American Poetry* (1937) through Nathaniel Huggins's 1971 *The Harlem Renaissance* to today, rely on anthologies. Even James Emanuel, in his 1975 *Black World* essay on sonnets of the 1920s, selects his examples—about thirty—from the pages of four key anthologies.[5] By the time the *Norton Anthology of African American Literature* appears in 1997, every sonnet included has been previously anthologized. So while anthologies have kept the most characteristically African American sonnets in circulation for a century, even Emanuel's backward glance in 1975 could not discern sonnet influence over time if he had tried.

The African American poetry volumes that followed Johnson's *Book of American Negro Poetry* include Robert T. Kerlin's *Negro Poets and Their Poems* (1923); Newman Ivey White and Walter Clinton Jackson's *An Anthology of Verse by American Negroes* (1924); Countee Cullen's *Caroling Dusk* (1927); V. F. Calverton's *An Anthology of American Negro Literature* (1929); Otelia Cromwell, Lorenzo D. Turner, and Eva B. Dykes's *Readings from Negro Authors for Schools and Colleges* (1931); Beatrice F. Wormley and Charles W. Carter's WPA anthology, *An Anthology of Negro Poetry by Negroes and Others* (1937); Beatrice M. Murphy's *Negro Voices: An Anthology of Contemporary Verse* (1938); Sterling Brown, Arthur P. Davis, and Ulysses Lee's *The Negro Caravan* (1942); Beatrice M. Murphy's *Ebony Rhythm: An Anthology of Contemporary Negro Verse* (1948); Langston Hughes and Arna Bontemps's *The Poetry of the Negro, 1746–1949* (1949); Herman Dreer's *American Literature by Negro Authors* (1950); Arna Bontemps's *American Negro Poetry* (1963); Herbert Hill's *Soon, One Morning: New Writing by American Negroes, 1940–1962* (1963); and Langston Hughes's *New Negro Poets U.S.A.* (1964), with a foreword by Gwendolyn Brooks.

Four important idiosyncratic collections of essays and poems also appeared: Alain Locke's volume *The New Negro* (1925); Charles Johnson's *Ebony and Topaz* (1927); Wallace Thurman's *Fire!!* (1927), and Nancy Cunard's *Negro: An Anthology* (1934), all of which published essays and artworks alongside literary works. Table 1 presents the twentieth-century anthologies of African American poetry published from *BANP* through 1967, listing the sonnets included in these anthologies. Table 2 lists the anthologies between 1968 and 1973; new sonnets will be discussed in chapter 6.

TABLE 1. Sonnets from the Twentieth-Century Anthologies of African American Poetry, 1922–1967

James Weldon Johnson, ed., *The Book of American Negro Poetry*. Harcourt Brace, 1922.
    BENJAMIN BRAWLEY: "Chaucer"
    JAMES W. JOHNSON: "Mother Night"
    JAMES CORROTHERS: "Paul Laurence Dunbar," "The Negro Singer"
    LESLIE PINCKNEY HILL: "Tuskegee"
    CLAUDE MCKAY: "The Lynching," "If We Must Die," "White Fiends,"
        "Harlem Dancer," "Tired Worker"
    ALICE DUNBAR-NELSON: "Sonnet"
    PLACIDO: "Despida a Mi Madre"

Richard Kerlin, ed., *Negro Poets and Their Poems*. Associated Publishers, 1923.
    JAMES CORROTHERS: "Paul Laurence Dunbar," "The Negro Singer"
    ALICE DUNBAR-NELSON: "Sonnet"
    WILLIAM MOORE: "Expectancy," "As the Old Year Passed"
    CLAUDE MCKAY: "The Lynching," "In Bondage," "The Harlem Dancer,"
        "If We Must Die," "The Negro"
    LESLIE PINCKNEY HILL: "Mater Dolorosa," "To a Caged Canary"
    JAMES W. JOHNSON: "The Black Mammy"
    LUCIAN WATKINS: "The New Negro"
    CARRIE CLIFFORD: "An Easter Message"

Newman Ivey White and Walter Clinton Jackson, eds., *Anthology of Verse by American Negroes*. Trinity College Press, 1924.
    PAUL LAURENCE DUNBAR: "Slow Through the Dark"
    T. THOMAS FORTUNE: "Lincoln"
    WM. STANLEY BRAITHWAITE: "This Is My Life"
    BENJAMIN BRAWLEY: "Chaucer," "The Bells of Notre Dame"
    JAMES CORROTHERS: "The Negro Singer," "Paul Laurence Dunbar"
    GEORGE MARGETSON: "Time" (To the Recent Graduates), "Resurrection"
        (On the Discovery of Pharoah's Tomb. February 1923),
    JAMES W. JOHNSON: "Mother Night"
    JOSEPH SEAMON COTTER, JR.: "Sonnet to Negro Soldiers"
    LESLIE PINCKNEY HILL: "Tuskegee," "Freedom," "So Quietly," "To the Smartweed"
    CLAUDE MCKAY: "Spring," "In Bondage," "The Lynching," "Baptism"

Alain Locke, ed., *The New Negro*. Simon & Schuster, 1925.
    CLAUDE MCKAY: "White Houses," "Baptism," "Like a Strong Tree,"
        "Subway Wind," "Russian Cathedral," "To the Entrenched Classes"

Wallace Thurman, ed., *FIRE!!* Negro Universities Press, 1927.
    COUNTEE CULLEN: "From the Dark Tower"

Countee Cullen, ed., *Caroling Dusk: An Anthology of Verse by Negro Poets*. Harper & Brothers, 1927.
    JAMES W. JOHNSON: "My City"
    WM. STANLEY BRAITHWAITE: "October XXXIX 1795" (Keats's Birthday)
    JAMES EDWARD MCCALL: "The New Negro"
    ANNE SPENCER: "Substitution"

ALICE DUNBAR NELSON: "Sonnet"

CLAUDE MCKAY: "America," "Russian Cathedral"

JEAN TOOMER: "November Cotton Flower"

LEWIS G. ALEXANDER: "Africa," "The Dark Brother"

STERLING BROWN: "Salutamus," "Challenge," "Return"

GWENDOLYN BENNETT: "Sonnet I," "Sonnet II"

COUNTEE CULLEN: "Protest," "Yet Do I Marvel," "From the Dark Tower"

GEORGE LEONARD ALLEN: "To Melody"

HELENE JOHNSON: "Sonnet to a Negro in Harlem"

WESLEY CURTWRIGHT: "The Close of Day"

Charles Johnson, ed., *Ebony and Topaz: A Collectanea.* Ayer, 1927.

LOIS AUGUSTA CUGLAR: "Consecration"

HELENE JOHNSON: "Sonnet to a Negro in Harlem"

CLARENCE F. BRYSON: "The Soudan"

V. F. Calverton, ed., *Anthology of American Negro Literature.*
Modern Library, 1929.

PAUL LAURENCE DUNBAR: "Robert Gould Shaw"

CLAUDE MCKAY: "If We Must Die," "The Harlem Dancer,"
    "The Lynching"

LEWIS G. ALEXANDER: "The Dark Brother"

Otelia Cromwell, Lorenzo Dow Turner, and Eva B. Dykes, eds., *Readings from Negro Authors for Schools and Colleges.* Harcourt Brace, 1931.

COUNTEE CULLEN: "From the Dark Tower"

CLAUDE MCKAY: "America"

ALICE DUNBAR-NELSON: "Sonnet"

ANGELA WELD GRIMKÉ: "To Dunbar High School: A Sonnet"

Nancy Cunard, ed., *Negro: An Anthology.* Continuum, 1934.

CARRIE W. CLIFFORD: "The Black Draftee from Dixie"

COUNTEE CULLEN: "From the Dark Tower"

Beatrice F. Wormley and Charles W. Carter, eds., *An Anthology of Negro Poetry by Negroes and Others.* Works Progress Administration, 1937.

PAUL LAURENCE DUNBAR: "The Path"

JAMES D. CORROTHERS: "Paul Laurence Dunbar"

FENTON JOHNSON: "These Are My People"

WM. STANLEY BRAITHWAITE: "Thanksgiving"

GEORGE MARGETSON: "Time"

CLAUDE MCKAY: "America"

LESLIE PINCKNEY HILL: "To a Caged Canary in a Negro Restaurant," "Tuskegee"

WILLIAM MOORE: "As the Old Year Passed," "Expectancy"

RAYMOND G. DANDRIDGE: "Time to Die"

COUNTEE CULLEN: "From the Dark Tower"

LEWIS G. ALEXANDER: "Africa"

LUCIAN WATKINS: "The New Negro," "A Prayer of the Race That God Made Black"

Beatrice M. Murphy, ed., *Negro Voices: An Anthology of Contemporary Verse.* Henry Harrison, 1938.

LEWIS G. ALEXANDER: "Southland"

CONRAD CHITTICK: "Torches"

MARCUS B. CHRISTIAN: "Spring in the South"

EDYTHE MAE GORDON: "Sonnet for June"
JOHN E. HALL: "Justice"
CALVIN S. LAMBERT: "Lock Lomond"
OCTAVE LILLY, JR.: "The Worker"
ELEANOR MCDUFFIE: "If You Forget"
BEATRICE MURPHY: "Hatred"
LUCIA MAE PITTS: "Challenge," "Requiem"
MELVIN B. TOLSON: "The Wine of Ecstasy"
EUGENE B. WILMAN: "Lament of the Farm," "Song of the Maimed Soldier"

Sterling Brown, Arthur Davis, et al., *The Negro Caravan*. Citadel/Dryden Press, 1942.
PAUL LAURENCE DUNBAR: "Robert Gould Shaw," "Harriet Beecher Stowe"
LESLIE PINCKNEY HILL: "So Quietly," "Tuskegee"
CLAUDE MCKAY: "Baptism," "America," "White Houses," "If We Must Die," "The
Lynching"
COUNTEE CULLEN: "From the Dark Tower"
GEORGE LEONARD ALLEN: "Pilate in Modern America," "To Melody"

Beatrice M. Murphy, ed., *Ebony Rhythm: An Anthology of Contemporary Negro Verse*.
Exposition Press, 1948.
WALTER G. ARNOLD: "Entreaty," "Interrogation"
ALPHEUS BUTLER: "Primrose and Thistle," "Maid and Violinist," "Portrait of a Poet"
MARCUS B. CHRISTIAN: "Selassie at Geneva," "Go Down, Moses!," "The Craftsman"
YLESSA DUBONEE: "Departure"
JOHN W. FENTRESS: "Booker T. Washington," "Abraham Lincoln"
GEORGIA DOUGLAS JOHNSON: "Black Recruit"
LUTHER GEORGE LUPER, JR.: "Sonnet Spiritual"
CONSTANCE NICHOLS: "Civil Service"
LUCIA PITTS: "If Ever You Should Walk Away," "Before a Monument"
ALEXANDER YOUNG: "Love's Helplessness"

Langston Hughes and Arna Bontemps, eds., *The Poetry of the Negro, 1746-1949*.
Doubleday, 1949.
JAMES D. CORROTHERS: "Paul Laurence Dunbar"
JAMES WELDON JOHNSON: "My City"
ALICE DUNBAR NELSON: "Sonnet"
WM. STANLEY BRAITHWAITE: "The House of Falling Leaves,"
"The Arsenal of the Lord"
LESLIE PINCKNEY HILL: "Tuskegee"
MARCUS B. CHRISTIAN: "The Craftsman," "McDonogh Day in
New Orleans," "Sonnets 1 and 2"
GWENDOLYN BENNETT: "Yet Do I Marvel"
COUNTEE CULLEN: "From the Dark Tower"
JONATHAN H. BROOKS: "Muse in Late November"
HELENE JOHNSON: "Remember Not"
ROBERT HAYDEN: "Frederick Douglass"
MARGARET WALKER: "For Mary McLeod Bethune," "Love Note II: Flags"
GWENDOLYN BROOKS: "The Birth in a Narrow Room," "Mentors,"
"Piano after War," "Sonnet," "America"
ALFRED DUCKETT: "White Houses"
CLAUDE MCKAY: "If We Must Die," "Baptism," "Russian Cathedral"

Herman Dreer, ed., *American Literature by Negro Authors*. Macmillan, 1950.
  CLAUDE MCKAY: "America," "The Tired Worker"
  LESLIE PINCKNEY HILL: "Freedom"
  LORENZO D. BLANTON: "I Wonder"
  STERLING BROWN: "Return"
  GEORGIA DOUGLAS JOHNSON: "Foregather"
  FREDERICK W. BOND: "To a Whippoorwill"
  JEAN TOOMER: "November Cotton Flower"
  GWENDOLYN BROOKS: "Love Note. I. Surely," "The Progress"

Arna Bontemps, ed., *American Negro Poetry*. Hill & Wang, 1963.
  CLAUDE MCKAY: "Outcast," "St. Isaac's Church, Petrograd,"
    "If We Must Die," "The White House"
  MARCUS B. CHRISTIAN: "McDonogh Day in New Orleans"
  LANGSTON HUGHES: "Pennsylvania Station"
  GWENDOLYN BENNETT: "Sonnet I," "Sonnet II"
  COUNTEE CULLEN: "Yet Do I Marvel"
  HELENE JOHNSON: "Sonnet to a Negro in Harlem"
  ROBERT HAYDEN: "Frederick Douglass"
  FRANK YERBY: "You Are a Part of Me," "Calm after Storm," "Weltschmerz"
  GWENDOLYN BROOKS: "Flags," "Piano after War"
  ALFRED A. DUCKETT: "Sonnet"

Herbert Hill, ed., *Soon, One Morning: New Writing by American Negroes, 1940–1962*. Knopf, 1963.
  GWENDOLYN BROOKS: "Intermission"
  LEROI JONES: "The Turncoat"

Langston Hughes, ed., *New Negro Poets U.S.A.* Indiana University Press, 1964.
  SOLOMON EDWARD: "Shoplifter"
  LEROI JONES: "Epistrophe"

If a small group of newspaper editors was responsible for the publication of sonnets by African American poets, a different small group of editors was responsible for crafting the black poetry tradition through the editing of anthologies. The most influential anthology editors were well-known male writers and editors from New York and Washington, D.C.: Johnson, Locke, Cullen, Thurman, Bontemps, Charles Johnson, Calverton, and Hughes. The lesser-known Beatrice M. Murphy, from Washington, D.C., was the book review editor for the *Afro-American*. Kerlin, White, Jackson, Davis, Lee, Cromwell, Turner, Dykes, Wormley, and Carter were all academics and educators. Cunard was an heiress and political activist. The sonnets included in each of these anthologies speak to the tastes and preferences of the anthologizers. And while Hughes, noted for his largely free verse/jazz idiom–inflected verse, is regularly contrasted in essays and scholarship with Cullen, noted for his formal poetry, Hughes was the more energetic anthologizer of sonnets.[6]

Some notable patterns emerge in looking at the sonnets sifted out from the black press archives and the various poetry anthologies before 1967. A group of five to seven sonnets published by McKay before 1925 continues to appear, joined by one or two sonnets by Cullen and, occasionally, by Dunbar, Corrothers, Leslie Pinckney Hill, Helene Johnson, Alice Dunbar-Nelson, Lewis G. Alexander, and some others. These sonnets reflect the social and publishing landscape of the era: most were first published in *Opportunity* or the *Crisis*. After 1929, Alexander, Benjamin Brawley, T. Thomas Fortune, George Margetson, and Lucian Watkins disappear from anthologies. After 1942, sonnets by Marcus Christian, Robert Hayden, and Gwendolyn Brooks appear more regularly and sonnets by Dunbar, Corrothers, Hill, and Johnson appear sporadically. Fewer radical sonnets by McKay appear in mid-century teaching anthologies but will return in force after Dudley Randall's 1971 anthology, which includes ten sonnets by McKay. With the exception of two anthologies by Murphy that include sonnets not published in any other anthologies (many by women), nearly all of these collections include influential sonnets by McKay and Cullen that will continue to appear into the twenty-first century (see table 1).

❀ ❀ ❀

In his preface to the *Book of American Negro Poetry*, Johnson, seeking to lay the foundation for an intellectual tradition characterizing black poetry and evaluating its features, called on poets to find a form that expresses "racial spirit" without dialect, a form "capable of voicing the deepest and highest emotions and aspirations, and allow of the widest range of subjects and the widest scope of treatment."[7] Johnson praises artistic styles that are entirely African American in origin: Uncle Remus stories, spirituals or slave songs, cakewalk, and ragtime. But Johnson also included twelve sonnets, including his own, "Mother Night."

Kerlin's *Negro Poets and Their Poems* (1923) and Newman Ivey White and Walter Clinton Jackson's *An Anthology of Verse by American Negroes* (1924) both take an academic and sociological approach to their selection; their goal is to promote understanding of African American culture. Kerlin targeted students of literature and sociology. "Recognition of real literary merit will be accorded by the one class of students, and recognition of new aspects of the most serious race problem of the ages will be forced upon the second."[8] Kerlin's sources are newspapers; his is the only anthology to include sonnets by William Moore, a poet and critic from Chicago whose sonnets had been published in T. Thomas Fortune's *New York Age*.

Kerlin's most significant sonnet selection was Lucian G. Watkins's "The New Negro" (1923):

> He thinks in black. His God is but the same
> John saw—with hair "like wool" and eyes "as fire"—
> Who makes the vision for which men aspire.
> His kin is Jesus and the Christ who came
> Humbly to earth and wrought His hallowed aim
> 'Midst human scorn. Pure is his heart's desire;
> His life's religion lifts; his faith leads higher.
> Love is his Church, and Union is its name.
>
> Lo, he has learned his own immortal role
> In this momentous drama of the hour;
> Has read aright the heavens' Scriptural scroll
> 'Bove ancient wrong—long boasting in the tower.
> Ah, he has sensed the truth. Deep in his soul
> He feels the manly majesty of power.[9]

In Watkins's finely crafted Italian sonnet that uses only four rhymes, the speaker describes a black god and a humble son who, like the black speaker, lived "'midst human scorn." He is aspiring, upright, productive of Union. In the sestet, he recognizes that the truth is power and power is "manly majesty." "The New Negro" is not double-voiced, not ambivalent—somewhat in the manner of Dunbar's sonnet to Booker T. Washington—but its singular vision demonstrates resolve rather than bullheadedness. Watkins's sonnet celebrates the ideal individual, the "New Negro" unfettered by the past (the "ancient wrong") and embracing the future. It is a striking poem for its moment, particularly the opening half line "He thinks in black."[10]

Watkins's sonnet launched a tradition of sonnets on an ideal individual to include Helene Johnson's "Sonnet to a Negro in Harlem" (below). Watkins's "The New Negro" sonnet appears in the 1937 WPA anthology; Eugene Redmond in 1976 twice notes the power of the Watkins's first sentence, "He thinks in black."[11] Cullen's "From the Dark Tower" can be seen echoing the optimism of Watkins's sonnet, and even many of Gwendolyn Brooks's sonnets, offering glimpses of the inner thoughts of individual figures, resemble Watkins's here.[12]

Like Kerlin, in selecting poems for inclusion, White and Jackson are interested primarily in charting the "progress" of African American poetry. "Already a number of Negroes have produced poetry good enough to induce reputable publishers to assume the financial risk of publication," the editors proclaim. "It is therefore no longer to be doubted that the Negro will make his contribution to American poetry."[13] Readers are to consider the poems included as representative samples of each poet's work. Influence isn't mentioned. As with Kerlin, many of the poems in White and Jackson, such as George Margetson's sonnet to King Tut, "Resurrection," were published first in newspapers. Often, as in the case with "Resurrection," clippings were sent to the editors by the authors and the original publication date is lost.

Kerlin and White and Jackson were motivated by social and political concerns, as Vilma Potter emphasizes.[14] Both of these anthologies circulated widely but did not receive much critical notice. Yet both kept influential sonnets in circulation—Dunbar's "Slow Through the Dark," Corrothers's "The Negro Singer" and "Paul Laurence Dunbar" (included in both), McKay's "In Bondage" and "The Lynching" (in both), and lynching sonnets by Hill. Most subsequent black poetry anthologies rely almost entirely on poetry previously published in book form, including previous anthologies, rather than newspapers.

Alain Locke's March 1925 issue of *Survey Graphic*, "Enter the New Negro" (republished almost immediately as a volume, *The New Negro*), is more of a manifesto than anthology, although it features poetry alongside essays introducing the "New Negro" movement. Locke's influential introductory essay proclaims that it is "of" rather than "about" black America, "embodying the first fruits of the Negro Renaissance." Locke draws on metaphors of building and constructing to consider the idea of black literature and the base of the structure is broad and deep. He is not interested in the influence of one poet on another. *The New Negro* features five sonnets by McKay, including two new ones: "Like a Strong Tree" and "Russian Cathedral," neither of which are racialized.[15] The success of the anthology, Rampersad argues, "is its creation of a noble but credible portrait of black America just as black America was entering the modern world."[16] Locke enraged McKay by changing the name of his sonnet "The White House" to "White Houses" as a less politically charged title.[17] Locke included some rhymed verse by Cullen, who was then a new poetic voice in Harlem, but none of his sonnets.

Cullen had appeared on the scene in 1924 as a "boy wonder," as Gerald Early calls him, publishing poems and winning literary prizes and contests.[18] His poems were everywhere, the *Crisis* noted: "With four poems published simultaneously in four leading magazines, Countee Cullen takes his place as our leading poet."[19] Most of these poems were written when Cullen was a student at New York University, where he wrote an undergraduate thesis on Edna St. Vincent Millay. Cullen, like McKay, worked in traditional forms. Cullen's first collection of poetry, *Color*, was published to widespread acclaim in 1925. It was reviewed more widely than any other book of the era, and the reviews were almost all positive.[20] In part validated by the fact that *Color* appeared the same year as Locke's *The New Negro*, Cullen was soon the new voice of African American poetry, as Early argues:

> [T]he New Negro Movement, by the time Locke became its spokesman and Cullen its exemplar, ceased to be a search purely for a race-conscious ideology...[and] had become purely a movement where the Negro, like the white immigrants before him, could construct a migratory myth of freedom, so that he could become an American by, in effect, being reborn and having a new past that would free him from the burdens of slavery.[21]

During this time Cullen launched a column titled "The Dark Tower" for *Opportunity*, guest-edited an issue of *Palms*, and was given the opportunity to edit his own anthology, *Caroling Dusk* (1927).

Cullen introduced his anthology by emphasizing the importance of poetry in the development of a culture but insisting that his anthology was "an anthology of verse by Negro poets rather than an anthology of Negro verse," since "the attempt to corral the outbursts of the ebony muse into some definite mold to which all poetry by Negroes will conform seems altogether futile and aside from the facts."[22] For Cullen, poets who have inherited the English language have also inherited its forms and most likely have more to gain from their English and American heritage than from "any nebulous atavistic yearnings toward an African inheritance." In other words, he acknowledged multiple influences. *Caroling Dusk* features twenty-one sonnets, including two by McKay and two of Cullen's most influential: "From the Dark Tower" (chapter 2) and "Yet Do I Marvel" (1924):

> I doubt not God is good, well-meaning, kind
> And did He stoop to quibble could tell why

The little buried mole continues blind,
Why flesh that mirrors Him must some day die,
Make plain the reason tortured Tantalus
Is baited by the fickle fruit, declare
If merely brute caprice dooms Sisyphus
To struggle up a never-ending stair.
Inscrutable His ways are, and immune
To catechism by a mind too strewn
With petty cares to slightly understand
What awful brain compels His awful hand.
Yet do I marvel at this curious thing:
To make a poet black, and bid him sing![23]

"Yet Do I Marvel" is a marvel of twoness, coupling and opposing, offering multiple moments of double-voicedness. Using a Shakespearean rhyme scheme, Cullen's sonnet is composed of three sentences: one for the entire octave, the second for the third quatrain, and the third for the final couplet. The two sentences end precisely at the two voltas offered by the Shakespearean rhyme scheme. Ambivalence is performed from the opening phrase, where "I doubt not" signals doubt, followed by a mildly ironic list of God's attributes. In the second quatrain, the allusions to figures from Greek myth, Tantalus (always reaching without grasping) and Sisyphus (eternally laboring without completion), widen the scope to include a new mythological realm. The image of climbing up the endless stair evokes Dunbar's sonnet "Slow Through the Dark."

Cullen's sestet, made up of three couplets, begins with the word "inscrutable" to describe God, followed by "petty," "awful," and "awful." God is unknowable and immune to instruction by mere humans. The final, unforgettable couplet: "Yet do I marvel at this curious thing: / To make a poet black, and bid him sing!" is both ironic and abruptly optimistic and uplifting, engaging with the Shakespearean tradition of self-authorization and immortality to mock it. Can there be an immortal black poet? Cullen's sonnet hopes that the answer is yes.

Early argues that Cullen's poetry is "quaint and old fashioned," with "the added burden of being written in strict metrical forms like...the Petrarchan sonnet (Longfellow's favorite form)" without acknowledging McKay's contemporary stature.[24] Cullen, like McKay, resisted racial designations for his poetry, claiming that he wanted to be known as a "Poet," not a "Negro Poet."[25] Early attributes Cullen's decline to the fact that intellectual elites "were no longer impressed by a black man's manipulation of white poetic forms," sidelining the formal verse of Dunbar, Hill, and McKay as mere manipulation rather than innovation.[26] Cullen's sonnets, like Dunbar's and McKay's, grapple with the particular dilemma of being black in America. "If you asked any Negro what he found in Cullen's poetry," Owen Dodson observes, "he would say: all my dilemmas are written here—the hurt pride, the indignation, the satirical thrusts, the agony of being black in America."[27] Dunbar and McKay showed Cullen that the sonnet is an ideal vehicle for black poetry.

Cullen included in *Caroling Dusk* one of the most influential sonnets to appear in 1927, Helen Johnson's "Sonnet to a Negro in Harlem," published also in *Ebony and Topaz*:

> You are disdainful and magnificent—
> Your perfect body and your pompous gait,
> Your dark eyes flashing solemnly with hate;
> Small wonder that you are incompetent
> To imitate those whom you so despise—
> Your shoulders towering high above the throng,
> Your head thrown back in rich, barbaric song,
> Palm trees and mangoes stretched before your eyes.
> Let others toil and sweat for labor's sake
> And wring from grasping hands their meed of gold.
> Why urge ahead your supercilious feet?
> Scorn will efface each footprint that you make.
> I love your laughter, arrogant and bold.
> You are too splendid for this city street![28]

In what could be seen as a response to Watkins's "New Negro" sonnet, Johnson's speaker describes in the Italian octave a charismatic figure in terms that simultaneously admire, mock, and fully apprehend him. He is tall, strong, proud, exotic. He is solemnly hateful and unable to conform. The speaker exhibits some ambivalence as the sestet turns to others who labor for survival and asks why the "supercilious" figure should bother striving when his impact will be erased. The period at the twelfth line leaves the last two lines exposed as an unrhymed couplet; Johnson takes full advantage of the Italian form's rhyme scheme for a double-voiced, qualified nonresolution. The figure is "too splendid" to survive.

Emanuel appreciated Johnson's remarkable sonnet "for its satire—an early but slowly developing tradition in Black poetry—and it is further noteworthy for the in-group quality of the satire." Johnson was writing for a black audience, not intending for patronizing white readers to laugh at the "pompous gait" of this young man "confronting racism by means of much Black pride and life-style but little vocational skill."[29] Sharon Lynette Jones observes that Johnson's sonnet "illustrates the tendency of Harlem writers to employ traditional poetic forms, such as the sonnet"; clearly Johnson saw the sonnet's capacity to express qualified, ambivalent praise.[30]

Indeed, the tendency to write sonnets about the New Negro ideal was contagious, as James Edward McCall's sonnet "The New Negro" (1927) suggests:

> He scans the world with calm and fearless eyes,
> Conscious within of powers long since forgot;
> At every step, new man-made barriers rise
> To bar his progress—but he heeds them not.
> He stands erect, though tempests round him crash,
> Though thunder bursts and billows surge and roll;
> He laughs and forges on, while lightnings flash
> Along the rocky pathway to his goal.
> Impassive as a Sphinx, he stares ahead—
> Foresees new empires rise and old ones fall;
> While caste-mad nations lust for blood to shed,
> He sees God's finger writing on the wall.
> With soul awakened, wise and strong he stands,
> Holding his destiny within his hands.[31]

Evoking both Watkins's and Johnson's sonnets, McCall's sonnet describes in a Shakespearean octave a powerful, fearless figure who heeds not dangers as he forges on to his goal. If Watkins's "New Negro" is pure and faithful and Johnson's is "disdainful and magnificent," McCall's is "calm and fearless," without irony. Echoes of Dunbar's "Slow Through the Dark" can be heard in the "rocky pathways" as well as of Tennyson's "The Eagle" (though not a sonnet). The final couplet recalls the final couplet of McKay's "America" (where it contends with Shelley's "Ozymandias"): "Beneath the touch of Time's unerring hand, / Like priceless treasures sinking in the sand." Like Watkins's sonnet and unlike Johnson's, McCall's is not ambivalent. The speaker simply turns to stand still in the sestet, revealing no emotion as he stares ahead, contemplating the future, in control of his destiny.

These three "New Negro" sonnets demonstrate that in a single generation of African American sonnet writing a pattern of influence is beginning to emerge: black sonnet writers can be seen contending with the sonnet tradition and poems circulating in the newly established African American canon simultaneously. Sonnets by a young Sterling A. Brown, anthologized in *Caroling Dusk* five years before Brown published his acclaimed volume, *Southern Road* (1932), offer further evidence of influence, in particular "Salutamus" (1927):

> —O Gentlemen the time of Life is short.
> *Henry IV*, Part I

> The bitterness of days like these we know;
> Much, much we know, yet cannot understand
> What was our crime that such a searing brand
> Not of our choosing, keeps us hated so.
> Despair and disappointment only grow,
> Whatever seeds are planted from our hand,
> What though some roads wind through a gladsome land?
> It is a gloomy path that we must go.
> And yet we know relief will come some day
> For these seared breasts; and lads as brave again
> Will plant and find a fairer crop than ours.
> It must be due our hearts, our minds, our powers;
> These are the beacons to blaze out the way.
> We must plunge onward; onward, gentlemen. . . .

The epigraph is a line spoken by Henry Percy, "Hotspur," one of the manliest (if unsuccessful) heroes in English literature. Using an Italian rhyme scheme (rather than the expected Shakespearean), Brown's sonnet speaker speaks in first-person plural, as a spokesman for a hated, branded people. The opening couplet, "The bitterness of days like these we know; / Much, much we know, yet cannot understand," evokes the opening couplet of Dunbar's "Douglass": "Ah, Douglass, we have fall'n on evil days, / Such days as thou, not even thou didst know." Brown's sonnet speaker is, like Dunbar's, mournful, all-seeing, and determined, yet resolute, in the manner of McKay's "If We Must Die," without the outrage. Brown's seeds recall Cullen's seeds in "From the Dark Tower" as well as the dark path from Dunbar's "Slow Through the Dark." The sestet appears to turn to optimism. If in the octave the speaker differentiates knowledge from understanding, in the sestet the speaker *knows* that the future will be fruitful. He speaks for faith in future generations who will "plunge onward." And yet, optimism is tempered by knowledge that Shakespeare's Hotspur failed in battle.

Brown was widely read, reared on Longfellow, Burns, and Dunbar, and valedictorian at Dunbar High School in 1918, writing a prizewinning essay, "The Comic Spirit in Shakespeare and Molière."[32] While Mark Sanders sees Brown modeling his sonnets largely on "Milton's renovation of the overly ornate Elizabethan sonnet," Blyden Jackson apprehends other black sonnet writers, even as he characterizes sonnet writing as a hobby, not an influence: "Brown did, upon occasion, resort to traditional white ways of writing poetry. Like McKay and Cullen, for example, he tried his hand at sonneteering. But whereas in McKay's and Cullen's sonneteering one may find suggestions of non-Negro influences too binding upon them for the good of the New Negro cause, in Brown the sonnets constitute a conscious holiday from his major interest."[33]

But Brown's sonnets clearly show the impress of Dunbar's sonnets as well as McKay's and Cullen's. Brown saw Dunbar's "dignified sonnets to Harriet Beecher Stowe, Robert Gould Shaw, the militant Douglass and the unmilitant Booker T. Washington" as "race conscious poetry."[34] Dunbar's sonnets had an impact. Joanna Gabbin writes that it is "one of the great paradoxes of American literature" that Brown, "who has done as much as any one man to identify the foundations of the Black aesthetic tradition, has been so little studied."[35] Two scholars who have written recently on Brown's sonnets also suggest that sonnet writing was a matter of "indulging" Victorian convention.[36] While scholarship on Brown's dialect verse in relation to Dunbar's continues to advance, the influences on Brown's sonnets deserve closer study. Two additional sonnets by Brown appear in *Caroling Dusk*, "Challenge" and "Return." Sonnets by Brown appear in Dreer's *American Literature by Negro Authors* (1950) but not again until Michael Harper's 2000 anthology, *Vintage Book of African American Poetry*.

The balance of the sonnets that appear in *Caroling Dusk* are George Allen's prizewinning and sentimental "To Melody," Wesley Curtwright's "The Close of Day," and Gwendolyn Bennet's "Sonnet 1" and "Sonnet 2," as well as Braithwaite's sonnet on Keats's birthday. Braithwaite's inclusion is primarily a matter of respect. Wallace Thurman described Braithwaite as "best known as a student and friend of poets and poetry rather than a poet," partly because of his avoidance of racial themes but also because his sonnets were unremarkable.[37] Braithwaite's sonnets would not be anthologized again until the twenty-first century.

Charles Johnson's collection *Ebony and Topaz* (1927) and Wallace Thurman's anthology *Fire!!* (1927) are notable primarily for their art and essays rather than their poetry, but both republished influential sonnets. Helene Johnson's "Sonnet to a Negro in Harlem" appears in *Ebony and Topaz* along with two less notable sonnets; Cullen's "The Dark Tower" appears in *Fire!!* and is notably the only poem in the collection that uses a political "we"—the only poem that positions itself as speaking for black solidarity. While Thurman would famously praise McKay's "If We Must Die" for its muscular potency ("There is no impotent whining here, no mercy-seeking prayer to the white man's God, no mournful jeremiad, no 'ain't it hard to be a nigger', no lamenting of or apologizing for the fact that he is a member of a dark-skinned minority group"),[38] the poetry in *Fire!!* is remarkably conservative. Provocatively, Locke's observation in an essay titled "Our Little Renaissance" that new writers "are just beginning perhaps to shake off the artifices of that relatively early stage; so to speak the Umbrian stiffness is still upon us and the Florentine ease and urbanities looms just ahead" suggests an optimism that more sonnets in the manner of Helene Johnson and Cullen will appear.[39]

V. F. Calverton's *Anthology of American Negro Literature* (1929), with its relatively small poetry section, emphasizes that his selections are representative. "This does not mean that an attempt has not been made in every case to choose work of merit, but that in a number of instances it has been necessary to include material because of its representational value, though it is without fine, literary distinction."[40] Calverton includes Dunbar's "Robert Gould Shaw," several sonnets by McKay, and Lewis G. Alexander's sonnet "The Dark Brother," which opens, "Lo I am black but I am comely too," and closes with "Though I am black my heart through love is pure, / And you through love my blackness shall endure!" Sonnets that expressed the "black but comely" sentiment increasingly fell out of favor.

In their preface to *Readings from Negro Authors for Schools and Colleges* (1931), editors Otelia Cromwell, Lorenzo Dow Turner, and Eva B. Dykes emphasize that their volume is not an anthology but rather a collection of "worth-while productions of Negro authors," in service of a teacher's duty to students "to form in them a taste for good reading." The editors add that "no unique method or approach, no special interpretation of the rules of craftsmanship" are needed "because the standards of literary form are based upon universal principles."[41] The sonnets included by McKay, Cullen, and Dunbar-Nelson were well known, as well as Angela Weld Grimke's sonnet "To Dunbar High School." The volume was reviewed favorably: "[S]omehow the path from Phyllis Wheatley to Countee Cullen seems perfectly forthright. It represents a literature gradually more and more absorbed in challenging realities, approaching nearer and nearer to greatness of perception, divining more and more clearly its own increasing worth."[42] In other words, the editors saw a growing stream of African American poetry but not a stream of influence.

Sonnets appear in two poetry anthologies from the 1930s that did not circulate widely at the time: Nancy Cunard's *Negro: An Anthology* (1934) features Carrie W. Clifford's "The Black Draftee from Dixie" and Countee Cullen's "From the Dark Tower." A 1937 Works Progress Administration publication, *An Anthology of Negro Poetry by Negroes and Others*, edited by Beatrice F. Wormley and Charles W. Carter, features fifteen sonnets, including Dunbar's "The Path," Hill's "To a Caged Canary in a Negro Restaurant," and Lucian Watkins's "The New Negro." The volume was critiqued in the *Crisis* for leaning heavily on but not acknowledging Johnson's *Book of Negro American Poetry*, although it includes more sonnets from Kerlin than from Johnson.[43]

Beatrice M. Murphy's 1938 anthology *Negro Voices: An Anthology of Contemporary Verse* includes fourteen sonnets, including Lewis G. Alexander's "Southland," Conrad Chittick's "Torches," and an early sonnet by Melvin Tolson, "The Wine of Ecstasy." Notable as a new voice offering a novel and distinctively African American sonnet is Marcus Christian's "Spring in the South" (1934):

> A Resurrection whisper runs along
> The world's cold pulse and earth grows warm again.
> Green flames leap up and birds break into song,
> A feeling of half-ecstasy—half-pain
> Grips hard the body—shakes the soul from sleep,
> Song inarticulate dams up the mouth,
> Green fire runs from plots to thickets deep:
> The kindling breath of Spring has kissed the South.
> When every green thing yearns, I must not yearn
> To test the sun—because my skin is black;
> Reluctantly, my dragging feet I turn
> To kindlier lands. And I shall not come back.
> Self-exiled, fronting Hate—Fear claiming fee,—
> This is the last of Southern Springs for me.[44]

In the Shakespearean octave, Christian's speaker describes spring as a hot, animating force: a Resurrection, flames, fire, kindling. Spring is enlivening but frightening, and terms such as "pain," "runs," and "plots to thickets deep" raise the specter of lynching. In the sestet the resigned speaker, now using the personal pronoun "I," will exile himself from where he belongs. Like "Southern Share-Cropper," Christian's "Spring in the South" contends directly with McKay's sonnets, notably "Outcast" ("song inarticulate dams up the mouth," "self-exiled") and "America" ("fronting Hate," "yet as a rebel fronts a king in state"). Christian's sonnet speaker will not love an America that casts him out from his own land, land that he has tilled. Christian, a poet and educator-activist, lived most of his life in New Orleans. One of the few scholars to write about Christian, Tom Dent, argues that Christian "had a tendency to be a little too tied to nineteenth-century English form, to the detriment of his Afro-American sensibility."[45] Yet the more contemporary influence on Christian is clearly McKay. Murphy did not include any sonnets by McKay in her anthology so a comparison would not have been convenient.

Alexander's "Southland" (1927) sonnet resonates with McKay's sonnets as well:

> A carnival where souls of black men dance,
> Free as the air we breathe, the sun that shines;
> Coal swathed and lithe as steeds decked for the prance
> Flaunting their body charms like concubines,
> Beneath a moon seductive as the eyes
> Of whores worn by too many nights of flesh;
> Where clouds hang heavy in the drooping skies
> Like bellies pregnant with a season's mesh.
> O land that lured me like a dark eyed slave,
> Into the vortex of your beauty's hold;
> But to repay the largesse which you gave
> I've come, but ah the advent is untold.
> The southland still is but a virgin womb,
> With hurried treasures like an unearthed tomb.

With its ninth line, "Oh land that lured me like a dark eyed slave," and its provocative final couplet, "The southland still is but a virgin womb, / With buried treasure like an unearthed tomb," the sonnet shows influences of multiple traditions. Both Alexander's and Christian's sonnets are double-voiced, distinctively southern and black, of the land and destroyed by the land, pushing back against McKay's urbanity.

In 1942 Sterling Brown, Arthur Davis, and Ulysses Lee published *The Negro Caravan* for students' and classroom use. The anthology includes twelve well-known (by now) sonnets: two by Dunbar, two by Hill, five by McKay, and one by Cullen. Sonnets by George Allen will not be anthologized again. *The Negro Caravan* also includes selections from Albery Whitman's long poem in Spenserian stanzas, "Rape of Florida."

Murphy's 1948 anthology, *Ebony Rhythms*, features seventeen sonnets, including five sonnets demonstrating the influence of earlier African American sonnets: three by Christian, one by Georgia Douglas Johnson, and one by Alexander Young. While Murphy drolly characterizes her collection as "something like a box of mixed chocolates" that have been selected according to "what appeared to be the best of that submitted, regardless of subject matter," Murphy's selection sensibility must have involved resonance, although she did not engage with questions of influence in her introduction. Georgia Douglas Johnson's unexpectedly good sonnet "Black Recruit" (1948), for example, is clearly in conversation with other works by black poets:

> At home, I must be humble, meek,
> Surrendering the other cheek;
> Must be a coward over here,
> And yet, a brave man—over there.
>
> This sophistry is passing strange,
> Moves quite beyond my mental range—
> Since I must be a hero there,
> Shall I prepare by crawling here?
>
> Am I a faucet that you turn
> To right—I'm cold—to left—I burn!
> Or but a golem wound to spring
> This way or that—a soulless thing!
> He surely is a master-man
> Who formulated such a plan.

Written in iambic tetrameter couplets rather than pentameter, lines in the second quatrain, "This sophistry is passing strange / Moves quite beyond my mental range," evoke Othello's "passing strange" as well as the final couplet from Langston Hughes's sonnet "Ph.D.": "And all the human world is vast and strange— / And quite beyond his Ph.D.'s small range." The tone of Johnson's sonnet and especially the final couplet, "He surely is a master-man / Who formulated such a plan," evokes the tone and final couplet from Cullen's "Yet Do I Marvel." The resonances with Hughes and Cullen are apparent because of Johnson's quasi-sonnet form, which indicates that Johnson has been reading the work of her fellow poets closely.

Somewhat less overtly, Alexander Young's "Before a Monument," which first appeared in the *Pittsburgh Courier* in 1940, before America entered World War II, is also a sonnet in conversation with Cullen and Dunbar:

> Before a monument to one unknown
> And martyred Negro soldier once I stood,
> And thought of all the ills that since have grown
> From that last conflict for the common good.
> If he could see another war to make
> The world safe for democracy and find
> Oppressors rising in its early wake
> To deal despondency to humankind . . .
> I wonder, would this unknown soldier hold
> His life ill-spent to have such evils ensue?
> And would he leave his home and friends behind
> To seek a rendezvous with death's dank dew?
> I think that he might lift his hand and cry,
> "Let those who made this war go forth and die!"[46]

Like Dunbar's sonnet to Robert Gould Shaw, Young's sonnet asks if martyrdom in war is worth it if war doesn't accomplish what it is supposed to. Young's sonnet, structured on a Shakespearean rhyme scheme, features a speaker standing before a monument to a black World War I soldier, pondering the ills that have risen "in its early wake." In the sestet, Young's speaker wonders more bluntly than Dunbar's if the solder would have chosen not to leave home and friends to fight, had he known the evils that would ensue. The phrase "rendezvous with death" evokes Alan Seeger's poem and, by extension, Cullen's prizewinning poetic answer to it, "I Have a Rendezvous with Life."

Murphy remarks that a critic of the 1938 volume expressed disappointment "because the work of the Negro poets was not dissimilar to that of any other race" and adds that "we are sure some will be just as disappointed here."[47] Murphy aimed her anthology at a postwar readership, whose literary tastes reflected growing numbers of college-educated citizens. James Smethurst suggests that these readers had a strong sense of the sonnet:

For the "Middle-class" American, black and white, with a reasonable amount of formal education, the sonnet as a literary form epitomized "high" culture. If an American of that era (or this one) were asked to name a type of poem (and could), he or she would almost certainly name the sonnet....In short, the sonnet as a form could be seen as a popular-culture emblem of "high" culture (and in turn a sort of commercial marketing strategy) in much the same way as the name "Shakespeare."[48]

While for readers sonnets may represent high culture, the specific sonnets Murphy selects, notably by Christian, Johnson, and Young, are contending with ideas of high culture rather than embodying high culture. More importantly, Murphy's selections demonstrate a much broader landscape of poetic influence than is usually acknowledged. These poets were clearly reading each other.

John W. Parker, reviewing *Ebony Rhythms* in *Phylon*, faintly praised the volume as "useful" and "something of an index to post-war Negro poetry."[49] Parker's primary concern is poetic politics (including formal politics) rather than influence:

It is perhaps worth noting that no one of the poems in the "protest" group follows the thinking of a writer with left-wing tendencies....Absent too, for the most part, are poems about fallen Negro women, hard luck Charlie, Harlem after midnight....Despite the generous sprinkling of sonnets fashioned after the traditional English and Italian patterns and the recurrent appearance of the four-line stanza, the book shares the current trend in the direction of variegated poetic forms; free verse similar to that found in Hughes' *One Way Ticket* abounds throughout the volume.[50]

But as a matter of establishing an African American sonnet tradition, Murphy's two anthologies are particularly significant for publishing new sonnets and demonstrating connections that would otherwise be hard to see.

Langston Hughes's and Arna Bontemps's anthology, *The Poetry of the Negro, 1746–1949* (1949), was also designed as an educational volume. By the late 1940s Hughes had reconsidered his remark to Carl Van Vechten in 1926: "If I ever get in the school books then I know I'm ruined."[51] Getting into the classroom was key to Hughes's longevity. Elizabeth Alexander observes that "Hughes-as-anthologizer" saw his task as both participating "in the making of the context in which his own work would be read" and exhibiting "responsibility to the literary community."[52] As the preface claims:

> The Negro in Western civilization has been exposed to overwhelming historical and sociological pressures that are bound to be reflected in the verse he has written and inspired. The fact that he has used poetry as a form of expression has also brought him into contact with literary trends and influences. How one of these forces or the other has predominated and how the results may be weighed and appraised are among the questions to which the poetry itself contains answers.[53]

The Poetry of the Negro was criticized for devoting space to white poets. "Tributary Poems by Non-Negroes" includes Elizabeth Barrett Browning's "The Runaway Slave at Pilgrim's Point" (which had been anthologized in *Ebony and Topaz*), Wordsworth's sonnet "To Toussaint L'Ouverture," and several poems (including sonnets) on racial themes by poets known to the editors.

Hughes and Bontemps include thirty-nine sonnets by African American poets. Theirs was the first anthology to include sonnets by Robert Hayden, Margaret Walker, and Gwendolyn Brooks, all of whom, in interviews, acknowledged their sonnet influences. Eighteen sonnets, including five by Claude McKay, are grouped under "The Caribbean," at the end of the volume, with the result that McKay's influence on Christian (it is the first time they are together in the same volume) remains difficult to see.[54]

Hayden's sonnet "Frederick Douglass," published in the *Atlantic Monthly* in February 1947, appears in a slightly different version than the final 1966 version that would become a staple of African American poetry volumes:

> When it is finally ours, this freedom, this liberty, this beautiful
> and terrible thing, needful to man as air,
> usable as earth; when it belongs at last to our children,
> when it is truly instinct, brain matter, diastole, systole,
> reflex action; when it is finally won; when it is more
> than the gaudy mumbo jumbo of politicians:
> this man, this Douglass, this former slave, this Negro
> beaten to his knees, exiled, visioning a world
> where none is lonely, none hunted, alien,
> this man, superb in love and logic, this man
> shall be remembered—oh, not with statues' rhetoric,
> not with legends and poems and wreaths of bronze alone,

but with the lives grown out of his life, the lives
fleshing his dream of the needful, beautiful thing.[55]

In two sentences and no structured rhyme scheme, Hayden crafts a sonnet that allows his speaker to break nearly every sonnet convention—meter, line length, rhyme, volta—except the convention that sonnets allow
the breaking of every convention to demonstrate freedom. Only the general shape and its fourteen-line length indicate that it is a sonnet—perhaps the most notable African American sonnet since Dunbar's "Douglass." The two sonnets are not at all alike as a matter of diction, except for
the "oh" in the eleventh line, and yet both speak to a Douglass that is very
much present. Both poems express a personal relationship with Douglass, a melancholy intimacy. Both poems express a need for liberty that
Douglass is seen as filling—not Douglass the man but rather his guiding
arm (for Dunbar) and his example (for Hayden). Hayden's sonnet is undoubtedly influenced by and contending with Dunbar's sonnet.

Hayden's first version of "Frederick Douglass," published in a short-
lived African American newspaper in 1945 alongside sonnets to Harriet Beecher Stowe, William Lloyd Garrison, Sojourner Truth, and Abraham Lincoln, is an entirely different poem.[56] Hayden revised "Frederick
Douglass" while reading the sonnets of Gerard Manley Hopkins, whose
concepts of "inscape" and "instress," Pontheolla Williams argues, help
Hayden achieve the effect of Douglass's vividness and presence.[57] There is
no hint at all of Dunbar's influence in the earlier poem, although Hayden
in his youth read Dunbar along with Hughes and Cullen and "tried to
write dialect verse the way Dunbar did."[58] Yet as with Sterling Brown,
Dunbar's sonnets were most likely as influential as his dialect verse, and
Hayden clearly revisited Dunbar's sonnet in his recrafting of "Frederick
Douglass." Timo Müller notes Hopkins's influence on Hayden's sonnet
without noting that Dunbar too wrote a sonnet to Douglass.[59]

"Hayden has his cake and eats it too," Fred Fetrow argues, "as he di-
vests himself of practically all of the traditional formal conventions associated with the sonnet yet successfully retains the reinforcement relationship between form and meaning." Fetrow sees Hayden as joining
"a group of twentieth-century poets who experimented with the sonnet
structure for a variety of rhetorical effects and thematic purpose: Wilfred
Owen, e. e. cummings, Edna St. Vincent Millay, John Wheelwright, W. H.
Auden, Dylan Thomas, and John Berryman, to name a few."[60] Absent on
this list is any black sonnet writer, most notably Brooks, who had begun

an era of dramatic sonnet innovations that would continue through the 1960s and whose sonnets were already widely circulating. Brooks's "The Sundays of Satin Legs Smith" (in iambic pentameter, though a sonnet) influenced Hayden's "Witch Doctor" and "Mourning Poem for the Queen of Sundays," which appear in sequence in Hayden's *Collected Poems*.[61] Hayden's poetry—like most poetry—is rich with influences. "Frederick Douglass" evokes Hayden's earlier twenty-line "We Have Not Forgotten," from his first volume of poetry, *Heart-Shape in the Dust* (1940), which Smethurst argues is itself a response to Sterling Brown's "Children's Children."[62]

The Poetry of the Negro was the first anthology to include a sonnet by Margaret Walker, with "For Mary McLeod Bethune":

> Great Amazon of God behold your bread
> washed home again from many distant seas.
> The cup of life you lift contains no less,
> no bitterness to mock you. In its stead
> this sparkling chalice many souls has fed,
> and broken hearted people on their knees
> lift up their eyes and suddenly they seize
> on living faith, and they are comforted.
> Believing in the people who are free,
> who walk uplifted in an honest way,
> you look at last upon another day
> that you have fought with God and men to see.
> Great Amazon of God behold your bread.
> We walk with you and we are comforted.

Using a hybrid Italian-Shakespearean rhyme scheme, Walker's sonnet is an apostrophe to Bethune in the manner of "New Negro" sonnets, updated for a particular woman—one of the best-known black political figures of her day—rather than a representative ideal. In the octave, Walker's speaker portrays Bethune as "Great Amazon of God," an African Christ figure or priest, who feeds "broken hearted people on their knees" and comforts them. There is no ambivalence expressed, no double-voicedness, but rather doubleness: the thirteenth line repeats the first. The fourteenth line begins the long awaited "We" as the pronoun turns from third to first person and confirms that the speaker is one of the comforted.

Margaret Walker had won the Yale University Younger Poets award in 1942 for her volume, *For My People*, which includes several sonnets (in-

cluding "Childhood" and "Whores") alongside with verse in more innovative forms. After 1970, Walker's sonnet "For Malcolm X" (chapter 6) will
be regularly anthologized, but her earlier sonnets not again. Blyden Jackson thought the form was not characteristic for Walker, suggesting that
"[h]er world is an intensely racial universe (in spite of the fact that she
sometimes writes a sonnet)."[63] But Walker, like Wordsworth, understood
the freedom of a small space:

> Sometimes the only quiet and private place I could write a sonnet was
> in the bathroom, because that was the only room where the door could
> be locked and no one would intrude. I have written mostly at night in
> my adult life and especially since I have been married, because I was
> determined not to neglect any member of my family; so I cooked every
> meal daily, washed dishes and dirty clothes, and I nursed sick babies.[64]

Walker's sense of freedom in her sonnets is clear from her fresh diction in a sonnet such as "Childhood": "I also lived in low cotton country /
where moonlight hovered over ripe haystacks, / or stumps of trees, and
croppers' rotting shacks / with famine, terror, flood, and plague near by"
in which meter is simply spoken language that seems to happen to fit a
ten-syllable line.

The Poetry of the Negro was also the first African American poetry anthology to include sonnets by Brooks, already well known for *A Street
in Bronzeville* (1945) (which had been highly praised by *Poetry*, the *New
Yorker*, and elsewhere), and who had won prizes including the *Mademoi-
selle* Merit Award for Distinguished Achievement (1945), a Guggenheim
fellowship (1946), and the American Academy of Arts and Letters Award
(1946). The following year, 1950, she would become the first African American to win a Pulitzer Prize for her volume *Annie Allen*. Hughes included
three sonnets, "love note II: flags," "Mentors," and "Piano after War," as
well as the thirteen-line "Kitchenette Building" and the fifteen-line "The
Birth in a Narrow Room."

In the context of an African American sonnet tradition, Brooks's sonnets on black soldiers might be seen in conversation with—but entirely
unlike—Cotter's "Sonnet to Negro Soldiers," Clifford's "The Black Draftee
from Dixie," and Johnson's "The Black Recruit." Rather than tributes or
political punditry, Brooks's sonnets feature black soldiers speaking in
their own voices, as the speaker of "Mentors" does, after the war:

> For I am rightful fellow of their band.
> My best allegiances are to the dead.

I swear to keep the dead upon my mind,
Disdain for all time to be overglad.
Among spring flowers, under summer trees,
By chilling autumn waters, in the frosts
Of supercilious winter—all my days
I'll have as mentors those reproving ghosts.
And at that cry at that remotest whisper,
I'll stop my casual business. Leave the banquet.
Or leave the ball—reluctant to unclasp her
Who may be fragrant as the flower she wears,
Make gallant bows and dim excuses, then quit
Light for the midnight that is mine and theirs.[65]

In a hybrid Shakespearean-Italian rhyme scheme, Brooks's speaker is a veteran contemplating his fallen comrades. He lists seasons poetically, evoking high culture (a ball, gallant bows) and Shakespeare (ghosts, banquet, midnight). Race is neither mentioned nor implied. Brooks mandated that "Mentors" must always be paired with "Piano after War" as poems that spoke together about existence changed utterly by war.[66] Like "Piano after War," which gestures to Wordsworth's sonnet "Surprised by Joy" (both about a sudden turn from joy to pain—Brooks's "But suddenly, across my climbing fever / Of proud delight—a multiplying cry" evoking Wordsworth's "Oh! with whom / But Thee, long buried in the silent Tomb") Brooks's goal is simultaneously acknowledging her influences and situating the sonnet in her own time and place.

The scholarship on Brooks, as it is on McKay and Cullen, is extensive. Relatively little, however, involves the influence of other black sonnet writers on Brooks or of Brooks on later sonnet writers. D. H. Melhem argues that "the sonnet form was not an eccentric choice for Brooks. It had already been favored by many Harlem Renaissance…poets such Claude McKay, Countee Cullen, and Langston Hughes" but does not look for intertextual influence.[67] Francini argues that "Brooks also brings us to the heart of the European lyric tradition, mediated once again by the sonnet sequences of the English Renaissance, from Shakespeare's to John Donne's."[68] Karen Jackson Ford notes that Brooks read Robert Hillyer's *First Principles of Verse* (1938) avidly and demonstrates her understanding of how the sonnet form has a kind of agency that enables it to argue with itself and its history. "What reading Hillyard would have shown Brooks, perhaps inadvertently," Ford argues, is "that sonnets can *think*. This is precisely what gave the sonnet its political force."[69]

More than any other African American sonnet writer, Brooks's sonnets contend with sonnet history as they engage with a local and particular moment, as the quasi-sonnet "The Birth in a Narrow Room" does, published for the first time in the Hughes/Bontemps anthology:

> Weeps out of western country something new.
> Blurred and stupendous. Wanted and unplanned.
>   Winks. Twines, and weakly winks
> Upon the milk-glass fruit bowl, iron pot
> The bashful china child tipping forever
> Yellow apron and spilling pretty cherries.
> Now, weeks and years will go before she thinks
> "How pinchy is my room! how can I breathe!
> I am not anything and I have got
> Not anything, or anything to do!"—
> But prances nevertheless with gods and fairies
> Blithely about the pump and then beneath
> The elms and grapevines, then in darling endeavor
> By privy foyer, where the screenings stand
> And where the bugs buzz by in private cars
> Across old peach cans and jelly jars.[70]

With an unorthodox rhyme scheme and two extra lines, reminiscent of the sixteen-line sonnets of George Meredith,[71] Brooks's sonnet begins with an unrhymed sestet that introduces a "blurred and stupendous" being encountering objects. In the ten lines that follow—each finally resolving the sestet's rhymes—"she" breaks free of her "pinchy" room and prances blithely around the yard and empty fruit cans and jars. The sonnet form is not simply an emblem of Gwendolyn Brooks's mastery, Leonard argues, but "an emblem of the interaction between will and circumstance that constitutes the social agency of the existential imagination." Off-line couplets, Leonard observes, "defy the common resolution potentially available in the final quatrain and couplet of the Shakespearean sonnet or the intricate closure of the Italian sonnet in deference to the 'off-rhyme situation,' leaving the possible self-assertion at the end as yet unresolved."[72] More recently, Cummings argues that "Brooks's dependable, if too brief, presence in American literature anthologies" is a function of her status as the first African American Pulitzer winner and "her poems' accessibility and (teachable) focus on race, gender, and class."[73]

In a 1972 *New York Times* review of a new collection of her works, *The World of Gwendolyn Brooks*, Addison Gayle describes arguing with Brooks in a taxicab about the sonnet form when they stopped to attend to the African cabdriver shouting slang:

> To contain and retain the symbolic fury of such an idiomatic expression, to capture its vibrancy of tone and meaning, mandated forms different from those handed down to the Western mind from Petrarch and Shakespeare; it mandated a poetry that, in the Pulitzer Prize winner's words, said something meaningful to black people about their lives, spoke to Afro-Americans on the street corners and in colleges as well.[74]

New forms were needed for the new era, Gayle insisted. Yet Gayle's review is ambivalent, emphasizing Brooks's turn away from traditional form even while acknowledging that the sonnet has always been "indispensible" to her success and noting that poems such as "the sonnet series, 'Children of the Poor,' are models for the younger poets, metaphors of their strivings as concrete as that of the new birth in the opening lines of 'The Birth in a Narrow Room.'"[75] The pressure on Brooks to move away from the sonnet is treated further in chapter 6.

Two additional influential sonnets are included in Hughes and Bontemps's anthology. The first is Nicolás Guillén's sonnet "Two Weeks"; the second is Alfred A. Duckett's "Sonnet," which will be anthologized for the next several decades before disappearing:

> Where are we to go when this is done?
> Will we slip into old, accustomed ways,
> finding remembered notches, one by one?
> Thrashing a hapless way through quickening haze?
> Who is to know us when the end has come?
> Old friends and families, but could we be
> strange to the sight and stricken dumb
> at visions of some pulsing memory?
> Who will love us for what we used to be
> who now are what we are, bitter or cold?
> Who is to nurse us with swift subtlety
> back to the warm and feeling human fold?
> Where are we to go when this is through?
> We are the war-born. What are we to do?

Structured on a Shakespearean rhyme scheme and clearly influenced by World War I poets, Duckett's sonnet speaker ponders the fate of soldiers after war, his insistent questions evading and yet making clear why he is asking them. In the octave the speaker is far from "old, accustomed ways," far from "remembered notches," "old friends and families," worried that he will be "stricken dumb at visions" when he returns. The line "thrashing a hapless way through quickening haze" evokes Wilfred Owen's "Dulce et Decorum Est" (1920). In the sestet, Duckett's speaker continues questioning, describing himself and others finally as "bitter and cold," wondering if they will be loved and nursed "back to the human fold." The "we" are "the war born," he states in the final line. "What are we to do?"

Duckett's sonnet, published in 1947, can be read as expressing universal concerns of all soldiers returning from any conflict as well as black soldiers returning from World War II. His refusal of particularity in his repetition of "this" as the only referent for his current plight allows his plea "Where are we to go when this is through?" to represent the cry of African Americans in the long battle for freedom and equal civil rights. Like McKay's "If We Must Die," the double-voicedness of Duckett's sonnet is produced in part by its simultaneous universality and its particularity as a sonnet written by an African American poet. The applicability of Duckett's sonnet to the black struggle was noted by *Negro Digest*, reviewing Arna Bontemps's 1963 anthology and closing with the question, "What are we to do?"

In his review of *The Poetry of the Negro* for *Phylon*, Alain Locke singled out Walker, Brooks, and Hayden—all sonnet writers—as important new voices, without regard to genealogy or influence:

> Poetic creativeness seems on a slow upswing after a serious decline from the heyday of Cullen, Hughes, McKay, and Sterling Brown. Now, with a difference, it may be on the march again, and the significant difference is the rise of the universalized theme supplementing but not completely displacing the poetry of racial mood and substance. The Negro poet is of course basically a modern poet and an American poet. But conversely, too, he must be at the proper time and in the proper way a Negro poet, a spokesman for his innermost experiences.[76]

Locke's integrationist view of literature was the standard view expressed by *Phylon* writers at the time and would not be seriously challenged until the Black Arts movement of the late 1960s.

Herman Dreer's anthology from the following year, *American Literature by Negro Authors*, designed as a textbook that avoided texts "unsuitable for classroom use," was accordingly criticized for being insufficiently political and sociological. Even McKay's "If We Must Die" is left out; the sonnets included are far milder. "Unfortunately, however, the volume contains all too little of the vigorous and convincing treatment of American social problems from the standpoint of the Negro which belongs to the last three decades," one reviewer wrote. "In other words, the writings in which the Negro begins to find himself widely effective in our time are neglected."[77] And as much as these early anthologies loom so large for scholars of the period and for the poets who read these volumes in school, it is important to recall that their reach was limited largely to black educators and black readers. A reviewer in the *School Review* writes that the anthology is, "so far as this reviewer knows…a first attempt to produce an anthology of American literature by Negro authors."[78] Influence, under these circumstances, is difficult to perceive.

Arna Bontemps does not specify selection criteria for his 1963 anthology *American Negro Poetry*, simply listing important authors and awards in his introduction with the implication that the volume is a collection of greatest hits. Most of the sonnets had been previously anthologized; new were a sonnet by Marcus Christian, sonnets by the best-selling author Frank Yerby, and a sonnet by Hughes: "Pennsylvania Station," first published as "Terminal" in 1932. Hughes's 1927 remarks disparaging conventional poetic forms—"I fail to see why I should be expected to copy someone else's modes of expression when it amuses me to attempt to create forms of my own"—had been mostly tongue in cheek, of course.[79] Hughes wrote sonnets and published several in *Opportunity* in the 1930s, although he did not include them in his collected works. Rampersad describes Hughes striving to overcome writer's block in the late 1920s and trying everything he could. "For a poet of Hughes's rhythmic originality, however, this was a backward step in almost every way," Rampersad argues, rationalizing that "perhaps it was a class exercise for his course in the art of poetry."[80] Perhaps. Read alongside the sonnets of Dunbar, James Weldon Johnson, Cullen, and McKay, however, Hughes's "Pennsylvania Station" shows their influence:

> The Pennsylvania Station in New York
> Is like some vast basilica of old
> That towers above the terrors of the dark
> As bulwark and protection to the soul.
> Now people who are hurrying alone
> And those who come in crowds from far away
> Pass through this great concourse of steel and stone
> To trains, or else from trains out into day.

And as in great basilicas of old
The search was ever for a dream of God,
So here the search is still within each soul
Some seed to find to nourish earthly sod.
Some seed to find that sprouts a holy tree
To glorify the earth—and you—and me.[81]

Using a Shakespearean rhyme scheme, Hughes's speaker, in the octave, ponders a grand building and those who pass through it. The use of the term "basilica" evokes classical halls of justice as well as Christian churches, suggesting that the station is protective of legal rights as well as souls. The sestet repeats the comparison to "great basilicas" but expresses a new mood, from hurrying to dreaming and searching. The seeds in Hughes's sestet evoke the "agonizing seeds" from Cullen's "From the Dark Tower," although in Cullen's poem the seeds are being tended, not sought for; here the search is for seeds rather than for soil to plant them in. It is tempting to think of Hughes's search for seeds as the search for a poetic theme and that Hughes structured that search as a sonnet. Emanuel groups Johnson's "My City" and McKay's "Russian Cathedral" sonnets together as urban works with only "slight adaptability to the racial program."[82] Had Emanuel known of Hughes's sonnet he might have included it. These city sonnets are not racialized, focusing rather on the modern individual among grand buildings and crowds.

The best-selling novelist Frank Yerby had written poetry in his youth; Bontemps included three sonnets by Yerby, including "You Are a Part of Me":

You are a part of me. I do not know
By what slow chemistry you first became
A vital fiber of my being. Go
Beyond the rim of time or space, the same
Inflections of your voice will sing their way
Into the depths of my mind still. Your hair
Will gleam as bright, the artless play
Of word and glance, gesture and the fair
Young fingers waving, have too deeply etched
The pattern of your soul on mine. Forget
Me quickly as a laughing picture sketched
On water, I shall never know regret
Knowing no magic ever can set free
That part of you that is a part of me.[83]

First published in the *Fisk Herald* magazine in 1937, "You Are a Part of Me" uses a Shakespearean rhyme scheme and is reflective of a student's interest in Keats. The sonnet is remarkable for its absence of any end punctuation. Yerby's sonnets will not be anthologized again.

Negro Digest reviewed Bontemps's anthology in 1963, noting the "old familiars, such as Paul Laurence Dunbar and James Weldon Johnson" and "newcomers such as Dudley Randell." Not all the poetry is excellent, the reviewer acknowledges, but "it is good to read again Countee Cullen's 'Heritage,' especially in the context of Africa's new influence on her children in this land."[84] Still, discussions of poetic influence on each other would have to wait.

❀ ❀ ❀

Meanwhile, between 1923 and 1967 new sonnets continued to be published in the *Crisis, Opportunity,* and the *Messenger,* as well as in the pages of journals whose archives have had somewhat less critical attention, including *Carolina Magazine,* the *Colored American,* the *Voice of the Negro,* and scores of others.[85] The techniques and craft of formal poetry were discussed in black literary journals from the *Crisis* and *Opportunity* in the 1920s and 1930s to *Phylon Quarterly* in the 1940s and 1950s to *Negro Digest* in the 1960s.[86]

The influential essays of the era arguing for the definition and contours of African American poetry touched on the sonnet but without advocating for its inclusion or exclusion.[87] For example, Du Bois in "The Criteria of Negro Art" argues for artworks with political muscle that use "all the methods that men have used before."[88] George Schuyler assumes that the work of most black artists would be "identical in kind with the literature, painting, and sculpture of white Americans: that is, it shows more or less evidence of European influence."[89] Cullen's "Dark Tower" columns in *Opportunity* support poetry in standard poetic forms. Hughes's 1926 essay "The Negro Artist and the Racial Mountain" advises that the black artist need not go "outside his race" to find material "to furnish a black artist with a lifetime of creative work," but Hughes does not define black culture *against* European culture, nor does he mention sonnets specifically.[90] Franklin Frazier, in *Ebony and Topaz,* wonders about cultural assimilation as a sociological phenomenon, not an aesthetic one: "[I]t still remains an open question how far the Negro group can escape the adoption of the cultural forms of America."[91] Zora Neale Hurston in "Characteristics of Negro Expression" argues that even "in the midst of a white civilization," all black art is innovative; "everything that he touches is re-interpreted for his own use."[92] Richard Wright, in "Blueprint for Negro Writing," offers a conception of black culture that is less about race than class, that is opposed to "a rising Negro bourgeoisie, parasitic and mannered," and that "Eliot, Stein, Joyce, Proust, Hemingway, and Anderson; Gorky, Barbusse, Nexo, and Jack London no less than the folklore of the Negro himself should form the heritage of the Negro writer."[93] Most do not rule specifically on the question of the appropriate form for black poetry, although Thomas L. G. Oxley criticizes Phillis Wheatley for never sounding "a native note" as well as for never writing a sonnet "to laud the Nubian skin of her people."[94] None consider poetic influence.

Occasionally, essays will address sonnets. Charlotte Taussig's "The New Negro as Revealed in His Poetry," for example, agues that black poets need "to find a form that will express the racial spirit by symbols from within, rather than symbols from without, such as the mere mutilation of English spelling and pronunciation."[95] Taussig presents McKay's 1925 sonnet "Like a Strong Tree" (published a month earlier in Locke's *Survey Graphic* "Enter the New Negro" issue) as "indicative of his powers," but without noting that it is a sonnet. On the following page, she introduces Cullen, who has "taken the new movement a step beyond even the strength displayed by Claude McKay," to write poems without bitterness that "are beautiful in form." She then introduces "Yet Do I Marvel," without commenting on form or influence.

In 1963 the *Saturday Review* published back-to-back essays on poetry by LeRoi Jones and Hughes under the headline "Problems of the Negro Writer." Hughes worries about the problem of getting paid. But Jones sets the stage for his later scorched earth critiques. "The mediocrity of what has been called 'Negro literature' is one of the most loosely held secrets of American culture," Jones argues; with a few "notable exceptions, in most fields of 'high art' in America the Negro contribution has been—when any existed at all—one of impressive mediocrity."[96] Only in the field of music, "blues, jazz, and spirituals—'Negro music'—has there been a significant contribution," Jones adds.

The question of "contribution" is key here. Jones does not define the term. More importantly, he limits what scholars should consider worthy of study among the works of black poets past. In arguing for the primacy of music as "the only way for the Negro artist to provide his version of America, from that no man's land outside the mainstream,"[97] a poem such as Hughes's sonnet "Search" (1937) may be missed:

> All life is but the climbing of a hill
> To seek the sun that ranges far beyond
> Confused with stars and lesser lights anon,
> And planets where the darkness reigneith still.
> All life is but the seeking for that sun
> That never lets one living atom die—
> That flames beyond the circles of the eye
> Where Never and Forever are as one.
> And seeking always through this human span
> That spreads its drift of years beneath the sky
> Confused with living, goeth simple man
> Unknowing and unknown into the Why—
> The Why that flings itself beyond the Sun
> And back in space to where Time was begun.[98]

Evoking Dunbar's "Slow Through the Dark" sonnet in its description of climbing and planets, Hughes's sonnet speaker, in the Italian octave, twice describes life as a matter of seeking the sun. In the sestet, the speaker suggests that "simple man" confuses seeking and living, and that the Why of it all is eternally impossible to know. While perhaps emblematic of Jones's "impressive mediocrity" label, Hughes's sonnet, like "Pennsylvania Station" above, can be seen in conversation with his fellow poets. This influence matters in the building of a tradition.

Consider how Cullen's 1929 sonnet "Black Majesty" might be read as yet another response to Dunbar's "Slow Through the Dark":

> These men were kings, albeit they were black,
> Christophe and Dessalines and L'Overture;
> Their majesty has made me turn my back
> Upon a plaint I once shaped to endure.
> These men were black, I say, but they were crowned
> And purple-clad, however brief their time.
> Stifle your agony; let grief be drowned;
> We know joy had a day once and a clime.
> Dark gutter-snipe, black sprawler-in-the-mud,
> A thing men did a man may do again.
> What answer filters through your sluggish blood
> To these dark ghosts who knew so bright a reign?

"Lo, I am dark, but comely," Sheba sings.
"And we were black," three shades reply, "but kings."[99]

No, Cullen's sonnet speaker responds to Dunbar: the race is not on an upward climb but has fallen into the gutter and mud from previous heights. Using the multiple turns offered by the change of rhymes in the Shakespearean rhyme scheme, he emphasizes his restatement at the beginning of the second quatrain ("These men were black, I say") in turning from statement to exhortation: "Stifle your agony; let grief be drowned." The sestet addresses a figure—the speaker or the sprawler—and moves firm resolution, repeating the first line in the reverse: "we were black…but kings." Cullen is also responding to Alexander's "The Dark Brother."

When Jones critiques the "paternalism of Charles Chesnutt and his 'refined Afro-American' heroes," by which he means heroes who quote Western literature, and when he argues that "the Negro remains an integral part of [Western] society, but irrevocably outside it, a figure like Melville's Bartleby," Jones simultaneously acknowledges and prefers not to see the significance of literary allusion or influence.[100] But clearly, there is influence. The foundations of an African American sonnet tradition laid down by Dunbar, McKay, and others before 1922 were built on robustly by Cullen, Christian, Hughes, Walker, Hayden, Brooks, and many others by the 1960s. Aldon Lynn Nielson tells the story of the modernist and postmodernist influences quietly operating among and around black poets, black poetics, and black poetry anthologies in the decades after World War II.[101] A similar narrative emerges for poets writing in the sonnet form, demonstrating the long-hidden influences on twenty-first-century sonnet writers. The "old familiars" quietly remained influential.

TABLE 2. Sonnets from the Twentieth-Century Anthologies of African American Poetry, 1968–1973

Amiri Baraka and Larry Neal, eds., *Black Fire: An Anthology of Afro-American Writing*. William Morrow, 1968.
    No sonnets.
Clarence Major, ed., *The New Black Poetry*. International Publishers, 1969.
    No sonnets.
June Jordan, ed., *Soulscript: Afro-American Poetry*. Zenith Books, 1970.
    CLAUDE MCKAY: "The White House," "If We Must Die"
    JEAN TOOMER: "November Cotton Flower"
    COUNTEE CULLEN: "Yet Do I Marvel," "From the Dark Tower"
    ROBERT HAYDEN: "Those Winter Sundays," "Frederick Douglass"
    ALFRED A. DUCKETT: "Sonnet"

Arthur P. Davis and Saunders Redding, eds., *Cavalcade: Negro American Writing from 1760 to the Present*. Houghton Mifflin, 1971.
>   JAMES CORROTHERS: "Paul Laurence Dunbar," "The Negro Singer"
>   CLAUDE MCKAY: "If We Must Die," "The White House," "America"
>   COUNTEE CULLEN: "Yet Do I Marvel"
>   ROBERT HAYDEN: "Frederick Douglass"
>   GWENDOLYN BROOKS: "Intermission/Deep Summer"

Dudley Randall, ed., *The Black Poets*. Bantam Books, 1971.
>   PAUL LAURENCE DUNBAR: "Harriet Beecher Stowe"
>   CLAUDE MCKAY: "Harlem Dancer," "The Tired Worker," "The White City," "Enslaved," "Tiger," "If We Must Die," "The Negro's Tragedy," "Truth," "The Pagan Isms," "I Know My Soul"
>   COUNTEE CULLEN: "From the Dark Tower," "Yet Do I Marvel"
>   MELVIN TOLSON: "A Legend of Versailles"
>   GWENDOLYN BROOKS: "What Shall I Give My Children," "The Rites for Cousin Vit," "A Lovely Love"
>   MARGARET WALKER: "For Malcolm X"
>   DOUGHTRY LONG: "Ginger Bread Mama"

Arnold Adoff, ed., *The Poetry of Black America: Anthology of the 20th Century*. Harper Collins, 1973.
>   CLAUDE MCKAY: "If We Must Die," "Outcast," "America," "In Bondage," "The Lynching," "To the White Fiends," "St. Isaac's Church, Petrograd," "The White House"
>   COUNTEE CULLEN: "From the Dark Tower," "Yet Do I Marvel," "Black Majesty," "Brown Boy to Brown Girl"
>   ALICE DUNBAR NELSON: "Sonnet"
>   LESLIE PINCKNEY HILL: "So Quietly"
>   RAYMOND G. DANDRIDGE: "Time to Die"
>   JOSEPH SEAMAN COTTER JR.: "Sonnet to Negro Soldiers"
>   GWENDOLYN BENNETT: "Sonnet I," "Sonnet II"
>   ROBERT HAYDEN: "Frederick Douglass"
>   MARGARET WALKER: "Childhood," "For Malcolm X"
>   GWENDOLYN BROOKS: "Egg Boiler"
>   ALFRED A DUCKETT: "Sonnet"
>   ETHERIDGE KNIGHT: "For Black Poets Who Think of Suicide"
>   HENRY DUMAS: "Black Trumpeter"
>   DOUGHTRY LONG: "Ginger Bread Mama"

Stephen Henderson, ed., *Understanding the New Black Poetry*. William Morris, 1973.
>   CLAUDE MCKAY: "Baptism," "If We Must Die"
>   COUNTEE CULLEN: "Yet Do I Marvel"
>   ROBERT HAYDEN: "Frederick Douglass"
>   MARGARET WALKER: "For Malcolm X"
>   JAMES EMANUEL : "Freedom Rider: Washout"

CHAPTER 6

Power Lines:
The Black Aesthetic and
the Black Sonnet

Free verse is a club.
If it batters long enough,
It may crush a breastplate.

A sonnet is an arrow.
Pointed and slim, it pierces
The slit in the armor.

—DUDLEY RANDALL, "Verse Forms," 1980

The political movement to create and define the African American literary canon after 1967 swept aside formal poetry. Yet sonnets somehow survived. While the study of black poetry changed (the term "Negro" disappeared from the title of African American poetry anthologies after 1971), sonnets were still being written. Even advocates of the Black Arts movement calling for new creative traditions to work in concert with the Black Power movement, which would "expose the enemy, praise the people," and "reflect and support the Black Revolution," occasionally wrote sonnets, including Amiri Baraka, Dudley Randall, Eugene Redmond, and Lorenzo Thomas.[1] Yet the most decorated African American poet, Gwendolyn Brooks, was being actively pressured to renounce her early works in traditional forms. Critics of the Black Aesthetic worried about the movement becoming too mainstream, limiting younger poets to narrow channels of how to signify blackness, of marginalizing innovation, of forestalling resistance.[2]

Editors of poetry collections continued to be the key figures in shaping the canon of African American poetry after 1967, joined by editors of journals such as *Negro Digest/Black World*, the *Liberator*, and *Journal of Black Poetry*; the essayists who published in these journals; and academics who would decide what would be read and taught and how in newly formed black studies programs around the country.[3] While African American literature had been taught in historically black colleges and universities for decades, new courses on black literature and poetry in predominantly white colleges and universities demanded new texts to define and explain African American poetry. The aesthetic and political goals for inclusion—the nature of blackness, authenticity, essentialism, and particularity—became central to the study of black poetry rather than issues of influence. Baraka and Larry Neal's 1968 collection *Black Fire: An Anthology of Afro-American Writing* refused all rhymed verse.[4] Anthologizers whose poetic sensibilities departed from the mainstream were discouraged. Nikki Giovanni, in a 1969 *Negro Digest* review of Beatrice Murphy's *The Rocks Cry Out*, critiques Murphy for failing to see herself as part of a community suffering racial violence, seeming "to just miss the whole point of being Black in the beginning of Blackness."[5] Would new poets write to fit these new standards?

Sonnets on overtly racial themes or militant works, such as McKay's "If We Must Die," remained in circulation in comprehensive poetry anthologies still used in the classroom, as Emanuel's *Black World* essay demonstrates. But the sonnet was still perceived as a prestigious "European" form, at odds with the new emphasis on art that was particularly black. McKay's use of the sonnet form "to portray anger and protest," Gayle argues, indicated that his generation "lacked an aesthetic which might have given form and direction to their art."[6] Emanuel's appeal that black sonnets are "racial treasures" that "wherever found, must be scrupulously protected for the benefit of later generations hopefully not beleaguered by the peculiar enormities of our times" reveals the pressure that the sonnet form was under. "The revolutionary spirit of the Seventies is a legacy, not a sudden notion," Emanuel pleads.[7] But political opposition was firm.

If in the 1950s the category of black literature could include William Faulkner's new novel *Intruder in the Dust*, efforts toward cultural assimilation were put aside in the 1960s.[8] Louis D. Rubin, Jr., saw traditional poetic forms to be "a poetic mode that was hardly congenial for imagining the experience of a segment of the American population whose life and thought was neither abstract nor genteel, and was not to be depicted in tones of bloodless ideality."[9] The new goal was nationalism, and the loudest voices called for a distinct canon of African American poetry involving black forms and black themes, voicing the particular, unique history of Africans in America on an individual, local, and historical dimension. Addison Gayle argued for "an art which maximizes the differences between White and Black culture."[10] Art should speak to black concerns and issues, and reach inside the community for inspiration, whatever the form, but the right voice and the right forms for black art were jazz, improvisation, innovation, and African influences.

Forms that black poets had worked in for years were overnight suddenly seen as "white." James T. Stewart argued that black poets "must construct models which correspond to his own reality. The models must be nonwhite. Our models must be consistent with a black style, our natural aesthetic styles, and our moral and spiritual styles."[11] Brooks's friend Don Lee (later Haki R. Madhubuti) proclaimed that "black poets will be examples of their poems, and if their poems are righteous the poet will be righteous and he will be a positive example for the black community."[12] Blyden Jackson saw the black poet's challenge as a search "for the right language as a medium of appropriate diction through which he can represent himself without demeaning his own concept of what he is and, even so, still manage to speak persuasively to non-Negroes, many of whom may be indifferent, if not hostile, to any positive picture of a black."[13]

Past borrowing of "white" forms was characterized as "developmental stage" writing: a clean break from the past, a demythologizing of the "Harlem Renaissance." George E. Kent characterized poets from the precursor Dunbar (who "retained in his sensibility too much of the nostalgic glow for the lost plantation days") through Cullen as "'bourgies' lacking relevance to the people whose struggles and qualities they were to portray." Kent saw the poets of the 1920s and 1930s as "the father of many children whose features are likely to be looked upon suspiciously by the offspring."[14] All of the sonnet's historical baggage became a problem again. Moreover, as Nathan Huggins argued, "The creation of Harlem as a place of exotic culture was as much a service to white need as to black."[15] Their formal poetry was seen as compromised.

Even the notion of double consciousness was under attack.[16] The First International Conference of Black Writers and Artists, in Paris in September 1956, emphasized African cultural unity and "negritude." Self-alienation was an American phenomenon that should be rethought. Franz Fanon questioned all literature and art produced in colonial regimes, "the culture of culture."[17] Aimé Césaire argued for black singularity:

> One fact that is paramount in my eyes is this: we, men of colour, at this precise moment in our historical evolution, have come to grasp, in our consciousness, the full breadth of our singularity....The singularity of our "situation in the world," which cannot be confused with any other. The singularity of our problems, which cannot be reduced to any other problem. The singularity of our history, constructed out of terrible misfortunes that belong to no one else. The singularity of our culture, which we wish to live in a way that is more and more real.[18]

In the 1960s thinking internationally was preferable to mythologizing Harlem writers from a bygone era. The reinvigorated embrace of a radically Black Aesthetic recast the "Negro Art" essays by Du Bois, Hughes, and others as explicitly advocating for black poets to seek black traditions and to avoid assimilation. These essays, plucked out of their sonnet-rich context, became foundational to the project of defining and evaluating black literature and became the basis of the intellectual tradition for the study of African American literature in black colleges and universities and, later, in black studies departments in "mainstream" colleges and universities after 1968.

LeRoi Jones (after 1967, Imamu Amiri Baraka) was the new hero, the "charismatic leader of the black arts movement," as Abby Arthur Johnson and Ronald Maberry Johnson call him.[19] Labeling Western culture the "beast" from the *Book of Revelation*, Baraka characterized the black poet as "priest." His blank verse poem "Black Art" (which begins, "Poems are bullshit unless they are / Teeth or trees or lemons piled / On a step") was the movement's poetic manifesto. The battlefield was poetry; the altar was poetry. Yet Baraka was ambivalent about the sonnet. "I'm not interested in writing sonnets, sestinas or anything...only poems," he claimed in 1960, but "if the poem has got to be a sonnet (unlikely tho) or whatever, it'll certainly let me know."[20] As a serious poet, the past could not be avoided.

A few years earlier, Baraka had in fact published two sonnets, though neither is formally identified as a sonnet. "The Turncoat," from *Preface to a Twenty Volume Suicide Note* (1961), unmistakably contends with multiple sonnet traditions:

The steel fibrous slant & ribboned glint
of water. The Sea. Even my secret speech is moist
with it. When I am alone & brooding, locked in
with dull memories & self hate, & the terrible disorder
of a young man.

I move slowly. My cape spread stiff & pressing cautiously
in the first night wind off the Hudson. I glide down
onto my own roof, peering in at the pitiful shadow of myself.

How can it mean anything? The stop & spout, the
wind's dumb shift. Creak of the house & wet smells
coming in. Night forms on my left. The blind still
up to admit a sun that no longer exists. Sea move.

I dream long bays & towers... & soft steps on moist sand.
I become them, sometimes. Pure flight. Pure fantasy. Lean.

Without a defined meter or rhyme scheme, Jones's poem still embraces its sonnet form. The double-voiced, disordered, self-hating speaker of the octave broods over secret speech and ponders his own shadow, the sonnet cage evoked by the lines "locked in / with dull memories." The sestet turns, performing the volta, asking, "How can it mean anything?" "The stop & spout" evokes each line of a sonnet; "the / wind's dumb shift" wryly evokes the rhyme scheme. The sonnet is too creaky; the sun no longer exists. "Pure flight. Pure fantasy" is preferable. "Lean" is provocatively ambiguous—meaning either without fat or tilting away from tradition. Baraka did not include the sonnet in his later collections, but it appears, along with Gwendolyn Brooks's "Intermission," as one of two sonnets anthologized in Herbert Hill's 1963 anthology *Soon, One Morning: New Writing by American Negroes, 1940–1962.*

The sonnet form is clearly a compelling foil for Baraka, who also uses it for "Epistrophe (for yodo)":

It's such a static reference; looking
out the window all the time! the eyes' limits . . .
On good days, the sun.

& what you see. (here in New York)
Walls and buildings; or in the hidden gardens
of opulent Queens: profusion, endless stretches of leisure.

It's like being chained to some dead actress;
& she keeps trying to tell you something horribly maudlin.

> e.g. ("the leaves are flat & motionless.")
>
> What I know of the mind
> seems to end here;
> Just outside my face.
>
> I wish some weird looking animal
> would come along.[21]

As with "The Turncoat," Baraka's speaker begins looking out the window. The sun is again evoked, as well as walls, hidden gardens, and limits. The speaker is immediately contending with sonnet tropes and traditions; the line "It's like being chained to some dead actress" suggests the "fair maidens" of sonnet tradition that he cannot break from. Just after the eighth line and a volta, the parenthetical ("the leaves are flat & motionless") evokes the "dead leaves" of Keats's sonnet (chapter 2). The last two lines, as with "The Turncoat," express longing for a new form, some "weird looking animal." "Epistrophe" appears in Hughes's 1964 anthology *New Negro Poets U.S.A.*, with its foreword by Brooks.

Baraka's sonnets are startling in their robust engagement with sonnet tradition, with its structural doubleness, its conflicted and deliberative nature, and its capacity for transcendent and spiritual expression. Both "The Turncoat" and "Epistrophe" are as knowingly innovative as Brooks's "To a Winter Squirrel" (chapter 2). And yet rather than see a kinship with Brooks in their poetic projects—rather than name their shared work in wrenching the best-known poetic form from the European tradition, building on the work of black poets from Dunbar and McKay onward, and transforming it into an African American poetic form—Baraka turned his back on her. He was among the forces that made Brooks renounce sonnet writing. He never claimed his own verse as sonnets.[22]

Other poets defended the sonnet form. Robert Hayden's sonnet "The Performers" (1972) can be read as a pointed engagement with Baraka's sonnets:

> Easily, almost matter-of-factly, they step,
> two minor Wallendas, with pail and squeegee along
> the wintry ledge, hook their harness to the wall
> and leaning back into a seven-story angle of space
> begin washing the office windows. I
> am up there too until straps break
> and iron paper apple of iron I fall
> through plate glass wind onto stalagmites below.

But I am safely at my desk again by the time
the hairline walkers, high-edge
balancers end their center-ring routine
and crawl inside. A rough day, I remark,
for such a risky business. Many thanks.
Thank *you*, sir, one of the men replies.[23]

Hayden's sonnet avoids strict iambic pentameter or a perceivable rhyme scheme, particularly in the octave, where the only rhyme is "wall/fall." The speaker describes two window washers outside the office windows; the speaker joins them and "iron paper apple of iron," he falls. There is a clear volta, signaled by the "But," and in the sestet the speaker is "safely" at his desk where he thanks the window washers—presumably for giving him a clearer view.

Hayden's sonnet is provocatively in conversation with the opening of "Epistrophe": "It's such a static reference; looking / out the window all the time! the eyes' limits… / On good days, the sun," as well as the "glide down" of "The Turncoat," which for Hayden's speaker is a violent fall. The window washers are artist-poets ("minor Wallendas"); if Hayden's speaker tried what they were doing, he would fail. He will play it safe, outside the center ring. "Thank *you*, sir," Hayden's speaker is told.

Hayden rejected the politics of the Fisk conference, advocating for poetry outside "crude propaganda," and he was rejected in turn as "outmoded" and "a form of treachery," as Arnold Rampersad put it.[24] If I read this history into "The Performers" it is only because Hayden's sonnet has invited it—his sonnet recognizes that Jones was calling for one thing and doing another, and Hayden will have none of it.

While Hayden kept writing formal poetry, Brooks opted for change. She was the dominant African American poet in postwar America and a celebrated sonnet writer. If the Black Aesthetic required a clean break from established poetic practices, that meant either a clean break from Brooks or an effort to get Brooks to break with her previous work and aspirations. And the effort succeeded—for many years, Brooks openly repudiated the sonnet form, as did June Jordan and others.

Without Brooks's stature there may not have been debates about the sonnet. It may not have been as necessary. In 1968 essayists in *Negro Digest* still called out Louis Simpson, a white *New York Herald Tribune* reviewer, for his criticism five years earlier of Gwendolyn Brooks's *Selected Poems* (1963), observing that "I am not sure it is possible for a Negro to write well without making us aware he is a Negro," citing an early poem, "the ballad of chocolate Mabbie."[25] Simpson's sentiment enraged and aroused many readers in part because *Selected Poems* was far from a radical volume of race poetry. While her sonnets could be characterized as political, Brooks herself was not a political figure; she did not inject herself into the race-leader power struggles of the era, and her sonnets were not militant race-protest sonnets in the manner of McKay. Her politics in the 1940s and 1950s were Cold War politics and self-representation, James Smethurst argues.[26] But she was the black poet white critics knew best. After requoting Simpson's review of Brooks in 1968, Hoyt Fuller jumps quickly to Simpson's more recent review of Arnold Adoff's new poetry anthology, *I Am the Darker Brother*, and his disparagement of black poets who attempt to use traditional forms.[27] The point of his essay is clear: black poets should be doing something new.

Joanne V. Gabbin argues that what Brooks absorbed from the urgent voices of the 1967 writers' conference at Fisk University (including Baraka, John Killens, and Hoyt Fuller) and back in Chicago (Etheridge Knight, Don L. Lee) was "their cogent awareness of the importance of cultivating and speaking directly to a black audience, and their reliance upon new poetic forms that reflected the rhythms, texture, and richness of folk music and speech."[28] Brooks understood that the sonnet was "one of the white forms that had to be shelved after 1967," Karen Jackson Ford argues. "Indeed, it became *the* white form to be 'chased out,' because it symbolized all of the other 'Western measures, rules, models' she and her contemporaries eschewed." Ford adds that Brooks's "constant swearing off of sonnet writing after 1967 may be a measure of how difficult it was for her to abandon the form."[29]

In her 1972 autobiography, Brooks describes her poetry prior to 1967 as "work that was conditioned to the times and the people." In his preface to the volume, Don Lee repeats this idea—or rather claims it first, since the reader encounters his voice first. "The early years reaped with self awareness," he writes, "even though at times the force of her poetic song is strained in iambic pentameter, European sonnets, and English ballads. Conditioned!"[30] In a 1975 essay, "Of Flowers and Fire and Flowers," Brooks recounted:

> The forties and fifties were years of high poet-incense; the language-flowers were thickly sweet. Those flowers whined and begged white folks to pick them, to find them lovable. Then the '60s: Independent fire! Well, I don't want us to creep back to the weaker flowers of the old yes-

terday. I don't want us to subscribe, again, to Shelley or Pound-Eliot or Wallace Stevens. I don't want us to forget the Fire. Baldwin's announced "Next Time" is by no means over. I want us to "advance," yes, to experiment, yes, to labor, yes. But I don't want us to forget the Fire.[31]

And in 1979, Brooks sighed that she would leave haiku to the Japanese and the sonnet to Miltons. "If we keep on concentrating on Shakespearean sonnets we'll continue to estrange ourselves from the discoveries we need to make."[32] Yet in an interview with Claudia Tate, Brooks remarks, "I'm fighting for myself a little bit here because I believe it takes a little patience to sit down and find out that in 1945 I was saying what many of the young folks said in the sixties. But it's crowded into language like this: 'The pasts of his ancestors lean against / Him.'"[33] In the 1990s Brooks recalled growing up with Cullen's *Caroling Dusk*, reading Hughes, Sterling Brown, and both Cotters—Joseph Cotter, Sr. and Jr.—and Dunbar.[34]

What is most remarkable about the scholarly criticism of Brooks then and still now is how difficult it seems to be to see her as part of a tradition of African American poetry, to see her as a continuation of black sonnet voices from Dunbar onward. In 1972 Houston Baker begins his assessment of Brooks by situating her in a white male poetic community:

> Miss Brooks writes tense, complex, rhythmic verse that contains the metaphysical complexities of John Donne and the word magic of Apollinaire, Eliot, and Pound.... [Her style], however, is often used to explicate the condition of the black American trapped behind a veil that separates him from the white world. What one seems to have is "white" style and "black" content—two warring ideals in one dark body.[35]

Baker understands the sonnet as particularly appropriate for Du Boisian double consciousness; in fact, he describes her as "[b]eset by a double consciousness" and argues that "she has kept herself from being torn asunder by crafting poems that equal the best in the black and white American literary traditions." He remarks that her early poetry "fits the white, middle-class patterns Imamu Baraka has seen as characteristic of 'Negro literature.'" Baker notes that she admired Langston Hughes and that "We real cool" could be by Hughes or Sterling Brown, but he won't acknowledge the existence of previous sonnets. Yes, of course, she read Dunbar and "Harlem Renaissance" writers, but, he concludes, "Gwendolyn Brooks represents a singular achievement."[36] This is how erasure works.

Baker's influential critique disturbs Keith Leonard, who argues that Baker "accepts the premise that the forms of the Anglo-American tradition are almost exclusively the cultural province of white people and that all a black person can do with those forms is to insert black cultural content." Yet even in arguing that "combining the aesthetic power and social validity of traditional formalist artistry with the complexities of African American experience, culture, and heritage" allowed African American formalist poets to inhabit a "middle ground," Leonard clarifies what disturbed so many Black Arts movement advocates about Brooks's poetry: there should be no middle ground.[37] Never considered was the idea that Brooks was drawing on the black sonnet writing tradition to turn the sonnet into a black form.

Gladys Williams argues that Brooks's virtuosity with the sonnet is the expected result of poetic seriousness and the notion that every serious English language poet wrote sonnets. "She knows the ways in which Shakespeare, Spencer, Milton, Donne, Keats, Wordsworth juxtaposed intense emotion against the rigid iambic pentameter line of the sonnet, creating patters of pull and push among its elements. She knows the ways in which moderns like Pound, Eliot, Yeats, and Frost break traditional poetic patterns."[38] Both Melhem and Henderson note Brooks's modernist influences, including John Crowe Ransom, Joyce, Eliot, Frost, and Merrill Moore, but not the influence of other black poets.[39]

Gary Smith too notes that Brooks's sonnets are "more in the style of the modernist poets, Robert Frost, Ezra Pound, e. e. cummings, who experimented beyond the sonnet's traditional diction and structure."[40] He acknowledges McKay and Cullen but argues that Brooks's "Gay Chaps at the Bar" sonnets surpass them by adapting the sonnet form more radically. Smith and others often point specifically to "The white troops had their orders but the Negroes looked like men" (1945):

> They had supposed their formula was fixed.
> They had obeyed instructions to devise
> A type of cold, a type of hooded gaze.
> But when the Negroes came they were perplexed.
> These Negroes looked like men. Besides, it taxed
> Time and the temper to remember those
> Congenital iniquities that cause
> Disfavor of the darkness. Such as boxed
> Their feelings properly, complete to tags—

A box for dark men and a box for Other—
Would often find the contents had been scrambled.
Or even switched. Who really gave two figs?
Neither the earth nor heaven ever trembled.
And there was nothing startling in the weather.

Structured on an Italian rhyme scheme, Brooks's speaker inhabits the minds of white soldiers tasked with "boxing" the remains of Negro soldiers. Both the octave and the sestet engage with conventional sonnet tropes of containment and ambivalence. Smith notes that unlike Cullen, Brooks does not use the final Shakespearean sonnet couplet to transcend or sidestep a racial dilemma. Rather, Smith argues, Brooks "strategically places her volta in the tenth line: 'Who really gave two figs?' At this point, the question of racial discrimination is not transcended, nor does Brooks provide a resolution of the sonnet's ordeal."[41] The off rhyme Other/weather further attenuates the already fragile sense of resolution. All dead soldiers go home dead.

Marcellus Blount sees that in "Gay Chaps," Brooks "must have had McKay's poetry in mind" even while she "challenges the gender assumptions of McKay's call to male arms by subverting the male ideal of war," using the voices of black soldiers contemplating the changes brought by war.[42] Williams too attends closely to the ways that meter, syntax, and word order contribute to the martial sound of the sonnets in "Gay Chaps." But still Williams apologizes for Brooks's choice of form: "The sonnet form would seem, almost without one's thinking about it, too limited in compass, too artificial and demanding in its making, and therefore too intellectual in the tensions that must be made to obtain between depth of emotion and rigidity of form, to be an appropriate genre for this subject matter."[43] Melhem labels sonnets as "a white form" even while praising "the dynamic confluence of black and white poetic energy" and adds, "Brooks turned away from the sonnet, symbol of conventional form and the past, to a 'tom-tom hearted' present."[44]

Like previous critics, Elizabeth Alexander argues more recently that while the first black sonnet writers faced pressure to write "expertly within prescribed European forms," Brooks pushed the sonnet form further than Dunbar and Cullen, who merely "spread their wings elegantly within" the sonnet and mostly followed the rules. Brooks was freer to make the sonnet her own. Alexander too notes Brooks's off rhymes in the "Gay Chaps" series, to signal "the profound contradiction these soldiers faced, fighting for their country but knowing all along that they would remain second-class citizens."[45] Yet once again, in arguing for Brooks's innovations, she too overlooks the conditions that allowed Brooks's apprenticeship, including the many years publishing unremarkable sonnets in the pages of the *Chicago Defender* in the 1930s. The popularity of the sonnet form in African American newspapers encouraged Brooks's writing and her innovations.

In short, despite decades of critical attention to Brooks's sonnet writing, Baker's early critique is remarkably influential: Brooks is not often seen as a key part of an African American sonnet tradition except insofar as her sonnets are more formally innovative than previous black poets such as McKay or Cullen. While Smethurst notes that "it is worthwhile to link" Brooks's sonnets to earlier black sonnet writers (and scolds Melhem for leaving out Dunbar as a possible influence), Smethurst himself simply suggests that Brooks's sonnets "are formally quite different from those earlier sonnets." He too notes off rhymes in "the white troops had their orders." But then he repeats an assertion he has made several times that sonnets are "the popular middle-class icon of 'high' literature," even while the sonnet form was "especially favored by African-American writers in the twentieth century until at least the early 1950s."[46] And Maria K. Mootry reads Brooks's sonnet innovations solely alongside Melvin Tolson, arguing that "in their use of the sonnet form in their initial volumes, Brooks and Tolson had played off its conventions and stanzaic structures, rhyme, meter, and poetic argument against their own creative practices."[47]

Yet Brooks herself saw herself as part of a longer continuum of sonnet writers, as Ford notes. "Disavowing the sonnet required a strenuous effort...because the form symbolized not simply white aesthetics but black poetic achievement....When the Black Arts Movement determined that the sonnet was no longer useful to African Americans, it had to deny a valuable aspect of the very African American past it was reclaiming."[48] Brooks had in her corner her friend Dudley Randall, poet and Broadside Press publisher, who had won a sonnet-writing contest at age thirteen and who walked a fine line between uncritical praise and harsh disparagement of previous generations of black poets.[49] He published several sonnets, including the love sonnet "Anniversary Words" and, here, "The Dilemma" (1956):

My poems are not sufficiently
obscure to please the critics.
—RAY DUREM

I'd like to sing (but singing is naïve)
To express emotion freely and unveiled,
(But should I wear my heart upon my sleeve,
And as a lush Romantic be assailed?)
And sometimes I would like to make a plain
Unvarnished statement bare of metaphor,
(But to speak simply is to be inane;
A man of the world should never be a bore.)
And so I cultivate my irony
And search strange books for the recondite allusion.
The time's confused, so I must also be,
and in the reader likewise plan confusion.
So, though no Shelley, I'm a gentleman
And if not Attic, Alexandrian.[50]

The epigraph from Ray Durem's poem "I Know I'm Not Sufficiently Obscure" (1962; not a sonnet, included in Randall's anthology *The Black Poets*)
was clearly added afterward. In this sonnet, which uses a Shakespearean
rhyme scheme, Randall's speaker is literally of two minds in the octave,
wondering how to express himself and what the critique of his form will
be. The sestet continues the theme and is perhaps even more tongue-in-
cheek. It is not an excellent sonnet.

Note also Eugene Redmond's little-known poem, "Sonnet Serenade/
Soulo Beauty for Gwendolyn Brooks" (1972):

Behold! the forms and rhythms of my face
Choral trees and soulos limbly bowing
Greenhiss grasslow and moanful in sparkspace
Caught crying, caroling and know-howing
Sometimes in gusty soulsoliloquys
Within vastvalleys and mountainous songs
Or much iterated with ah's and me's
Short-circuited or shattered against gongs
A lord-length voice invades these jungle sparks
Neoning drumscripting a passion-rain
Which seeds tear-tunes and in the drumpath marks
A cool mellow maid of song and a main
Squeeze close-held in sound-arms, in hip song-rap
Whose love, buttoned in gold, is your lyre-lap.[51]

Redmond remarked that the nature of the sonnet fascinated him and called this "a problem-solving sonnet." I include Redmond's and Randall's sonnets simply to illustrate that sonnets continued to be written even while essays in journals—*Negro Digest/Black World*, the *Liberator*, *Soulbook*, *Black Dialogue*, and the *Journal of Black Poetry*—militated for the role of radical poetry in the Black Power movement and calling for new forms.[52] In the January 1969 issue of *Negro Digest*, Carolyn Fowler Gerald lauded "the deliberate desecration and smashing of idols, the turning inside-out of symbols, to which black writers are now proceeding with a vengeance."[53] In July Gayle praised proponents of a Black Aesthetic rightly calling "for a set of rules by which Black literature and art is to be judged and evaluated."[54] And in September two sonnets appear in an issue proposing new categories of poetry, including "teachin'" poems, "mindblower" poems, and "shoutin'" poems.[55] One sonnet is Sarudzai's "Pan Africa" (chapter 1) and the other, "Heritage" by Octave Lilly, Jr.:

> It is not true that we have suddenly
> discovered that our skin is black, or known
> that we are cast in classic ebony:
> before our ancestors were chained and thrown
> in slaveships by crusading, kindly saviors—
> and loved with Christian whips to found empires—
> our fathers taught conservancy with mirrors,
> and burnt our spirit free in prideful fires.
> And later Woodson and Du Bois taught
> us pride, and opened misty eyes to see
> the naked truth: how outraged black men fought
> the architects of stolen liberty—
> with tooth and nail against the fiendish odds
> designed in hell by alien Western gods.[56]

Within a Shakespearean rhyme scheme, Lilly's speaker evokes several McKay sonnets ("The Lynching," "Outcast") to argue for a long history of black pride, beginning with ancestors and "later" with the assistance of Woodson and Du Bois. Lilly was not new to sonnet writing; he published several in *Opportunity* in the 1930s. "Heritage" harks back to early twentieth-century sonnet-writing practice: while it is concerned with race and borrows terms from other African American sonnet writers, it is not double-voiced, and it does not knowingly contend with sonnet tradition or the particular moment. "Heritage" is solely about African American heritage, not sonnet heritage. It appears in *Negro Digest* solely for its race consciousness but is not anthologized. Nor is "Pan Africa."

What reading scholarly criticism and poring over issues of *Black World/Negro Digest* and *Journal of Negro Poetry* reveal is that while sonnets continued to be written and published as a kind of new sonnet-writing practice, anthologies remain the key instrument for transmitting the canon of influential African American sonnets from one generation to the next. New sonnets by Brooks, Hayden, and others are added, and while the sonnet canon remains consistently good (sonnets such as Lilly's, Randall's, and Redmond's above are not included), it also remains consistently overlooked for evidence that sonnet writers are influencing each other.

In the next few years, nearly a dozen new anthologies appear, including June Jordan's *Soulscript: Afro-American Poetry* (1970), Arthur P. Davis and Saunders Redding's *Cavalcade: Negro American Writing from 1760 to the Present* (1971); Dudley Randall's *The Black Poets* (1971); Arnold Adoff's *The Poetry of Black America: Anthology of the 20th Century* (1973); and Stephen Henderson's *Understanding the New Black Poetry* (1973).[57] All will include "If We Must Die" and at least one other sonnet by McKay, Cullen's "Yet Do I Marvel," and usually Hayden's "Frederick Douglass," as well as sonnets by Brooks, Duckett's "Sonnet," and Margaret Walker's "For Malcolm X":

> All you violated ones with gentle hearts;
> You violent dreamers whose cries shout heartbreak;
> Whose voices echo clamors of our cool capers,
> And whose black faces have hollowed pits for eyes.
> All you gambling sons and hooked children and bowery bums
> Hating white devils and black bourgeoisie,
> Thumbing your noses at your burning red suns,
> Gather round this coffin and mourn your dying swan.
>
> Snow-white moslem head-dress around a dead black face!
> Beautiful were your sand-papering words against our skins!
> Our blood and water pour from your flowing wounds.
> You have cut open our breasts and dug scalpels in our brains.
> When and Where will another come to take your holy place?
> Old man mumbling in his dotage, crying child, unborn?

As in Hayden's "Frederick Douglass," Walker's speaker seems to overspill the standard ten-syllable line, speaking in the sonnet's octave to "you violated ones," "violent dreamers," "gambling sons" who are gathered around the coffin of Malcolm X, a "dying swan." The speaker turns in the sestet to the dead man, praising his "sand-papering words" as beautiful, seeing "our" blood in his wounds. Rhymes and off rhymes are apparent, occasionally resolving (sons, bums, suns; face, place) but usually only almost (wounds, brains; swan, unborn). The sonnet form creates the possibility of resolution and enables formal ambivalence. Toying with the sonnet form "signals Walker's engagement with literary modernism," Smethurst argues, "where the overt engagement with and evasion from the formal expectations of the sonnet was a common move of literary modernists both black and white."[58] Margaret Walker tried "problematically" in 1942 "to adapt the sonnet for a poetry of social conscience," and as Nelson argues, she succeeds here.[59]

Doughtry Long's "Ginger Bread Mama" (1971) appears in two collections and is less about modernist engagement than simply signifying:

> i love you ginger bread mama
> ginger bread mama
>   all sweet and brown
> love you
>   more than tired boys
> love collard greens and candied yams
> more than new watermelons
>   do the sun.
> before you,
> i was older
>   and owned a sky of sleep
> and not even cowboy dreams
> were poets enough to wish me you.
> now in brownness warm
> everything is everything and
> our forms move in soft affirmations.
> trying not to wake up the sun.

A playful love sonnet in the tradition of Petrarch and Elizabeth Barrett Browning, perhaps also gesturing to Baugh's "There's a Brown Girl in the Ring," Long's fourteen-line poem hews to no traditional sonnet rhyme scheme or meter, but it is clearly a sonnet. The speaker loves the beloved more than the love of boys and watermelons. While there is perhaps no strong ambivalence, the speaker turns from speaking of love metaphorically to a material present, where "everything is everything." The final couplet, "our forms move in soft affirmations / trying not to wake up the sun," ratifies its sonnetness.

And Lorenzo Thomas's sonnet "MMDCCXIII½" might be read as a commentary on Brooks's sonnets about kitchens:

> The cruelty of ages past affects us now
> Whoever it was who lived here lived a mean life
> Each door has locks designed for keys unknown
>
> Our living room was once somebody's home
> Our bedroom, someone's only room
> Our kitchen had a hasp upon its door.
>
> Door to a kitchen?
>
> And our lives are hasped and boundaried
> Because of ancient locks and madnesses
> Of slumlord greed and desperate privacies
>
> Which one is madness? Depends on who you are.
> We find we cannot stay, the both of us, in the same room
> Dance, like electrons, out of each other's way.
>
> The cruelties of ages past affect us now.[60]

Thomas's sonnet too avoids regular meter and rhyme scheme, although the many off rhymes and eye rhymes (unknown/home, room/door, boundaried/privacies) evoke the resolutions that do not quite come. The first seven lines engage with sonnet tropes of locked doors, enclosed spaces, and boundaries. The second seven move from the physical to the metaphysical, "our lives are hasped and boundaried / Because of ancient locks," before moving back to the reality of slumlord greed. The last line might be stronger, but it is a sonnet on sonnets, written by an Umbra poet.

❀ ❀ ❀

Houston Baker argues that the work of black American authors "has been molded largely by the white literary establishment."[61] Among the scholarly criticism of the sonnet form for black poetry, Baker's characterization of formal poetry as "mastered masks" has been the most influential: "I shall use the term 'form' to signal a symbolizing fluidity. I intend by the term a family of concepts or a momentary and changing same array of images, figures, assumptions, and presuppositions that a group of people (even one as extensive and populous as a nation) holds to be a valued repository of spirit. And the form most apt for carrying forward such notions is a *mask*."[62] Baker hastens to add that he means "mask" as a "center for ritual," and in fact that the form he has in mind is "minstrel mask." Thus form becomes equated to "minstrel mask."

"Mimicking" becomes another key term scholars use to describe sonnet writing by African American poets. Joseph McLaren argues that Cullen and McKay are "mimicking" "Eurocentric patterns and Standard English phrasings," not apprehending the influence of Dunbar.[63] Even if true, McLaren discounts Zora Neale Hurston's admonition that "[m]imicry is an art in itself."[64]

William Carroll argues that McKay uses the sonnet form for "far different" sentiments than Shakespeare and Petrarch did: while European sonnets of the Renaissance were a matter of human love, they were "tough love" for McKay.[65] While it is not quite clear what he means by this, the suggestion is that the sonnet is a punishment.

Much will change in the 1990s with Rita Dove's *Mother Love* and the sonnets of Yusef Komunyakaa. Therese Steffen notes that sonnet writing "has marked momentous personal and public turning points in African American careers. Countee Cullen uses the Shakespearean sonnet after the breakdown of his marriage, and Langston Hughes fights isolation and despair with a blues version of the form." McKay's "If We Must Die," she adds, expressed New Negro dignity with its "romantically inspired poetic structure with a theme that appears to cover revolutionary ground."[66] Dove herself noted that "some modern poets, women particularly, have rejected the sonnet form, calling it outdated, false, patriarchal, even fascist," but "I think that it is bogus to talk about patriarchal form in art."[67] For Steffens, Dove's sonnet use is a "talisman" and "sanctuary." For Francini, Dove's "singing 'in chains'" is a protest against "the pseudo-democracy of free verse, while the unorthodox forms of her sonnets become the objective correlative of a world where chaos and disintegration are inescapable." Dove's "violated" sonnets "suggest a way of organizing poetical material so as not to get lost in the chaos, the creation of a new order parallel to what happens in the natural world."[68]

Sonnet writing by African American poets at the turn of the twenty-first century will become a commonplace occurrence. But for how long will sonnet writers and scholars refer to the sonnet as a "received form"? The phrase demands the question: received from whom? Even Cary Nelson, who seeks to situate poets such as McKay in a broader leftist context, uses the phrase, arguing that "it is sometimes precisely the unresolvable conflicts between the connotations of a received form and the new anger it contains that make his poetry interesting."[69] The answer by now ought to be from the African American sonnet writers that have been using the form for more than a century. Roger Reeves, pondering sonnets by Terrance Hayes and Natasha Trethewey, uses the terms "received form, received poetic tradition" in speaking of the form. Focusing on Trethewey's "Native Guard" sonnet series specifically, Reeves sees the Trethewey's use of the sonnet form as

> a slave who writes the sequence in a diary that he stole from a plantation house. It's a palimpsest. However, Trethewey never allows the master's words, the former owner of the diary, to bleed through in the poem. We, the reader, are only aware of the former slave's words; thus, Trethewey makes the poem, the former enslaved's testimony visible through a disappearance. Concomitantly, Trethewey makes a meta-poetic statement about poets of African descent engaging with master narratives, forms, and traditions. Think: Audre Lorde and her question of can you use the master's tools to tear down the master's house. Think: Houston Baker, the literary critic, and his theorizing the deformation of mastery and the mastery of form in Harlem Renaissance (Modernist) poetry.[70]

When are the tools no longer the master's?

Kenneth Warren's argument that "African American literature was a post-emancipation phenomenon that gained its coherence as an undertaking in the social world defined by the system of Jim Crow segregation" does not focus on the influence of one African American writer on another. In arguing that African American literature "took shape" as a literature in the context of challenges to racial equality, he is in fact not really challenging the status quo. Coherence should involve influence.

Scholars looking backward could certainly find scattered critiques of standard European poetic forms for black poetry over the years: it was too bourgeois, too European, too international. Certainly the sonnet's reputation as sometimes too bourgeois (or genteel or middlebrow) was a matter of occasional impatience with nineteenth-century fustiness and reflected an aesthetic privileging of modernist and avant-garde poetics. But the popularity of modernist sonnets by Edna St. Vincent Millay, Robert Frost, e. e. cummings, Conrad Aiken, Merrill Moore, and Louise Bogan, among others, complicated arguments for Europeanness or gentility. The sonnet's popularity in the American labor movement in the early part of the twentieth century and its continued use by labor poet-activists such as Lola Ridge or Muriel Rukeyser through the 1930s demonstrated that the sonnet could embody radical leftist politics. The African American sonnet, as Brooks and Hayden showed, could be innovatively edgy and avant-garde.

The signal moments in establishing the African American literary tradition are studies mentioned by Houston Baker; Robert Stepto's 1979 *African American Literature: Reconstruction of Instruction*; all of Gates's works, including *Signifying Monkey*, *Black Literature and Literary Theory*, and *"Race," Writing and Difference*; works by Nellie McKay, Mary Helen Washington, and others establishing a literary tradition, beginning with the slave narrative; and Barbara Christian's *The Race for Theory*, as well as other works theorizing black literature. There have been decades of efforts to resurrect lost works by black women, raising up Nella Larsen, Zora Neale Hurston, Jessie Fauset. But not yet the sonnet.

African American participation in or opposition to the sonnet tradition has not been of particular interest to general sonnet anthologizers. David Bromwich's *American Sonnets: Anthology* (2007) does not acknowledge a black sonnet tradition.[71] The editors of *The Cambridge Companion to the Sonnet* (2011) treat sonnet race politics in the context of class politics.[72]

There are a number of reasons the fact of a sonnet tradition hasn't been recognized, let alone a genealogy of influence. One is that the first wave of anthologizing in the 1920s simply incorporated the important sonnets along with other verse forms, without differentiating sonnets as such. Until the late 1960s there was no specific aesthetic project beyond gathering and presenting representative works by African American writers. It may be that before Brooks the sonnet was not yet ready to be recognized as a form capacious enough, flexible enough, resilient enough to bend to the needs of African American poets, even though Dunbar showed it could. But it is only in certain settings that discourse about "movements" and the nature of traditions and a worldview become normalized. Black poetry scholars have had heuristics available to compare works, but sonnets have always been excluded, until now.

Perhaps the best understanding of the usefulness of the sonnet comes from outside the classroom. The rapper Jay-Z observes:

But even when a rapper is just rapping about how dope he is, there's something a little bit deeper going on. It's like a sonnet, believe it or not. Sonnets have a set structure, but also a limited subject matter: They are mostly about love. Taking on such a familiar subject and writing about it in a set structure forced sonnet writers to find every nook and cranny in the subject and challenged them to invent new language for saying old things. It's the same with braggadocio in rap. When we take the most familiar subject in the history of rap—why I'm dope—and frame it within the sixteen-bar structure of a rap verse, synced to the specific rhythm and feel of the track, more than anything it's a test of creativity and wit. It's like a metaphor for itself; if you can say how dope you are in a completely original, clever, powerful way, the rhyme itself becomes proof of the boast's truth.[73]

While Jay-Z may not have a thorough history of the sonnet traditions, he has no sense that the form is off limits or inappropriate.

Wrenched from any master it may have, long ago, the sonnet is now without question a black poetic form, as Tsitsi Jaji demonstrates in "Tell Me Something Good" (2018):

Who blessed the raucous cry of sparrows,
blaring out their call to prayer? As if
this gray were not, dead-tired, April's latest spit.
Who woke up this morning and, rose-shafted,
took light for a lucky charm, or worse, a
word from the Lord. Who, up at six, thinks
this is hope? Who can't afford to sleep?
When the radio croons, who slides on up,
hot body wired for a payday loan?
Who can't smell the coffee yet? There's no
one coming to celebrate a skirted cliff,
a missing mark. Snow bleeds out on tarmac. Cut.
Slow clot to black. This is America.
Now, let me hear you sing.[74]

ACKNOWLEDGMENTS

More than a decade of research and writing has gone into this book, and I find that I have an extensive list of individuals who have guided me at different moments over the past ten years. To begin, I am eternally grateful to Henry Louis Gates, Jr., Bill Gleason, Diana Fuss, Eric Gardner, Michael K. Johnson, Elizabeth Archibald, Jim Coleman, Peter Jelavich, Linda DeLibero, Doug Mao, Chip Wass, Meg Guroff, Andrew Talle, Tyler Cowen, and Robert Carson. All of you have read and supported my work for years in ways both professional and personal. My focus could not have been sustained without you. I am so very fortunate to know you and be guided by you.

This project could not have been finished without the support of National Humanities Center and the brilliant and generous minds I met there during my 2017–2018 fellowship year. Thank you to Robert Newman, Tania Munz, Lynn Miller, Brooke Andrade, Joe Milillo, all the staff, and all of my fellow Fellows. I give particular thanks to Stephanie Foote, Andreá Williams, Tera Hunter, Emily Levine, Tsitsi Jaji, Laura Murphy, Libby Otto, Sara Poor, Rian Thum, John Wilkinson, Maud Ellman, Ann Reynolds, Stephen Hall, Harleen Singh, Keith Howard, John McGowen, Hilde Hoogenboom, Mark Cruse, Therese Cory, John Smith, Valia Allori, and Mab Segrest.

I am grateful to Skip Gates, Abby Wolf, and the Hutchins Center for African and African American Research at Harvard University, which has twice awarded me a Du Bois Fellowship to work on book projects emerging from the Black Periodical Literature Project, with which I have been involved since 2004.

Thank you to the University of Maryland Local Americanists, particularly Bob Levine, Martha Nell Smith, Marilee Lindeman, and Zita Nunez, with whom I had many merry discussions about sonnets. Thank you to far-flung Americanist friends and colleagues: Bill Andrews, Janet Neary, Mark Sussman, Kim Gallon, Gretchen Gerzina, John Gruesser, Richard Ellis, Bryan Sinche, Priscilla Wald, Teresa Zackodnik, Lauri Scheyer, Paula Garrett, and Gregg Hecimovich.

Thank you to poets Lee Herrick, Nathaniel Mackey, Miriam Kotzin, Marilyn Nelson, Tomas Q. Morin, Gillian Conoley, Cody Ernst, Dora Malech, Jacob Bacharach, Andrew Motion, and Mary Jo Salter, who indulged my many sonnet questions.

I am grateful to many colleagues at the Center for Africana Studies during my years at Johns Hopkins, particularly Lester Spence, Nadia Nurhussein, Katrina McDonald, James Calvin, Floyd Hayes, Moira Hinderer, Jeanne-Marie Jackson, Sydney Van Morgan, Michael Hanchard, Amanda Gunn, Michael Degani, Debra Furr-Holden, Mieka Smart, and Ben Vinson.

I am grateful to Gabrielle Spiegel and the Mellon Fellows at Johns Hopkins who read and offered feedback on an early chapter; thank you especially to Leo Lisi, Emily Anderson, Rachel Galvin, Yi-Ping Ong, and Joshua Walden.

So many Hopkins colleagues offered ideas and support over the years it is hard to keep track, particularly as some of you have since decamped elsewhere. Thank you to Barbara Landau, Mark Thompson, Sharon Achinstein, Richard Halpern, Amanda Anderson, Chris Celenza, Pier Larson, Elizabeth Patton, Matt Roller, Phil Morgan, Barbara Morgan, Rob Lieberman, Jared Hickman, Lucy Sirianni, Christopher Nealon, Bret McCabe, Catherine Pierre, Thomas Dolby, Kathleen Beller, Susan deMuth, and Susan Baisley.

I am grateful to Rosemary Kegl at the University of Rochester for the invitation to give the Ford Lecture in 2014; thank you to Jennifer Grotz, James Longenbach, Katherine Mannheimer, Morris Eaves, and Jeffrey Tucker for generous and influential comments and conversation.

Thank you to my Princeton mentors and colleagues: in addition to Bill Gleason and Diana Fuss, I am grateful to Esther Schor, Susan Wolfson, Christopher Rovee, Paul Kelleher, Erwin Rosinberg, Julie Barmazel, Jay Dickson, and Dan Novak.

Thank you to the scholars and poets at the University of Colorado, Boulder, whose influence may be discerned in my close readings: Jeffrey Robinson, Elizabeth Robertson, and Nan Goodman.

I am most grateful to my many, many Peabody students who taught me as much about sonnets as I taught them. Can I name you all by name? I cannot but you know who you are and I hope you can still recite your sonnets by memory. Thank you also to my colleagues Sebastian Vogt, Mark Janello, Laura Protano-Biggs, Richard Giarusso, Monica Lopez-Gonzales, and the wonderful composers who put my sonnets to music.

A special thanks to Greg Britton, of the John Hopkins University Press, for directing me to Walter Biggins. Thank you Walter for your support and to everyone at The University of Georgia Press, including Lori Rider and Jon Davies. Thank you to Julie Wolf and Erica Tempesta for editing help when it was most needed.

Thank you to my many new colleagues at Sonoma State University for providing the rich intellectual culture I have found here.

Thank you stalwart friends for your unwavering support: Shannon Gifford, Kellyann Zuzulo, Martin Zuzulo, Wendy Goldberg, James Bowley, Sanford Zale, Sigal Ben-Porath, Louis Quagliato, and Heather Robbins.

And thank you finally to Ariel and Asher: your excellence inspires and amazes me.

NOTES

PROLOGUE

1. Wheatley, *Poems on Various Subjects*; Hammond, "Address to Miss Phillis Wheatly."

2. Braithwaite, *Anthology of Magazine Verse*, xiii.

3. Bloom, "Point of View," 32.

4. Bloom, *Anxiety of Influence*, 94.

5. James Weldon Johnson, *Book of American Negro Poetry*, xl–xli.

6. Gates, *Loose Canons*, 39.

7. Ellison, "The World and the Jug," 141. See also Hollander, *Work of Poetry*, a volume that solely treats white poets: "A poetic vocation consists partly in the discovery that although one has been born into a forceful and consequential biological and social family group, one is actually an imaginative foundling, or perhaps even a changeling" (6).

8. Neal, "Ellison's Zoot Suit," 105.

9. Brooks, Foreword, 13.

CHAPTER 1. TRACING TRADITION AND INFLUENCE

1. Du Bois, *Souls of Black Folk*, 364. First published as "Strivings of the Negro People," *Atlantic Monthly* (August 1897).

2. Spillers, "Crisis of the Negro Intellectual."

3. Gates, *Signifying Monkey*.

4. Chiles, "From Writing the Slave Self."

5. Langston Hughes, "Says Race Leaders," 8.

6. LeRoi Jones, "How You Sound?" 424–425; Larry Neal, "An Afterword," in Baraka and Neal, *Black Fire*.

7. Reed, "Can a Metronome Know?" 406.

8. Brooks, "Interview with Gwendolyn Brooks," 1–2. Brooks adds, "I still think there are things colloquial and contemporary that can be done with the sonnet form."

9. Brooks et al., "*GLR* Interview."

10. Gary Smith, "Black Protest Sonnet," 2.

11. Henderson, *Understanding the New Black Poetry*, 30–31.

12. Jordan, "Difficult Miracle," 252.

13. Wheatley, "Thoughts on the Works of Providence," in *Poems on Various Subjects*, 41.

14. William Shakespeare, *Othello* 1.3.160–166. Certainly the terms "passing" and "strange" gathered new meaning and resonances in the twentieth century. "Passing Strange" is the name of a Tony Award–winning rock musical by Stew and Heidi Rodewald, filmed by Spike Lee in 2008, a sort of black *Pilgrim's Progress*, which Hilton Als in "Young American" called a "hero's migration beyond the tenets of 'blackness" and toward selfhood." Martha Sandweiss titles her book *Passing Strange: A Gilded Age Tale of Love and Deception Across the Color Line.* Claude McKay uses the phrase in the third stanza of "The Years Between" (1934):

> This mood that seems to you so passing strange,
> This that you wrongly call a cynic smile,
> Is nothing but the sequence of a sea-change
> I have been running round a little while. (McKay, *Complete Poems*, 218)

15. Gates, *Signifying Monkey*, xxii–xxiii.

16. Ibid., 79.

17. Eliot, "Philip Massinger," 125.

18. Also the end of the speech:

> For he today that sheds his blood with me
> Shall be my brother; be he ne'er so vile,
> This day shall gentle his condition.
> And gentlemen in England now abed
> Shall think themselves accursed they were not here. (*Henry V*, 4.3.23–26)

19. Du Bois, "Triumph," 195.

20. Horace Gregory and Marya Zaturenska observe that "[n]o poet in America...more clearly reflected the immediate effects of Brooks's widely distributed influence than McKay." *History of American Poetry*, 394.

21. James Weldon Johnson, *Black Manhattan*, 264.

22. Quoted in North, *Dialect of Modernism*, 114.

23. Gary Smith, "Black Protest Sonnet," 3.

24. Braithwaite, "Negro in Literature."

25. Brawley, "Negro Literary Renaissance," 235.

26. Chace, "Development of Negro Poetry," 52.

27. Huggins, *Harlem Renaissance*, 220. Huggins thought McKay was too dependent on whites to be a voice of defiance, singling out Max Eastman, who apparently never invited McKay to his Martha's Vineyard summer home.

28. Myrdal, *American Dilemma*, 681.

29. *Anthology of Negro Poets in the U.S.A.*, a 1954 Folkways recording.

30. Emanuel, "Renaissance Sonneteers," 42.

31. See Cary Nelson, *Repression and Recovery*, 9–10. See also Dawson, "Foundational Myths."

32. Tolson, "Claude McKay's Art," 287.

33. See Jenkins, "'If We Must Die'," 333n10; "Radicalism and Sedition," 166n10, 166n335. McKay, who moved to London in 1919, lived and traveled outside the United States for most of the era known as the Harlem Renaissance.

34. Jackson and Rubin, *Black Poetry in America*, 46.

35. Randall, *Black Poets*, xxv.

36. Randall argues that the post-Renaissance generation, notably Brown and Walker, drew on folk materials, while "Robert Hayden, Gwendolyn Brooks, Melvin B. Tolson, and Margaret Danner brought black poetry abreast of its time by absorbing and mastering the techniques of T. S. Eliot, Hart Crane, Ezra Pound." Ibid., xxvi.

37. Redmond, *Drumvoices*, 173.

38. Emanuel, "Renaissance Sonneteers," 36.

39. Westover, "African American Sonnets."

40. Rampersad, *Life of Langston Hughes*, 160. Hughes's first result, "Barrel House: Chicago," was published in *Lincoln [University] News* in 1928.

41. Warren, *What Was African American Literature?*; Jarrett, *Representing the Race*. See also Thompson, "What Will Be African-American Literature?"

42. Warren, "Does African American Literature Exist?" *Chronicle of Higher Education*, February 24, 2011.

43. Henderson, *Understanding the New Black Poetry*, 9.

44. Bibby, "Disinterested and Fine."

45. Blount, "Caged Birds," 228.

46. George Kent notes that McKay's ability "to bend traditional forms to his purpose" was largely due to his understanding of sonnet traditions. Kent, "Patterns of the Harlem Renaissance," 20–21.

47. Bishop, *Edgar Allan Poe*, ix.

48. Redmond, *Drumvoices*, 12.

49. Hurston, "Characteristics of Negro Expression"; Langston Hughes, "Negro Artist"; Neal, "Black Arts Movement."

50. Appiah, "Structuralist Criticism and African Fiction," 170.

51. Marilyn Nelson, "Wreath for Emmett Till," 8–9.

52. Caplan, *Poetic Form*, 6.

53. Du Bois, *Souls of Black Folk*, chap. 6.

54. Blyden Jackson, "From One 'New Negro'," 49.

55. Easthope, *Poetry as Discourse*, 60, 24.

56. Major, introduction to *New Black Poetry*, 18–19.

57. Easthope, *Poetry as Discourse*, notes that in 1912 "Ezra Pound set himself

the principle of composing 'in the sequence of the musical phrase, not in sequence of a metronome.'...A generation later Brecht, in an essay of 1939, rejected 'the oily smoothness of the usual five-foot iambic meter'...and describes how he 'gave up iambic entirely and applied firm but irregular rhythms'" (53).

58. James, "Bloomsbury Atmosphere," 28.

59. The sonnet is said to have appeared in a volume titled *Pascall Bowled and Other Verses* (1922). The last four lines, apparently, are

> O Wilton St. Hill, Trinidadians' pride,
> A century and four came from your bat,
> And helped to win the victory for your side,
> But more than that you did, yea, more than that. (James, *Beyond a Boundary*, 90)

60. Greene, *Unrequited Conquests*, 2.

61. Francini, "Sonnet vs. Sonnet," 59–60.

62. Leonard, *Fettered Genius*, 3–8, quotations on 4.

63. Ibid., 2.

64. Gilroy, *Black Atlantic*, 90, 91.

65. Leonard, *Fettered Genius*, 3–8, quotations on 8; Baker, *Modernism and the Harlem Renaissance*, 85.

66. Marilyn Nelson, "Owning the Masters," x.

67. Benston, "Ellison, Baraka," 334–335.

68. *Negro Digest*, September 1969, 71.

69. McKay, *Long Way from Home*, 90.

70. Girard, "J. Saunders Redding," 286. "Millay was, in fact, one of Cullen's primary poetic influences. While at New York University, Cullen wrote his undergraduate thesis on Millay's poetry."

71. Sherman, *Invisible Poets*, xxix.

CHAPTER 2. SUFFERING, LOVE, BONDAGE, AND PROTEST

1. Caplan, *Poetic Form*, 74. See also Wolfson, "Sonnets Then and Now."

2. Tate, *Psychoanalysis and Black Novels*, 3–4.

3. Cousins and Howarth, introduction to *Cambridge Companion to the Sonnet*, 1.

4. Petrarch began writing the *Canzoniere* sonnets around 1336; he continued to add to, revise, and reorganize them throughout his life. The sonnets circulated among his friends in manuscript form; the first published edition appeared in 1358.

5. See Distiller, *Desire and Gender*, 98.

6. Translation by Mark Musa, in introduction to Musa, *Petrarch's Canzoniere*, xvii–xviii.

7. Spiller, *Development of the Sonnet*, 3.

8. Fussell, *Poetic Meter and Poetic Form*, 115–116.

9. Barbara Herrnstein Smith, *Poetic Closure*, 51.

10. Silver, *Intellectual Evolution of Ronsard*, 156.

11. Carozza and Shey, *Petrarch's Secretum*, 81.

12. Quitslund, "Spenser's Amoretti VIII," 256-276.

13. Translation by Dante Gabriel Rossetti, in Rossetti, *Early Italian Poets, 280*; Silver, *Intellectual Evolution of Ronsard*, 280-281.

14. Baugh, *Tale from the Rainforest*, 30.

15. Baugh's sonnet is also a response to Shakespeare's Sonnet 127, which begins as follows:

> In the old age black was not counted fair,
> Or if it were, it bore not beauty's name.
> But now is black beauty's successive heir,
> And beauty slandered with a bastard shame.

16. Cf. George Gascoigne [1535-1577], "Certayne Notes of Instruction," 38-39. See also Hanson, "Elegy, Ode," 310.

17. Quitslund, "Spenser's Amoretti VIII," 256-276.

18. Feldman and Robinson, *Century of Sonnets*, 6.

19. "Harlem Dancer," published with "Invocation" under the title "Two Sonnets," *Seven Arts* 2 (October 1917): 741.

20. Collier, "I Do Not Marvel," 80.

21. McKay, *Long Way from Home*, 88-89.

22. Dunbar, *Lyrics of Lowly Life*, 21.

23. Dunbar, Letter to Alice Moore, 403.

24. *Lyrics of the Hearthside*, 186.

25. Redmond, *Drumvoices*, 14.

26. Smethurst, *New Red Negro*, 187.

27. Easthope, *Poetry as Discourse*, 64.

28. Brooks, *Bean Eaters*, 21.

29. Washington, *Other Blacklist*, 198-199.

30. Donne, *Complete English Poems*, 14.

31. Henderson, *Understanding the New Black Poetry*, 237.

32. Cunningham, "Review," 71.

33. Merrit Y. Hughes, *Variorum Commentary*, 168. See also Sauer, "Tolerationism." Sauer suggests that Irish, French, and Italian Catholics were a "triple threat" against European Protestants. Cf. Petrarch's sonnet "On the Papal Court at Avignon," which begins as follows:

> Fountain of woe! Harbour of endless ire!
> Thou school of errors, haunt of heresies!
> Once Rome, now Babylon, the world's disease,
> That maddenest men with fears and fell desire!

34. "The Lynching," in McKay, *Harlem Shadows*.

35. McKay, *Long Way from Home*, 21. See chapter 2 for Milton's sonnet.

36. Jon Woodson, "Anti Lynching Poems," 30.

37. Redmond, *Drumvoices*, 174.

38. Gandhi, "On 'The Lynching,'" 101.

39. Jennifer Ann Wagner, *Moment's Monument*, 16.

40. Shelley, *Selected Prose and Poems*, 407.

41. Wordsworth, "There Is a Bondage," in Wordsworth, *Poems, in Two Volumes*, 132.

42. Cullen, "From the Dark Tower," in Cullen, *Copper Sun*, 3.

43. Collier, "I Do Not Marvel," 78.

44. Psalms and Proverbs as well as Galatians 6:7–8 and 2 Corinthians 9:6 refer to sowing and reaping.

45. Peppis, "Schools, Movements, Manifestos," 45.

46. Phelan, *Nineteenth Century Sonnet*, 14, 24.

47. Wordsworth later offered an appreciation of the sonnet's poetic heritage in "Scorn not the Sonnet" (1827).

48. Brooks, "To a Winter Squirrel," first published in *Sisters Today* (November 1965), later in *In the Mecca* (1968). See Melhem, *Gwendolyn Brooks*, 175.

49. Burt and Mikics, *Art of the Sonnet*, 311–312.

50. Elizabeth Alexander, *Black Interior*, 17, 56.

51. Quoted in Kent, *Life of Gwendolyn Brooks*, 165–167.

52. Ibid., 167.

53. Smethurst, *New Red Negro*, 177.

54. Dykes, *Negro in English Romantic Thought*, 69, 71. See also Gannon, *Skylark Meets Meadowlark*, 131.

55. *National Era*, January 22, 1852.

56. Leslie Pinckney Hill, *Wings of Oppression*, 21.

57. Steffen, "Rooted Displacement in Form," 60.

58. Edwin Arlington Robinson, *Children of the Night*, 67.

59. See Hollander, *Melodious Guile*, 101.

60. Joel Chandler Harris's wildly popular fictional character, the storytelling former slave Uncle Remus, first appeared in 1881. Mark Twain's *The Adventures of Huckleberry Finn* appeared in 1884 and *Pudd'nhead Wilson*, also set in prewar Missouri, in 1894.

61. Dickey, introduction to *Selected Poems*, by Edwin Arlington Robinson.

62. Sharp, *American Sonnets*, xxviii–xxxix.

63. Ibid., xxix–xxx. Sharp argues: "[N]ote how very small in quantity are the Shakespearian sonnets—the form that can be sweetest, most resonant, most impressive, when the favourite medium of a true poet" (xxxiii).

64. Keats, "If by Dull Rhymes," in *Complete Poetical Works*, 436.

65. Milnes, *Life and Letters*, 162. While this sonnet is not Shakespearean, Phelan argues that Keats's revival of the Shakespearean sonnet had an important influence on later English poets, who "came to see in Keats' isolated rediscovery of the Shakespearean sonnet a poignant anticipation of their own more wide-ranging attempt to revive the values and beliefs of the Renaissance." Phelan, *Nineteenth Century Sonnet*, 39.

66. Phelan quotes Hopkins: "[W]hen one goes so far as to run the rhymes of

the octave into the sestet a downright prolapsus or hernia takes place and the sonnet is crippled for life." Ibid., 115.

67. Dunbar, Lyrics of the Hearthside, 83.

68. Christian, "The Craftsman," in Murphy, *Ebony Rhythm.*

69. Hillyer, *First Principles of Verse,* 62. Hillyer, whom Gwendolyn Brooks drew on to form her poetic consciousness, suggests that the clearly recognizable fourteen-line stanza is an example of "the survival of the fittest."

70. Stewart, *Poet's Freedom,* 111. Stewart's study begins, "How free is the artist in making? Why is the artist, at least in Western cultures, but surely in others as well, a figure of freedom?" (11). Her volume does not consider poets without (or with limited) freedom of creation.

71. Blount, "Caged Birds," 228.

72. Cousins and Howarth, *Cambridge Companion to the Sonnet,* 235. Howarth's claims for poetic equality were slow to be fulfilled. Sharp does not include any African American poets in his 1910 anthology, *Sonnets of This Century.* Neither does Charles Crandall in his 1891 anthology, *Representative Sonnets by American Poets,* though to be fair, he would not have known Dunbar, who had not yet published any sonnets.

73. William Blake, preface to *Jerusalem: The Emanation of the Giant Albion* (1820), quoted in Lowell, "Consideration of Modern Poetry," 105.

74. North, *Dialect of Modernism,* 11.

75. Johnson had largely stopped writing dialect verse in 1922; he began having doubts about dialect verse after discovering Walt Whitman: "I got a sudden realization of the artificiality of conventionalized Negro dialect poetry; of its exaggerated geniality, childish optimism, forced comicality, and mawkish sentiments." James Weldon Johnson, *Along This Way,* 158–159.

76. North, *Dialect of Modernism,* 11.

77. Bibby, "Disinterested and Fine," 486.

78. George Hutchinson quoted in Morrissette, *James Weldon Johnson's Modern Soundscapes,* 148.

79. Lowell, *Tendencies in Modern American Poetry;* Untermeyer, *New Era in American Poetry;* Riding and Graves, *Survey of Modernist Poetry.* One important anthology, *A History of Modern Poetry: 1900–1940* (1946) devotes a section to "The Negro Poet in America," noting the work of Dunbar, James Edwin Campbell, Braithwaite, Johnson, McKay, Jesse Redmon Fauset, Hughes, Countee Cullen, Sterling A. Brown, and Margaret Walker. Gregory and Zaturenska, *History of American Poetry,* 387–397.

80. See Morrissette, *James Weldon Johnson's Modern Soundscapes.*

81. See, for example, Langdon Hammer's Open Yale Course in Modern Poetry (Engl 310), which approaches the idea of modern poetry almost entirely from a white, educated perspective. See http://oyc.yale.edu/english/engl-310. No mention is made of important African American publications such as the *Crisis* or *Opportunity.*

82. Pound, *ABC of Reading*, 157.

83. Both quoted in Cousins and Howarth, *Cambridge Companion to the Sonnet*, 226, 225.

84. William Carlos Williams, "Poem as a Field of Action," 236.

85. William Carlos Williams, "Merrill Moore's Sonnets, Present Total, Steadily Mounting, 50,000" (1938), in Williams, *Something to Say*, 92–93.

86. William Carlos Williams, "Poem as a Field of Action," 289. See also William Carlos Williams, "The Tortuous Straightness of Charles Henri Ford," in Williams, *Something to Say*, 88.

87. Cousins and Howarth, *Cambridge Companion to the Sonnet*, 225.

88. Müller, "Vernacular Sonnet," 261.

89. Santayana, "Shakespeare," 97.

90. See Du Bois, *Autobiography*; David Levering Lewis, *W. E. B. Du Bois*.

91. Santayana, "Shakespeare," 98.

92. Cary Nelson, *Repression and Recovery*, 23.

93. Giovannitti, *Arrows in the Gale*, 20.

94. Quoted in ibid., 10. See also Watson, *Bread and Roses*. The publication of Wordsworth's "Sonnets on the Punishment of Death" (1842) provoked renewed interest in capital punishment in America. See DeLombard, *In the Shadow*.

95. Monroe, "Reviews," 38.

96. Chaplin, *Bars and Shadows*, 36. The collection of thirty poems includes fifteen sonnets, one to Eugene Debs.

97. *Liberator*, July 1921, 24.

98. McKay, *Long Way from Home*, 103.

99. Cary Nelson, *Repression and Recovery*, 40.

100. McKay, *Harlem Shadows*, 45.

101. Francini, "Sonnet vs. Sonnet," 42.

102. *Colored American*, February 1905, 78.

103. Woodson, *Anthems, Sonnets, and Chants*, 134.

104. Bromwich, *American Sonnets*, xxi.

CHAPTER 3. ANTECEDENTS (1768–1889)

1. See William Henry Robinson, *Black New England Letters*.

2. The original title, "To the King's Most Excellent Majesty, On His Repeal of the Stamp Act," was pruned when the poem was published in London.

3. Engberg, *Right to Write*, 55–56.

4. Quoted in Feldman and Robinson, *Century of Sonnets*, 8.

5. Only an isolated handful of sonnets were published in seventeenth- and eighteenth-century America: a number of irregular sonnets by Anne Bradstreet, the one by Wheatley, and a formal sonnet or two by David Humphreys, one of the "Hartford Wits," a late eighteenth-century Yale literary society. See Sterner, "General Survey." Sterner observes that the Puritan New England atmosphere did not encourage sonnet writing.

6. Blyden Jackson, *History of Afro-American Literature*, 46. For Jackson, Wheatley was a neoclassical poet "in the manner and spirit of Pope" but without the biting satire (42).

7. Rezek, "Print Atlantic," 22.

8. See Dykes, *Negro in English Romantic Thought*, 66–75, and Falbo, "Henry Reed and William Wordsworth," 15. See also Martineau, *Martyr Age*; Deborah Anna Logan, *Writings on Slavery*.

9. See Southey, *Poetical Works, Collected by Himself*; Southey, *Poetical Works*. See also Richardson, "Darkness Visible?" Richardson is one of the very few recent scholars who note the fact of the revisions (143), but he does not explore the significance of the revisions for abolitionist poetry in the United States. See also Basker, *Amazing Grace*, 428–429. Basker calls the works "Miltonic both in choice of poetic form and in the supernatural grandeur of the language" but does not discuss the revisions. Dykes, *Negro in English Romantic Thought*, studies the revised (1842) sonnets but does not note that they advocate violent revenge more overtly than the 1797 versions (80).

10. Jon Woodson treats Dodson's sonnets in chapter 1 of *Anthems, Sonnets, and Chants*, but he does not mention Southey as an influence, only Keats.

11. Kitson, "Fictions of Slave Resistance," 113. Tim Morton reads the 1797 sequence in *Poetics of Spice*, noting that Sonnet I "creates a picture of how capitalism and violence are intertwined" but that Southey is "unsure of how he should be addressing his audience, or even who his audience is precisely" (197). Much of the scholarship on the sonnets focuses on Sonnet III and its economic implications.

12. Kitson, "Fictions of Slave Resistance," 113.

13. Ibid., 116.

14. This sonnet appears in Damroch, *Longman Anthology of British Literature*.

15. Bohls, *Romantic Literature and Postcolonial Studies*, 58, 59.

16. Wood, *Poetry of Slavery*, 214, 215.

17. Ibid., xli.

18. Campbell, *Pleasures of Hope*, 46.

19. Wordsworth, *Collected Poems*, 305.

20. Garrison, *Sonnets and Other Poems*, 68.

21. Emerson, review of *Sonnets and Other Poems*. "Mr. Garrison has won his palms in quite other fields than those of the lyric muse, and he is far more likely to be the subject than the author of good poems. He is rich enough in the earnestness and the success of his character to be patient with the very rapid withering of the poetic garlands he has snatched in passing. Yet though this volume contains little poetry, both the subjects and the sentiments will everywhere command respect."

22. A very similar translation appeared in Harper's *New Monthly Magazine*, 1821, 313. In a different translation it appeared in Samuel Richardson's *The History of Sir Charles Grandison* (1753); it was also translated by Leigh Hunt. William Dean Howells, in a critical review of Leigh Hunt's "The Book of the Sonnet,"

published in the *North American Review* (no. 215, April 1867), writes about the sonnet form: "Its extreme artificiality is at once a test and a temptation,—a test, since it is only a true poet who can make artificiality serve the purposes of art; and a temptation, since the artificial construction—the mere form—can be easily built up and filled out with words by the simplest handicraftsman in verse" (628).

23. "It came down from the slow sloping of the western hills; it wandered miles up Castle Hill way, through grove and meadow, and finally mirabile dictu it went right through my front yard. That brook had everything to delight a boy's soul, rushing falls, gurgling murmurs, placid bits of lakes on gravelly beds, trees, bushes and little waterfalls. It was a complete and long and magnificent brook, and it brought its waters down the hills and through the yards and across town and emptied them at last in triumph into the Housatonic." "Speech Given on July 21, 1930, at the Annual Meeting of the Alumni of Searles High School." (Du Bois was the class of 1884.)

24. Quoted in McHenry, *Forgotten Readers*, 52. See also Porter, "Organized Educational Activities."

25. Quoted in McHenry, *Forgotten Readers*, 54.

26. In other contexts in the early black press, C. L. R. refers to Charles Lenox Remond. Remond was a well-known writer but not a poet. See Ward, "Charles Lenox Remond"; Wallace, "Charles Lenox Remond."

27. Sherman, *Invisible Poets*, 29.

28. "Phoenixonian Society," 214–215. Debate appeared in the pages of *United States Magazine and Democratic Review*. "Extending the magazine's criticism of Wordsworth's *Sonnets* over two years, [editor John] O'Sullivan made capital punishment a matter of cultural as well as political concern, printing his own anti-gallows essays alongside similarly themed poetry and prose by the likes of Lydia Sigourney, John Greenleaf Whittier, James Russell Lowell, Walt Whitman and even Nathaniel Hawthorne" (ibid., 215).

29. Horton, *Poetical Works*, xvii–xix. See also Sherman, *Black Bard of North Carolina*.

30. Walser, *Black Poet*, 55.

31. Hentz and Stowe knew each other and belonged to the same literary group, the Semi-Colon Club, in Cincinnati.

32. Blyden Jackson argues, "No poet more enslaved, *de jure* and de facto, than Horton ever has written, or ever will write, poetry in America." *History of Afro-American Literature*, 84.

33. Bryant, "Poetry of Spanish America," 148. Bryant, an abolitionist, was editor of the *New York Evening Post*.

34. Ibid. "Prayer" refers to Placido's six-stanza "Prayer to God," which Bryant also translated, confessing that "it is difficult to convey into English words of fire and force of expression of this noble poem" (147).

35. "Literary Notices"; "Cuban Literature"; "Cuban Problem," 611.

36. Bryant, "Poetry of Spanish America," 153.

37. James Weldon Johnson, "Placido," 110–111.

> Despida a Mi Madre" *(En La Capilla)*:
> Si la suerte fatal que me ha cabido,
> Y el triste fin de mi sangrienta historia,
> Al salir de esta vida transitoria
> Deja tu corazon de muerte herido;
> Baste de llanto: el animo afligido
> Recobre su quietud; moro en la gloria,
> Y mi placida lira a tu memoria
> Lanza en la tumba su postrer sonido.
> Sonido dulce, melodioso y santo,
> Glorioso, espiritual, puro y divino,
> Inocente, espontaneo como el llanto
> Que vertiera al nacer: ya el cuello inclino!
> Ya de la religion me cubre el manto!
> Adios, mi madre! adios—El Peligrino.

38. Whitfield, "America." See also Whitfield, *Works of James M. Whitfield.*

39. Dion, "Glances at Our Condition."

40. McClellan's "A January Dandelion" is from his second volume of poetry, *The Path of Dreams.*

41. Looney, *Freedom Readers*, 9. Longfellow translated Michelangelo's sonnets and wrote his own on Dante and Milton. The connection between Dante and postwar black culture, Looney adds, "has its origins in the political links between abolitionists—the outspoken adversaries of slavery in the Americas— and Italian nationalists in the Risorgimento" (9). Garrison edited Italian nationalist Guiseppe Mazzini's works in 1872. Helen Hunt Jackson wrote a famous sonnet, "Mazzini," after his death in 1872.

42. Browne, *Bugle-echoes.* The sonnets are "Fredericksburg" [December 13, 1862] and "By the Potomac" by Thomas Bailey Aldrich, and "A Nameless Grave," by Henry Wadsworth Longfellow.

43. Marius and From, *Columbia Book.* The two sonnets are Dunbar's "Robert Gould Shaw" and "Douglass."

44. McGill, "Frances Ellen Watkins Harper," 69. Also quoted in Still, *Underground Railroad*, 779–780, and in "Lectures in Philadelphia."

45. Markus, *Dared and Done.*

46. Browning and Browning, *Brownings' Correspondence*, 128.

47. Loggins, *Negro Author*, 254.

48. Morris, "History and Development," 309–317, quotation on 310–311; Penn, *Afro-American Press.*

49. See Lerner, "Early Community Work."

50. Sherman, *Invisible Poets*, xxiv, xx.

51. Loggins, *Negro Author*, 253.

52. Bruce, *Black American Writing*, 1.

53. See Sterling Brown, *Negro Poetry and Drama*; Jackson and Rubin, *Black Poetry in America*.

54. Parrington, *Main Currents in American Thought*, 3:53–54. George Santayana described what he labeled "the genteel tradition" in 1911, in a speech before the Philosophical Union of the University of California, in which he lamented the stunted growth and staleness of American religion, literature, and moral emotions. Santayana, "Genteel Tradition in American Philosophy," 186–215.

55. Parrington, *Main Currents in American Thought*, 3:53–55.

56. Sedgwick, "*Atlantic Monthly*," 173. Sedgwick notes the confusion of the treasurer, James Murray Kay, under a later *Atlantic* editor, Bliss Perry, over the payment of twenty-five or thirty dollars for a sonnet "to fill a third of a page when the same fee would fill three solid pages of prose" (295).

57. See Price, "Charles Chesnutt," 257–274.

58. Braithwaite, *House of Falling Leaves*, 25.

59. James Weldon Johnson, *Book of American Negro Poetry*, xlii.

60. See Baker, *Blues, Ideology*, 114–115. See also William J. Simmons's *Men of Mark* (1887); Frank L. Mathers's *Who's Who of the Colored Race* (1915); and "A Call for Afro-American Authors of America."

61. James Weldon Johnson, *Book of American Negro Poetry*, xxvi. Johnson leaves two syllables out of the last line of the Spenserian stanza he quotes (what should be "The boatman sang it over when his heart was young" becomes "The boatman sang it when his heart was young") and has gone uncorrected since. Johnson does not note that "The Rape of Florida" is in Spenserian stanzas. The stanza quoted is from Canto XXXIII. Johnson studied Whitman's verse when a college student (Bruce, *Black American Writing*, 34).

62. Quoted in Sherman, *Invisible Poets*, 116.

63. Bruce, *Black American Writing*, 34.

64. Whitman, *Twasinta's Seminoles*, 8.

65. Loggins, *Negro Author*, 253.

66. Sherman, *Invisible Poets*, 127.

67. Rubin, "Search for Language," 11.

68. Sherman, *Invisible Poets*, 113.

69. Bruce, *Black American Writing*, 33.

70. Menard, *Lays in Summer Lands*, 59.

71. Sherman, *Invisible Poets*, 97, xxvi.

72. See Logan, *Negro in American Life*.

73. Peterson, "Commemorative Ceremonies and Invented Traditions," 37.

74. Cotter, *Rhyming*, 15.

75. See Pigman, "Versions of Imitation."

76. Charles H. Crandall's *Representative Sonnets by American Poets* (1891) includes sonnets by Bronson Alcott on Thoreau and Emerson, Aldrich on England, Holmes on Longfellow, Longfellow on Charles Sumner and Washington Irving, Lowell on Whittier, and Whittier on Bayard Taylor, among others. The volume includes William Lloyd Garrison's "Freedom of Mind."

CHAPTER 4. PERIODICAL SONNETS FROM
DUNBAR TO MCKAY, 1890-1922

1. The three most established journals were *Lippincott's Magazine*, founded in 1868, *Harper's* in 1850, and the *Atlantic Monthly* in 1857. Newer journals included *Century Magazine*, founded in 1881 as a continuation of *Scribner's Monthly*; the *Dial* (1880); *Scribner's* (1886, no affiliation with *Scribner's Monthly*); *McClure's Magazine* (1893); the *New Republic* (1914); and *Poetry* (1912). *Century* published Dunbar's later poems. See the indispensable Johnson and Johnson, *Propaganda and Aesthetics*.

2. In the 1930s Owen Dodson was assigned by his Bates College English professor to write a sonnet every week "until you write one as fine as Keats." See Jon Woodson, *Anthems, Sonnets, and Chants*, 35.

3. Griffin, *Ashes of the Mind*, 176.

4. Santayana, "Genteel Tradition in American Philosophy," 200. As Claudia Tate argues, the 1890s also saw the emergence of "domestic novels of black women. . . a special category of African-American fiction in which a virtuous heroine generally undergoes a series of adventures en route to marriage, family happiness, and prosperity." Tate, *Domestic Allegories of Political Desire*, 5.

5. Mencken, *American Language*, 305.

6. Parrington, *Main Currents in American Thoughts*, 3:54. Garrison edited *Joseph Mazzini: His Life Writings, and Political Principles* in 1872.

7. Parrington, *Main Currents in American Thoughts*, 3:51.

8. Goldsby, *Spectacular Secret*, 371n11. Dunbar's outraged essay on the rash of murders, including the shooting of an African American postmaster and his family in Wilmington, North Carolina, "Recession Never: Negro and the White Man" (sometimes reprinted as "The Race Question") appeared in the *Toledo Journal* on December 18, 1898. It begins with these lines:

> Loud, from the South, Damascan cries
> Fall on our ears, unheeded still.
> No helping powers stir or rise.
> Hate's opiate numbs the nation's will.
> Slumbers the north. (While honor dies!)
> Soothed by th' insidious breath of lies!

9. Howells, *Modern Italian Poets*, 7. Nine years later, Howells wrote the introduction to Dunbar's *Lyrics of Lowly Life* (1896).

10. Howells, "Life and Letters": "I do not think one can read his Negro pieces without feeling that they are of like impulse and inspiration with the work of Burns when he was most Burns, when he was most Scotch, when he was most peasant. When Burns was least himself he wrote literary English, and Mr. Dunbar writes literary English when he is least himself. But not to urge the mischievous parallel further, he is a real poet whether he speaks a dialect or writes a language," 85.

11. *Atlantic Monthly* 86, no. 516 (October 1900): 488.

12. Shaw, a Harvard-educated son of New England abolitionists, was the commander of the first all-black regiment, the 54th Massachusetts Infantry. He was killed in 1863.

13. William Dean Howells argued in 1899 that Riley was a more influential poet than Longfellow because Riley's dialect poetry "reaches the lettered as well as the unlettered." Howells, "New Poetry," 588.

14. Griffin, *Ashes of the Mind*, 189–191.

15. Brawley, *Negro in Literature and Art*, 71.

16. Flint, "Black Response to Colonel Shaw." Dunbar's sonnet was one of more than three dozen poems written to Shaw. Four were by black poets, including Dunbar and Cornelia Ray (both of whom capitalize the "L" in learning). The other black poets were Benjamin Brawley and an anonymous poet.

17. Brawley, *Paul Laurence Dunbar*.

18. Griffin, *Ashes of the Mind*, 199.

19. Flint, "Black Response to Colonel Shaw," 215. Flint sees Dunbar's sonnet as a precursor to Robert Lowell's poem "For the Union Dead" (1960) in its pessimism about war in general.

20. Dunbar, *Lyrics of Love and Laughter*, 127.

21. Noted by many scholars, including Westover, "African American Sonnets"; Savoie, "Dunbar, Douglass, Milton," 24–27.

22. Milton's invocation from Book 7 of *Paradise Lost* expresses his political precariousness. Byron alludes to this in his dedication to *Don Juan*: "If fallen in evil days on evil tongues, / Milton appealed to the avenger, Time." Jean Wagner compares Paul Laurence Dunbar's 1893 lyric "To Miss Mary Britton," about an antisegregationist schoolteacher, to Milton's sonnets. Jean Wagner, *Black Poets*, 101.

23. Arnold writes:

> Sophocles long ago
> Heard it on the Ægæan, and it brought
> Into his mind the turbid ebb and flow
> Of human misery.

24. Blount, "Caged Birds," 231–232.

25. *The Outlook*, November 3, 1900.

26. Crew, *History of Dayton, Ohio*, 240–241.

27. Dunbar, *Lyrics of Love and Laughter*, 135.

28. Dunbar, Letter to Alice Moore, 952.

29. Braithwaite, "Negro in Literature," 41.

30. Thurman, "Negro Poets and Their Poetry," 557. Thurman adds that Dunbar was "ambitious to experiment in more classical forms" but doesn't seem to have read Dunbar's sonnets (558).

31. Brown et al., *Negro Caravan*, 2:277.

32. Leonard, *Fettered Genius*, 66.

33. Loranger recognizes that Dunbar questions Shaw's choice to answer Fate's

call. "The sestet features a classic turn, with Dunbar concluding that Shaw would have been better off staying home in Boston than dying with his troops." This, to Loranger, is the end of the story. Loranger, "Outcast Poetics," 139–140.

34. Corrothers, *In Spite of the Handicap*, 226. Punctuation here is from the original, in *Century Magazine*, November 1912, 56.

35. Corrothers, In Spite of the Handicap, 228.

36. Ibid., 226.

37. "Bade Him Farewell." The anonymous author reported: "Speaking of the present condition of the South [Douglass] said: 'If the American people continue to tolerate the murders of Negroes in the South, there will come a day of vengeance. Beware how you pinion the arms of black men, tread ruthlessly on human breasts and scourge with cruel hands your brothers. God lives; and as a nation sows, so shall it reap.'" The *Chicago Tribune* reprinted this piece on December 6, 1983, with the headline "Fred Douglass Is Angry."

38. Corrothers, *In Spite of the Handicap*, 144.

39. The full poem reads:

> O'er all my song the image of a face
> Lieth, like shadow on the wild sweet flowers.
> The dream, the ecstasy that prompts my powers;
> The golden lyre's delights bring little grace
> To bless the singer of a lowly race.
> Long hath this mocked me: aye in marvelous hours,
> When Hera's gardens gleamed, or Cynthia's bowers,
> Or Hope's red pylons, in their far, hushed place!
> But I shall dig me deeper to the gold;
> Fetch water, dripping, over desert miles,
> From clear Nyanzas and mysterious Niles
> Of love; and sing, nor one kind act withhold.
> So shall men know me, and remember long,
> Nor my dark face dishonor any song.

40. James Weldon Johnson included Corrothers's two sonnets of "Paul Laurence Dunbar." These sonnets continue to be anthologized through 1971.

41. Dunn, "To Paul Lawrence Dunbar [*sic*]"; Grimké, "To the Dunbar High School"; "Paul Laurence Dunbar, (Upon reading the Introduction to *Lyrics of Lowly Life* by William Dean Howells)" in Clifford, *Widening Light*; Andrews, "Dunbar."

42. See Johnson and Johnson, *Propaganda and Aesthetics*.

43. The *Messenger* became increasingly radical, concerned with labor and trade unions, after 1921; it was effectively an organ of the Brotherhood of Sleeping Car Porters after 1925. It closed in summer 1928.

44. In September 1919 the *Messenger* reprinted McKay's "If We Must Die" alongside "Labor's Day" and published "Birds of Prey" in December 1919. Circulation of the *Messenger* was crippled by suspension of second-class mailing privileges by the Post Office because of the Espionage Act and scrutiny of McKay's sonnet. It was 26,000 in 1920.

45. Eastman also published James Weldon Johnson's "The Creation" in January 1920, after it was rejected by Harriet Monroe in 1919.

46. Looney, "Dante Abolitionist and Nationalist"; Looney, *Freedom Readers*. Dennis Looney focuses primarily on Ray's "Dante" (1885), which is not a sonnet, but a fifty-two-line poem in unrhymed iambic pentameter, or blank verse. For Looney, there is no contradiction involved in an African American poet writing about a European artist.

47. McKay, *Long Way from Home*, 27.

48. The poem is the eight-line "Scintilla" (1915), also included in *BANP*, which begins, "I kissed a kiss in youth / Upon a dead man's brow." The *Crisis* inexplicably republished this poem in its November 1970 issue.

49. McKay, *Long Way from Home*, 27.

50. Ray, *Poems*.

51. "All the efforts in patriotic verse that have come to our notice by Afro-Americans have been nearly if not fully failures, with the exception of H. Cordelia Ray's Lincoln Ode and the same writer's sonnet to Toussaint L'Ouverture." *New York Age*, August 16, 1890, 2; *Cleveland Gazette*, June 18, 1892, 1.

52. Fauset, "What to Read," 183.

53. In the *Colored American*, Ray's father's newspaper, Dante appears in articles on Turkish slavery (June 9, 1938), late learners (October 20, 1838, in an article that features Socrates, Cato, Plutarch, Franklin, and Dryden), and taciturn geniuses (March 7, 1840). Longfellow appears twice in 1841 (May 8 and December 25) in articles on music and the arts. Shakespeare appears a dozen times; Milton, two dozen.

54. Hallie Q. Brown, "Homespun Heroines." Brown writes: "Miss Ray came of the primitive Massachusetts stock, being a direct descendant of aboriginal Indian, English and of the first Negroes of New England. To find an ancestor of hers with unmixed blood, one would have to trace back from four or five generations. Emphasis is made of this fact as a vital disproof of the theory that a mixture of blood deteriorates all the component elements." Brown emphasizes Ray's education and culture: "Miss Ray...was well-born, well bred and enjoyed all the advantages accruing to her position in a family where birth, breeding and culture were regarded as important assets. The parents of the Ray Children could afford to give them all the intellectual advantages of the time. Those who lived were well educated and three of the girls were college graduates. Cordelia became proficient in French, Greek and Latin and was an English scholar" (172).

55. "Men of the Month," 292.

56. Ray, *Poems*, 20.

57. Morse, "Black Classical Ruins," 55.

58. Frederick Douglass reprinted long passages of "The Deaf Musician," from the journal *American Annals of the Deaf and Dumb* (vol. 2, no. 4, July 1849) on July 13, 1849.

59. 1877 Bülow-Lebert edition, notes translated by J. C. D. Parker.

60. Hull, *Color, Sex, and Poetry*, 161.

61. *Crisis*, May 1917; *Phylon Quarterly* 3, no. 2 (2nd Qtr. 1942): 116.

62. Braithwaite, introduction to *Heart of a Woman*, vii–ix; J. R. Fauset, review of *Heart of a Woman*, 467–468.

63. James Weldon Johnson, *Book of American Negro Poetry*, xlv.

64. *Messenger*, May 1923, 48.

65. Rampersad, *Life of Langston Hughes*, 1:106.

66. Leonard, *Fettered Genius*, 91.

67. The *Crisis* was named after James Russell Lowell's 1845 poem "The Present Crisis," which opens:

> When a deed is done for Freedom, through the broad earth's aching breast
> Runs a thrill of joy prophetic, trembling on from east to west,
> And the slave, where'er he cowers, feels the soul within him climb
> To the awful verge of manhood, as the energy sublime
> Of a century bursts full-blossomed on the thorny stem of Time.

68. A dinner on March 21, 1924, at the Civic Club in Manhattan to honor *Crisis* editor Jessie Fauset on the publication of her novel *There Is Confusion* is often cited as the start of the period called the Harlem Renaissance. See also Johnson and Johnson, *Propaganda and Aesthetics*.

69. "Radicalism and Sedition."

70. *Crisis*, December 1910; published earlier in the *Cleveland Gazette*, November 12, 1910, 2, which references earlier publication in the *Chicago Public*.

71. *Independent*, January 18, 1906.

72. "Blease Cites Higher Law."

73. Churchill et al., "Youth Culture," 75. The authors note that in the early decades, the great majority of poems published in the *Crisis* were traditional rhymed, metered forms.

74. Thomas Millard Henry wrote to W. E. B. Du Bois on July 11, 1930, to defend Dunbar against disparaging treatment in the *Crisis*: "The Crisis has driven all Negros to disregard Paul Laurence Dunbar's best works. This has been very unfortunate. The new idea that every line of verse which is not very musical must be very crude is false. By making poetry quite musical this idea has weakened the poetic message....I could see that before Dunbar's best salt had been tasted by his people the newly hatched scheme led the college trained group to regard him with indifference, and to regard poetry as being every apt-minded college man's toy. So insurgent has this movement been that it has attacked all of the poets of times past, even the foremost. To me this seemed tragic." Du Bois replied on July 24, 1930: "it is certainly untrue that *The Crisis* has disregarded Paul Lawrence [sic] Dunbar." Yet mostly, the *Crisis* ignored Dunbar.

75. The elder Cotter, Joseph Seamon Cotter (1895–1919), knew Dunbar. The younger Cotter famously admired Keats.

76. *Crisis*, special issue, "Soldiers Number," June 1918.

77. Cotter's reputation is mixed. Wallace Thurman differed from "most critics

in this field" who "alleged" that he "would have been a great poet had he lived but whose extant work belies this judgment." Thurman, "Negro Poets and Their Poetry," 558.

78. Bassett, *Harlem in Review*.

79. Gary Smith, "Black Protest Sonnet."

80. See Cooper, *Claude McKay*.

81. James Weldon Johnson, *Book of American Negro Poetry*, 135.

82. McKay, *Long Way From Home*, 26.

83. Thurman, "Negro Poets and Their Poetry," 559.

84. Caplan, *Poetic Form*, 77. In his later book, Caplan focuses on the sonnet form as elastic, able to express "racial solidarity as well as intraracial grieving." Caplan, *Questions of Possibility*, 14.

85. McKay, *Complete Poems*, xxxv–xxxvi.

86. Tolson, "Claude McKay's Art," 288.

87. Martin, *Literary Garveyism*, 133.

88. McKay, *Harlem Shadows*, 6.

89. Emanuel, "Renaissance Sonneteers," 39. Emanuel too notes the "Ozymandias" echoes.

90. Tolson, "Claude McKay's Art," 289, 288.

91. McKay, *Long Way from Home*, 28.

92. McKay's engagement with Garveyism is treated in Martin, *Literary Garveyism*.

93. James Weldon Johnson, *Book of American Negro Poetry*, xliii.

94. James Weldon Johnson, *Black Manhattan*, 264. Johnson updates his 1922 assessment, writing that McKay wrote protest poetry with "cynicism, bitterness, and invective. For this purpose, incongruous as it may seem, he took the sonnet form as his medium. There is nothing in American literature that strikes a more portentous note than these sonnet-tragedies" (264).

95. William Dean Howells, introduction to Dunbar, *Lyrics of Lowly Life*, xvi.

96. Max Eastman, introduction to McKay, *Harlem Shadows*, ix.

97. Allen Tate, preface to Tolson, *Libretto for the Republic of Liberia*, viii.

98. Cary Nelson, *Repression and Recovery*, 89.

99. Cullen, *My Soul's High Song*, 33.

100. Langston Hughes, "Says Race Leaders," 8.

CHAPTER 5. ANTHOLOGIES AND CANON FORMATION, 1923–1967

1. As Chace writes, "Edd Winfield Parks, in his *Southern Poets* includes not a single Negro, and even the spirituals are disparaged. In the sixteen volume *Library of Southern Literature* no Negro's work is to be found, and Pattee's *American Literature Since 1870* doesn't mention a Negro, though Edgar Guest is considered worthy of two pages!" "Development of Negro Poetry," 2.

2. Gates, *Loose Canons*, 26.

3. Braddock, *Collecting as Modernist Practice*, 23.

4. Walkowitz, "Shakespeare in Harlem," 497. "As 'Shakespeare in Harlem' points to Shakespeare's bawdy songs, it represents not 'low' Shakespeare so much as Shakespeare's own conjunction of high and low cultures. These songs were popular in his time; in his plays they are already in quotation. As his work brings high and low together, Shakespeare seems quite a bit like 'Shakespeare in Harlem.' One might say that Harlem can be found in Shakespeare, except that it is no longer clear just what Harlem is. Hughes has dismantled the opposition between high and low cultures that the poem's title seemed to offer." Ibid., 515.

5. James Weldon Johnson, *Book of American Negro Poetry*; Locke, *The New Negro*; Cullen, *Caroling Dusk*; Brown et al., *Negro Caravan*.

6. As Allison Cummings argues, "Certainly, Langston Hughes's and Countee Cullen's stylistic differences stem as much from different ideas of racial identity as from different wishes for audiences and literary posterity." Cummings, "Public Subjects," 4.

7. James Weldon Johnson, *Book of American Negro Poetry*, xl–xli.

8. Kerlin, *Negro Poets and Their Poems*, 2.

9. Lucian B. Watkins, "The New Negro," in ibid., 238.

10. Watkins's sonnets were influential; some weeks after his death, *Negro World* announced the formation of a poetry club in his honor. Thomas Millard Henry published "A Sonnet in Honor of Lucian B. Watkins," which begins: "What is so sad as when a poet dies / Whose song was sweet and bold, whose face was black, / Whose audience had not evolved, alack! / To cherish all he brought them from the skies?" Martin, Literary Garveyism, 66.

11. Redmond, *Drumvoices*, 134, 173.

12. For more on Watkins, see Martin, *Literary Garveyism*.

13. White and Jackson, *Anthology of Verse*, 1.

14. Potter, "Race and Poetry."

15. "Baptism" and "Subway Wind" appear in McKay's *Harlem Shadows*. In his foreword to *The New Negro*, Locke quotes the sestet of McKay's 1922 sonnet "To the Intrenched Classes" to illustrate the idea of being "on the right side of the country's professed ideals" (633).

16. Arnold Rampersad, introduction to Locke, *New Negro*, xxi–xxiii. *The New Negro* has been criticized for snobbery, exclusion of blues, deemphasizing jazz, ignoring Marcus Garvey, ignoring radical and socialist politics, and being generally conservative. Langston Hughes's short free-verse poem, "I, Too," appears, as well as several poems in ballad meter by Cullen. Arnold Rampersad's introduction to the 1992 *New Negro* anthology critiques Cullen as "conservative in his techniques and a conscious imitator of British romantic poets." Kenneth Warren argues that Locke's editorship made clear "that for all its celebration of the black rank and file, *The New Negro* laid out a plan of race-relations management directed by black elites." Warren, *What Was African American Literature?* 63.

17. In Locke's anthology, McKay's sonnet "Subway Wind" accompanies an essay on "The Tropics in New York" (649) emphasizing the urban nature of the New Negro movement. McKay's "Baptism" appears on 681, accompanying "Color Lines," by Walter F. White. See McKay, *Complete Poems*, for subsequent publication and variants.

18. Cullen, *My Soul's High Song*, 4. Cullen completed a master's at Harvard, where he studied with Robert Hillyer, whose *First Principles of Verse* (1938) was influential for Gwendolyn Brooks. Cullen won a prize for "I Have a Rendezvous with Life," a response to Alan Seeger's posthumous poem, "I Have a Rendezvous with Death." Seeger's poem is in praise of leaving a comfortable life—down pillows and apple blossoms—for the heroic duty as a soldier. Seeger's poem is twenty-four lines of iambic tetrameter sentiment. Cullen's "I Have a Rendezvous with Life" is fourteen lines in ballad stanza eschewing sentiment. Cullen won the John Reed Memorial Prize in 1925 for "Threnody for a Brown Girl."

19. *Crisis*, December 1924, 81. "The Browsing Reader" was Marvel Cooke. See Women in Journalism interview #3, Washington Press Club Foundation, October 30, 1989, http://www.wpcf.org/session-28/.

20. An exception was Benjamin Brawley, writing that Cullen "has not yet mastered the mechanics of his art.... We have read through [*Color*] twice and with a fair degree of care, and we regret that we can find in it not one quotable passage." Brawley, "Negro Literary Renaissance," 180. Brawley says of Hughes, "we have a sad case of a young man of ability who has gone off on the wrong track altogether" (181). More typical was Wallace Thurman: "For two generations Negro poets have been trying to do what Mr. Cullen has succeeded in doing. First, trying to translate into lyric form the highly poetic urge to escape from the blatant realities of life in America into a vivid past, and, second, fleeing from the stigma of being called a *Negro* poet, by, as Dunbar so desired to do, ignoring folk-material and writing of such abstraction as love and death" (182). Thurman praised Cullen's technique specifically, observing that "he has an enviable understanding of conventional poetic forms. Technically, he is almost precocious, and never, it may be added, far from academic." Thurman, "Negro Poets and Their Poetry," 559.

21. Cullen, *My Soul's High Song*, 37–38.

22. Cullen, *Caroling Dusk*. Republished as *Caroling Dusk: An Anthology of Verse by Black Poets of the Twenties* (Secaucus, N.J.: Carol, 1993).

23. First published in *Century Magazine* 109 (November 1924).

24. Cullen, *My Soul's High Song*, 6.

25. Sperry, "Countee P Cullen." Also reprinted in Cullen, *My Soul's High Song*, 23.

26. Cullen, *My Soul's High Song*, 36. See also Jackson and Rubin, *Black Poetry in America*, 47.

27. Dodson, "Countee Cullen," 20.

28. Helene Johnson, "Sonnet to a Negro in Harlem," in Charles Spurgeon Johnson, *Ebony and Topaz*, 148.

29. Emanuel, "Renaissance Sonneteers," 41.

30. Sharon Lynette Jones, "Poetry of the Harlem Renaissance," 204.

31. McCall, "New Negro," 211. McCall became blind at about age twenty after contracting typhoid fever; he abandoned his planned medical career and became a writer and editor, publishing the *Montgomery (Alabama) Emancipator* and, later, the *Detroit Independent*.

32. Brown recalls, "My mother read…Longfellow; she read Burns; and she read Dunbar—grew up on Dunbar!" Tidwell and Tracy, *After Winter*, 6. Brown elaborated on his influences in a speech at Williams in 1973: "Langston Hughes has meant much to me, Richard Wright, Claude McKay, Ralph Ellison, but I have learned also from people like Robert Frost." Quoted in Gabbin, *Sterling Brown*, 28. In "Negro Poetry and Drama", treating sonnet writers Braithwaite, Hill, Brawley, and McClellan, Brown writes that too often their poetry was "escapist and derivative, and although accomplished at times, was too often without vitality" (46).

33. Sanders, *Afro-Modernist Aesthetics*, 86; Jackson, "From One 'New Negro'," 61–62.

34. Sterling Brown, *Negro Poetry and Drama*.

35. Gabbin, *Sterling Brown*, 7.

36. Tidwell and Genoways, "Two Lost Sonnets." Brown wrote to Du Bois on March 28, 1927: "I have at hand a copy of the April *Crisis* in which I see included a poem of mine, *After the Storm* [sic]. I am properly thankful that you thought it worth publishing, but I am in the dark as to how it got into your hands. I hope you will understand the spirit in which this is written. I did not expect to see it, and still do not quite understand the publishing of it. That bit of mystery I am writing you to clear up for me. Would you send me the source from which you got it?" In the end, "he never received an adequate explanation of how Du Bois acquired his early poem" (742). Tidwell and Genoways suggest that these sonnets are "rebellions against conventional forms" (734), that Brown was rebelling not only against "Victorian conventions of poetry but also from the encumbrance of 'school' or 'movement' that, in his view, robbed the poet of individuality, of aesthetic uniqueness" (734–744).

37. Thurman, "Negro Poets and Their Poetry," 558.

38. Ibid., 559.

39. Alain Locke, "Our Little Renaissance," in Charles Spurgeon Johnson, *Ebony and Topaz*, 117. Locke continues: "It is a fiction that the black man has until recently been naïve: in American life he has been painfully self-conscious for generations—and is only now beginning to recapture the naïveté he once had."

40. Calverton, *Anthology of Negro Literature*, vii. In his introduction, "The Growth of Negro Literature," Calverton briefly surveys a long and rich African

cultural past, suggesting that early black art in America was more "genuine" because it was "untutored" and "artless" and produced under intense economic and psychological pressure" (4). "Life was a continuous crucifixion," as Calverton observes (5).

41. Cromwell et al., *Readings from Negro Authors*, iii.

42. Strong, review of *Readings from Negro Authors*, 383–387, quotation on 386–387.

43. *Crisis*, February 1938, 48.

44. Christian, "Spring in the South," 201.

45. Dent, "Marcus B. Christian," 26.

46. Young, "Before a Monument," 6; Murphy, *Ebony Rhythm*, 161–162.

47. Murphy, preface to *Ebony Rhythm*, n.p.

48. Smethurst, *New Red Negro*, 177.

49. Parker, "Song," 289.

50. Ibid.

51. Hughes letter to Carl Van Vechten, January 20, 1926, in Remember Me to Harlem, 35–36.

52. Elizabeth Alexander, "Black Poet as Canon-Maker," 24.

53. Hughes and Bontemps, *Poetry of the Negro*, xxiv.

54. See Nwankwo, "More than McKay and Guillén," 130.

55. *Atlantic*, February 1947, 124. There are three small differences between this version and the final 1966 version. Line 3 ends "at last to all." There is a new sentence before "Oh" in the tenth line (more like Dunbar's, in fact). And the last line reverses needful and beautiful: "of the beautiful, needful thing."

56. Chrisman, "Robert Hayden," 133–134. The first version, from "Five Americans: A Sequence from *The Black Spear*," which appeared in a World War II-era black publication *Headlines and Pictures*, May 1945, reads as follows:

> III. Frederick Douglass (1945)
> Such men are timeless, and their lives are levers
> that lift the crushing dark away like boulders.
> Death cannot silence them, nor history,
> suborned or purchased like the harlot's crass
> endearments, expatriate them. Like negatives
> held to the light, their weaknesses reveal
> our possible strength. Their power proves us godly,
> and by their stripes are we made whole in purpose.
> Douglass, O colossus of our wish
> and allegory of us all, one thinks
> of you as shipwrecked voyagers think of
> an island. Breasting waters mined with doubt
> and error, we struggle toward your dream of man
> unchained, of man permitted to be man. (Chrisman, "Robert Hayden," 135)

57. Chrisman, "Robert Hayden," 137; Pontheolla T. Williams, *Robert Hayden*, 87–88. See also Savoie, "Dunbar, Douglass, Milton."

58. "A Conversation with A. Poulin Jr.," in Goldstein and Chrisman, *Robert Hayden*, 30.

59. Müller, *African American Sonnet*, 86–90.

60. Fred M. Fetrow, "Robert Hayden's 'Frederick Douglass': Form and Meaning in a Modern Sonnet," in Goldstein and Chrisman, *Robert Hayden*, 272, 274.

61. Hayden, *Collected Poems*, 35–38.

62. Robert Hayden, "We Have Not Forgotten," in Hayden, *Heart-Shape in the Dust*, 10; Smethurst, *New Red Negro*, 191.

63. Blyden Jackson, "From One 'New Negro'," 69.

64. Quoted in Joyce Pettis, "Margaret Walker: Black Woman Writer of the South," in Graham, *Fields Watered in Blood*, 47.

65. In Brooks, *Street in Bronzeville*.

66. Melhem, *Gwendolyn Brooks*, 46.

67. Ibid., 41.

68. Francini, "Sonnet vs. Sonnet," 47.

69. Ford, "Sonnets of Satin-Legs Brooks," writes that it is not a coincidence "that two early poems about appropriate aesthetics are sonnets" (358). She considers "The Egg Boiler," published in *The Bean Eaters* (1960). "This Shakespearean sonnet stages an opposition between utilitarian and aesthetic poetry, a disagreement rendered in the voice of a decidedly Shakespearean fool whose nonsense proves wise" (362). It is a sonnet "whether the question of poetic form is debated in a highly formal environment that is itself an argument for the politics of form" (364).

70. Brooks would include "The Birth" subsequently in *Annie Allen* (1949).

71. See Meredith, *Modern Love and Poems*.

72. Leonard, *Fettered Genius*, 138.

73. Cummings, "Public Subjects," 13.

74. Gayle, "Making Beauty from Racial Anxiety," 4.

75. Ibid., 97.

76. Locke, "Wisdom de Profundis I," 11.

77. J. H. Nelson, "Brief Mention," 277.

78. Lide, "American Literature by Negro Authors," 59. "While certain of these selections will be a source of inspiration to individuals of every race, this collection will no doubt prove an especial incentive to the Negro, since the achievements and aspirations portrayed have been wrought by members of his own race" (59).

79. Langston Hughes, "Says Race Leaders," 8. "Certainly the Shakespearian sonnet would be no mould in which to express the life of Beale Street or Lenox Avenue....I am not interested in doing tricks with rhymes." Hughes denied that he ever wrote sonnets to his friend, the poet Nicolás Guillén: "*Yo tengo la suerte de no haber escrito nunca un soneto*" (Rampersad, *Life of Langston Hughes*, 1:180).

80. Three of the sonnets Rampersad refers to were "Barrel House: Chicago," which Hughes published in the *Lincoln News* in 1928. "I've never tried a stan-

dard form before," Hughes explained to Van Vechten; "the idea of putting a barrel house into a sonnet rather amuses me." Quoted in Rampersad, *Life of Langston Hughes*, 1:160. For discussion of McKay's "radicalism of political and racial thought, on the one hand, and, on the other, a bone-deep commitment to conservatism of form," see Rampersad, "Langston Hughes and Approaches," 55.

81. *Opportunity*, February 1932, 52; later republished as "Pennsylvania Station" in *Approach*, Spring 1962, 4.

82. Emanuel, "Renaissance Sonneteers," 94.

83. Yerby also published sonnets in Dorothy West's *Challenge* magazine in the 1930s.

84. "Books Noted," 52.

85. Ralph Pearson, "Combatting Racism with Art," argues that Johnson's editorial stance was based on the idea that in order for African Americans to simultaneously "uplift" the race and succeed as artists, they must draw on black life. "They had to free themselves from the hold white cultural values exercised upon their art, just as white artists had found it imperative to reject European standards as the arbiter of their work" (384). Johnson himself argued that "American Negroes, born into a culture which they did not wholly share, have responded falsely to the dominant patterns.... [T]heir expression has been, to borrow a term which Lewis Mumford employs in referring to Americans in relation to Europe, 'sickly and derivative, a mere echo of old notes.'" Charles S. Johnson, "Address to the Graduating Classes," 9–10.

86. In a 1927 "Dark Tower" review, appearing in *Opportunity*, of Louis Untermeyer's *The Forms of Poetry*, Cullen assumes his readers' interest in questions such as: "How many kinds of sonnets are there, and how do they differ from one another? What is the meaning of cliché, cadence, strophe, polyphonic prose, assonance, verse libre, rime royale, villanelle?" (118). Cullen proposed that Untermeyer's book would be helpful to anyone interested in the tools of the poetic craft: "[to] introduce you to, or reacquaint you with, some excellent poems which still retain their attraction despite the straight jacket of form they wear.... [Its] perusal would save many a young poet the error of writing twelve line sonnets" (188). The issue also features a J. Harvey L. Baxter sonnet "Paint Me a God." Reviewing Harvey Baxter's volume of poetry *That Which Concerneth Me*, James O. Hopson in the *Crisis* writes: "The output of poetry by Negro authors has been very scarce within the past few years. For this reason the coming of a new poetic figure should create more than a casual interest...[But among the weaknesses of] many of the sonnets the author does not follow the regular sonnet rhyme scheme thereby destroying the classical mold for which his words are intended" (313).

87. Schomburg, "Negro Digs Up His Past"; Schuyler, "Negro-Art Hokum"; Langston Hughes, "Negro Artist"; Du Bois, "Criteria of Negro Art"; E. Franklin Frazier, "Racial Self Expression," in C. S. Johnson, *Ebony and Topaz*; Hurston,

"Characteristics of Negro Expression"; Wright, "Blueprint for Negro Writing"; Redding, *To Make a Poet Black*; Gates and Jarrett, *New Negro*.

88. Du Bois, "Criteria of Negro Art."

89. Schuyler, "Negro-Art Hokum." In 1951, in the fortieth anniversary issue, George S. Schuler recollected that the *Crisis* had arrived in 1911: "Here for the first time with brilliance, militancy, facts, photographs and persuasiveness, a well-edited magazine challenged the whole concept of white supremacy then nationally accepted....It is no exaggeration to say that the early *Crisis* created an intellectual revolution." Schuyler, "Forty Years of *The Crisis*," 163; Wilson, "*Crisis*" *Reader*.

90. The *Nation*, like most journals that published poetry, regularly published sonnets in the 1920s (notably by Maxwell Bodenheim, Joseph Auslander, Frederick Goddard Tuckerman, Marie Luhrs, and Clement Wood) but not by any African American poets.

91. E. Franklin Frazier, "Racial Self Expression," in Johnson, *Ebony and Topaz*, 121. Yet "to turn within the group experience for materials for artistic creation and group tradition is entirely different from seeking in the biological inheritance of the race for new values, attitudes, and a different order of mentality" (121).

92. Hurston, "Characteristics of Negro Expression."

93. Wright, "Blueprint for Negro Writing," 60.

94. Oxley, "Survey of Negro Literature," 37; also quoted in Wilson, *Messenger Reader*, 300. Oxley, founder of the Colored Poetic League of the World and a poet himself, wrote a column titled "The Negro in the World's Literature," which appeared regularly in the *Amsterdam News* in the late 1920s. Oxley praises George Reginald Margetson as "the only poet of color to exhibit a remarkable perfection of the sonnet," but he offers examples that are not sonnets. Oxley's assertions were not always well founded. Arthur Schomburg wrote to the *Amsterdam News* to query Oxley's statement in his August 24, 1927, column that José María de Heredia, whom Oxley called a "celebrated French mulatto sonnetist," was a Negro (July 15, 1927). "I would like to know how Oxley performed the remarkable feat of painting this Heredia black when the singer of the 'Niagara' is and has been known as a Cuban of white descent" (July 30, 1927). Oxley was probably referring to Severiano de Heredia.

95. Taussig, "New Negro as Revealed," 108.

96. LeRoi Jones, "Myth of a 'Negro Literature'," 20; Langston Hughes's "The Bread and Butter Side," in the same issue of *Saturday Review*, focuses solely on the issue of racism—getting published, getting speaking engagements, having to use the "Colored" entrance in the Jim Crow South.

97. LeRoi Jones, "Myth of a 'Negro Literature'," 21.

98. "Search," *Opportunity*, July 1937, 207.

99. Cullen, "Black Majesty," in Cullen, *Black Christ and Other Poems*.

100. LeRoi Jones, "Myth of a 'Negro Literature'," 21.

101. Nielson, *Black Chant*.

CHAPTER 6. POWER LINES

1. Karenga, "Black Cultural Nationalism," 31. See also Redmond's *Drumvoices* and Henderson's *Understanding the New Black Poetry*.

2. hooks, *Yearning*, 111.

3. For discussion of John Johnson's *Negro Digest* and Hoyt Fuller's transformation of it into *Black World*, see Doreski, *Writing America Black*; see also Johnson and Johnson, *Propaganda and Aesthetics*, 165.

4. Baraka and Neal, *Black Fire*; Major, *New Black Poetry*.

5. Giovanni, "Rocks Cry Out," 97–98. See also Giovanni, "Black Poems, Poseurs and Power," 34.

6. Gayle, "Harlem Renaissance," 84.

7. Emanuel, "Renaissance Sonneteers," 36, 40.

8. Locke, "Wisdom de Profundis II." See also Johnson and Johnson, *Propaganda and Aesthetics*.

9. Rubin, "Search for Language," 2.

10. Gayle, "Harlem Renaissance," 82. Gayle praised Johnson's *Book of American Negro Poetry* for its preface's attacks on dialect poetry and praises *The Autobiography of an Ex-Colored Man*, observing that it is, "[l]ike James Joyce's *Portrait of the Artist*…the picture of an artist trapped between two worlds" (83).

11. James T. Stewart, "The Development of the Black Revolutionary Artist," in Baraka and Neal, *Black Fire*, 3.

12. Johnson and Johnson, *Propaganda and Aesthetics*, 171.

13. Jackson and Rubin, *Black Poetry in America*, xii.

14. Kent, "Patterns of the Harlem Renaissance," 13, 78.

15. Huggins, *Harlem Renaissance*, 11.

16. See Larry Neal, "And Shine Swam On," in Jones and Neal, *Black Fire*, 640–641; John O'Neeal, "Black Arts: Notebook," in Gayle, *Black Aesthetic*, 48–50; Hoyt W. Fuller, "The New Black Literature: Protest or Affirmation," in Gayle, *Black Aesthetic*, 348–350.

17. Jules-Rosette, *Black Paris*, 59.

18. Césaire, "Letter to Maurice Theroz."

19. Johnson and Johnson, *Propaganda and Aesthetics*, 171.

20. LeRoi Jones, "How You Sound?" 425.

21. In Wilentz, *Beat Scene*, 56.

22. Neither appears in Baraka, *SOS*.

23. "The Performers," in Hayden, *Collected Poems*, 117.

24. Arnold Rampersad, afterword to Hayden, *Collected Poems*, 201.

25. Louis Simpson, "Book Week," October 27, 1963, *New York Herald Tribune*, quoted in Stephen Wright, Gwendolyn Brooks, 23. Simpson adds, "Miss Brooks

must have had a devil of a time trying to write poetry in the United States, where there has been practically no Negro poetry worth talking about" (23).

26. Smethurst, *New Red Negro*, 164.

27. Fuller, "The Critics Will Learn," *Negro Digest*, November 1968, 53. See also *Negro Digest*, January 1968, 49.

28. "The Early Poetry of Gwendolyn Brooks," in Gabbin, *Furious Flowering*, 255.

29. Ford, "Sonnets of Satin-Legs Brooks," 354, 353.

30. Gwendolyn Brooks, *Report from Part One*, 14.

31. Gwendolyn Brooks, "Of Flowers and Fire and Flowers," in Madhubuti, *Say That the River Turns*, 1–2.

32. Brooks et al., "*GLR* Interview," 55.

33. Gwendolyn Brooks in Tate, *Black Women Writers at Work*, 42. Brooks adds, "I'm so sick and tired of hearing about the 'black aesthetic.' I thought that expression had been dispensed with, that it was one of our losses following the sixties. And I was glad of that loss" (45).

34. Brooks, "Conversation," 278.

35. Baker, "Achievement of Gwendolyn Brooks," reprinted in *Singers of Daybreak: Studies in Black American Literature* (Washington, D.C.: Howard University Press, 1974), 43.

36. Ibid.

37. Leonard, *Fettered Genius*, 2, 4.

38. William, "Gwendolyn Brooks's Way," 216.

39. Melhem, *Gwendolyn Brooks*, 21. Melhem calls the sonnet "a tamer form" (20).

40. Smith, "Black Protest Sonnet," 6. Smith adds, on Tolson and Hayden, "After their initial experiment with the sonnet form, both poets abandoned it as a means of poetic expression" (11).

41. Smith, "Black Protest Sonnet," 6.

42. Blount, "Caged Birds," 235.

43. William, "Gwendolyn Brooks's Way," 229.

44. Melhem, *Gwendolyn Brooks*, 187, 30–31.

45. Elizabeth Alexander, *Essential Gwendolyn Brooks*, xviii–xix.

46. Smethurst, *New Red Negro*, 177.

47. Mootry, "Creative Practice in War Sonnets," 146. See also Bérubé, "Masks, Margins," 58.

48. Ford, "Sonnets of Satin-Legs Brooks," 365.

49. Randall, *Black Poets*.

50. Randall, "The Dilemma," in Randall, *Roses and Revolutions*, 112. Brooks wrote "Love You Right Back" as a response to Dudley Randall's "Love You." Brooks, *Family Pictures*, 21.

51. Eugene Redmond, "Sonnet Serenade," 46. In an oral history interview from March 12, 2012, with Howard Rambsy II and Mary Rosee, Redmond ex-

plains his sonnet: "Well you introduce a problem or an issue in the first eight lines, and then in the second, they call it a sextet. I mean octet, excuse me. And then in the sextet, the second section, six lines, you answer it or reaffirm it. So you got all this stuff going on caught 'crying, caroling, and know-howing.' And then a 'lord-length voice invades these jungle sparks.' Yeah. You end up, and she's the 'mellow maid.' 'A cool, mellow maid of song,' in other words she comes into the forest, my forest—and I'm indebted to another poet for some of the thinking. E. E. Cummings? 'Cause he has a line, great love poetry. 'lady, through whose profound and fragile lips / the sweet, small, clumsy feet of April came / into the ragged meadow of my soul." [from "If I have made, my lady, intricate"] I used to quote that when I was a freshman."

52. See Johnson and Johnson, *Propaganda and Aesthetics*, 165. One sonnet is Wangara, "Fire This Time," 48.

53. *Negro Digest*, January 1969, 47.

54. Gayle, "Cultural Strangulation," 38.

55. Rogers, "Black Poetry—Where It's At," 7–16.

56. Lilly, "Heritage," 42.

57. June Jordan, *Soulscript*; Davis and Redding, *Cavalcade*; Randall, *Black Poets*; Adoff, *Poetry of Black America*; Henderson, *Understanding the New Black Poetry*.

58. Smethurst, *New Red Negro*, 186.

59. Cary Nelson, *Repression and Recovery*, 178.

60. In Thomas, *Chances Are Few*.

61. Baker, *Afro-American Poetics*, 55. He adds, on the question of free verse, "It is not free" (169).

62. Baker, *Modernism and the Harlem Renaissance*, 17.

63. McLaren, "African Diaspora Vernacular Traditions," 107.

64. Hurston, "Characteristics of Negro Expression," 28.

65. Carroll, "Sonnet Sequence for the Diaspora," 89.

66. Steffen, "Rooted Displacement in Form," 60.

67. Patricia Kirkpatrick, "The Throne of Blues: An Interview with Rita Dove," *Hungry Mind Review* 35 (1995), qtd. in Steffen, "Rooted Displacement in Form," 36.

68. Francini, "Sonnet vs. Sonnet," 56.

69. Cary Nelson, *Repression and Recovery*, 89. Nelson asks why "the poetry sung by striking coal miners in the 1920s is so much less important than the appearance of *The Waste Land* in *The Dial* in 1922" (68).

70. Reeves, "What Black Poets Are Doing."

71. Bromwich, *American Sonnets*.

72. Cousins and Howarth, *Cambridge Companion to the Sonnet*.

73. Jay-Z, *Decoded*, 26.

74. Tsitsi Jaji, "Tell Me Something Good," *Mother Tongues*.

BIBLIOGRAPHY

ANONYMOUS WORKS

"Alexander Pushkin." *National Era*, February 11, 1847.

Anthology of Negro Poets in the U.S.A. 1955 Folkways recording. https://folkways
.si.edu/arna-bontemps/anthology-of-negro-poets-in-the-usa-200-years
/african-american-spoken-poetry/album/smithsonian.

"Blease Cites Higher Law." *New York Times*, December 8, 1912.

"Books by Negro Authors in 1937." *Crisis*, February 1938.

"Books Noted: Review of 1963 Arna Bontemps, *American Negro Poetry*, Hill &
Wang, 1963." *Negro World*, September 1963.

"A Call for Afro-American Authors of America: To Meet with the American Association of Educators of Colored Youth, in Wilmington, N.C., December
27-30, 1892." Pamphlet in Frederick Douglass's Papers, MS division, Library
of Congress.

"Cuban Literature." *Chambers Edinburgh Journal of Popular Literature* 305 (November 1859).

"The Cuban Problem." *Republic* 3 (1873).

"Lectures in Philadelphia: A Letter from Grace Greenwood." *New York Independent*, March 15, 1866.

"Literary Notices." *The Knickerbocker, or New-York Monthly Magazine* 33 (1849):
159.

"Men of the Month." *Crisis* 11, no. 6 (April 1916).

"Our Race in Literature." *Chicago Defender*, December 22, 1923.

"Phoenixonian Society." *Colored American*, July 13, 1839, 214-215.

"Radicalism and Sedition among Negroes as Reflected in Their Publications."
Exhibit No. 10, Investigative Activies of the Department of Justice, Senate
Executive Documents, 66th Congress, 1st Session, Sen. Ex. Doc. 153, vol XII,
161-166.

"Review." *Dial* 4 (1844).

"Review." *National Era*, January 22, 1852.

"Some Race Books of the Day." *New York Age*, August 16, 1890.

"Writers Past and Present." *Chicago Defender*, May 27, 1922.

AUTHORED WORKS

Adoff, Arnold, ed. *The Poetry of Black America: Anthology of the 20th Century*. New York: Harper Collins, 1973.

Aldrich, Thomas Bailey. "Unguarded Gates." *Atlantic Monthly* 70 (July 1892).

Alexander, Elizabeth. *The Black Interior*. Minneapolis: Greywolf Press, 2004.

———. "The Black Poet as Canon-Maker: Langston Hughes and the Road to *New Negro Poets: USA*." In *The Black Interior: Essays*. New York: Graywolf Press, 2004.

———. *The Essential Gwendolyn Brooks*. New York: Library of America, 2005.

Alexander, Lewis G. "Southland." *Carolina Magazine*, April 1930.

Als, Hilton. "Young American." *New Yorker*, June 11, 2007.

Andrews, James Edward. "Dunbar." *Opportunity* 17, no. 1 (January 1939): 10.

Appiah, Kwame Anthony. "Structuralist Criticism and African Fiction: An Analytic Critique." *Black Textual Strategies, Volume 1: Theory*, special issue of *Black American Literature Forum* 15, no. 4 (Winter 1981).

Arion. "Sonnet—to the Housatonic." *Freedom's Journal*, September 5, 1828.

Baker, Houston A., Jr. "The Achievement of Gwendolyn Brooks." *CLA Journal* 20, no. 1 (September 1972).

———. *Afro-American Poetics: Revisions of Harlem and the Black Aesthetic*. Madison: University of Wisconsin Press, 1988.

———. *Blues, Ideology and Afro-American Literature: A Vernacular Theory*. Chicago: University of Chicago Press, 1984.

———. *Modernism and the Harlem Renaissance*. Chicago: University of Chicago Press, 1987.

Baraka, Amiri. *SOS: Poems, 1961–2013*. New York: Grove Press, 2014.

Baraka, Amiri, and Larry Neal, eds. *Black Fire: An Anthology of Afro-American Writing*. New York: Morrow, 1968.

Basker, James G. *Amazing Grace: An Anthology of Poems about Slavery*. New Haven, Conn.: Yale University Press, 2002.

Bassett, John E. *Harlem in Review: Critical Reactions to Black American Writers, 1917–1939*. Selinsgrove, Pa.: Susquehanna University Press, 1992.

Baugh, Edward. *A Tale from the Rainforest*. Kingston, Jamaica: Sandberry Press, 1965.

Baxter, Harvey. *That Which Concerneth Me*. Roanoke, Va.: Magic City Press, 1935.

Benston, Kimberly W. "Ellison, Baraka, and the Faces of Tradition." *Boundary* 6, no. 2 (Winter 1978).

Bérubé, Michael. "Masks, Margins, and African American Modernism: Melvin Tolson's Harlem Gallery." *African and African American Literature*, special issue of *PMLA* 105, no. 1 (January 1990).

Bibby, Michael. "The Disinterested and Fine: New Negro Renaissance Poetry and the Racial Formation of Modernist Studies." *Modernism/Modernity* 20, no. 3 (September 2013): 485–501.

Bishop, Elizabeth. *Edgar Allan Poe and the Jukebox*. Edited by Alice Quinn. New York: Farrar, Straus & Giroux, 2006.

Bloom, Harold. *The Anxiety of Influence: A Theory of Poetry*. 2nd ed. New York: Oxford University Press, 1997.

———. "The Point of View for My Work as a Critic: A Dithyramb." *Hopkins Review* 38, no. 2 (Winter 2009).

Blount, Marcellus. "Caged Birds: Race and Gender in the Sonnet." In *Engendering Men: The Question of Male Feminist Criticism*, edited by Joseph A. Boone and Michael Cadden. New York: Routledge, 2012.

Bohls, Elizabeth. *Romantic Literature and Postcolonial Studies*. New York: Oxford University Press, 2013.

Bontemps, Arna, ed. *American Negro Poetry*. New York: Hill & Wang, 1963.

Braddock, Jeremy. *Collecting as Modernist Practice*. Baltimore: John Hopkins University Press, 2012.

Braithwaite, William Stanley, ed. *Anthology of Magazine Verse*. New York: Schulte, 1917.

———. *The House of Falling Leaves: With Other Poems*. Boston: J. W. Luce, 1908.

———. Introduction to *The Heart of a Woman and Other Poems*, by Georgia Douglas Johnson. Boston: Cornhill, 1918.

———. "The Negro in Literature." *Crisis*, September 1924.

Brawley, Benjamin. "My Hero." *Crisis*, May 1915, 37.

———. *The Negro in Literature and Art in the United States*. New York: Dodd, Mead, 1934.

———. "The Negro Literary Renaissance." 1927. In *The New Negro: Readings on Race, Representation, and African American Culture, 1892–1938*, edited by Henry Louis Gates, Jr., and Gene Andrew Jarrett. Princeton, N.J.: Princeton University Press, 2007.

———. *Paul Laurence Dunbar*. Chapel Hill: University of North Carolina Press, 1936.

Bromwich, David, ed. *American Sonnets: An Anthology*. New York: Library of America, 2007.

Brooke, Rupert. "The Soldier." 1915. In *A History of Modern Poetry: 1900–1940*, edited by Horace Gregory and Marya Zaturenska, 394. New York: Harcourt, Brace, 1946.

Brooks, Gwendolyn. *Annie Allen*. New York: Harper & Brothers, 1949.

———. *The Bean Eaters*. New York: Harper & Brothers, 1960.

——. "Conversation: Gwendolyn Brooks and B. Denise Hawkins." In *The Furious Flowering of African American Poetry*, edited by Joanne V. Gabbin, 274. Charlottesville: University of Virginia Press, 1999.

——. *Family Pictures*. Detroit: Broadside Press, 1970.

——. Foreword to *New Negro Poets, USA*, edited by Langston Hughes. Bloomington: Indiana University Press, 1964.

——. "An Interview with Gwendolyn Brooks." *Contemporary Literature* 11, no. 1 (Winter 1970).

——. *Report from Part One*. Detroit: Broadside Press, 1972.

——. *A Street in Bronzeville*. New York: Harper & Brothers, 1945.

——. *The World of Gwendolyn Brooks*. New York: Harper & Row, 1971.

Brooks, Gwendolyn, Martha H. Brown, and Marilyn Zorn. "GLR Interview: Gwendolyn Brooks." *Women in the Midwest, special issue of Great Lakes Review* 6, no. 1 (Summer 1979): 48–55.

Brown, Hallie Q. *Homespun Heroines and Other Women of Distinction*. Xenia, Ohio: Aldine, 1926.

Brown, Sterling Allen. "The Negro Author and His Publisher." *Quarterly Review of Higher Education Among Negroes*, July 1941.

——. *Negro Poetry and Drama*. No. 7. New York: Holiday House, 1937.

Brown, Sterling Allen, Arthur Paul Davis, and Ulysses Lee, eds. *The Negro Caravan: Writings by American Negroes*. Vol. 2. New York: Citadel Press, 1941.

Browne, Francis Fisher, ed. *Bugle-echoes: A Collection of Poems of the Civil War, Northern and Southern*. New York: White, Stokes, & Allen, 1886.

Browning, Elizabeth Barrett, and Robert Browning. *The Brownings' Correspondence*. Vol. 8. Edited by Philip Kelley, Ronald Hudson, Scott Lewis, and Edward Hagan. Winfield, Kans.: Wedgestone Press, 1984.

Bruce, Dickson D. *Black American Writing from the Nadir: The Evolution of a Literary Tradition, 1877–1915*. Baton Rouge: Louisiana State University Press, 1992.

Bryant, William Cullen. "The Poetry of Spanish America." *North American Review* 68 (January 1849).

Burt, Richard. "'*Being Your Slave*'—Not Citing Sonnets 57 and 58 and the 'TraUmisSion' of Race in the United States." In *Shakespeare's Sonnets, for the First Time Globally Reprinted: A Quartercentenary Anthology*, edited by Manfred Pfister and Jürgen Gutsch. Dozwil, Switzerland: Signathur, 2009.

Burt, Stephen, and David Mikics. *The Art of the Sonnet*. Cambridge, Mass.: Harvard University Press, 2010.

C. L. R. "Sonnet." *Colored American*, November 28, 1840.

Calverton, V. F. *An Anthology of Negro Literature*. New York: Modern Library, 1928.

Campbell, Thomas. *The Pleasures of Hope and Other Poems*. London: Longman, 1820.

Caplan, David. *Poetic Form: An Introduction*. London: Pearson, Longman, 2007.
———. *Questions of Possibility*. New York: Oxford University Press, 2005.
Carozza, Davy A., and H. James Shey, eds. *Petrarch's Secretum: With Introduction, Notes, and Critical Anthology*. New York: Peter Lang, 1989.
Carroll, William. "A Sonnet Sequence for the Diaspora: The 'Angry Sonnets' of Claude McKay." *MAWA Review* 14, no. 2 (December 1999).
Césaire, Aimé. Letter to Maurice Theroz, Paris, October 24, 1956. Translated by Chike Jeffers. *Social Text* 28, no. 2 (Summer 2010): 152.
Chace, Eleanor Frances. "The Development of Negro Poetry in the Twentieth Century." Master's thesis, Boston University, 1940.
Chaplin, Ralph. *Bars and Shadows: The Prison Poems of Ralph Chaplin*. New York: Leonard Press, 1922.
Chatman, Seymour Benjamin, and Samuel R. Levin. *Essays on the Language of Literature*. Boston: Houghton Mifflin, 1967.
Chesnutt, Charles W. "Baxter's Procrustes." *Atlantic Monthly*, June 1904, 823–829.
Chiles, Katy. "From Writing the Slave Self to Querying the Human: The First Twenty-Five Years of *The Signifying Monkey*." *Journal of Early American Literature* 50, no. 3 (2015).
Chrisman, Robert. "Robert Hayden: The Transition Years, 1946–1948." In *Robert Hayden: Essays on the Poetry*, edited by Laurence Goldstein and Robert Chrisman. Ann Arbor: University of Michigan Press, 2001.
Christian, Marcus B. "Southern Share-Cropper." *Opportunity*, July 1937.
———. "Spring in the South." *Opportunity*, July 1934.
Churchill, Suzanne W., Drew Brookie Hall Carey, and Cameron Hardesty. "Youth Culture in *The Crisis* and *Fire!!*" *Journal of Modern Periodical Studies* 1, no. 1 (2010).
Clifford, Carrie Williams. *The Widening Light*. Boston: Walter Reid, 1922.
Collier, Eugenia W. "I Do Not Marvel, Countee Cullen." *College Language Association Journal* 11, no. 1 (1967).
Cooper, Wayne. *Claude McKay: Rebel Sojourner in the Harlem Renaissance*. Baton Rouge: Louisiana State University Press, 1996.
Corrothers, James D. *In Spite of the Handicap*. New York: George H. Doran, 1916.
———. "The Negro Singer." *Century*, November 1912.
———. "Paul Laurence Dunbar." *Century*, November 1912.
Cotter, Joseph Seamon, Jr. "Sonnet to Negro Soldiers." *Crisis*, June 1918.
Cotter, Joseph Seamon, Sr. *A Rhyming*. Louisville, Ky.: New South, 1895.
Cousins, A. D., and Peter Howarth. Introduction to *The Cambridge Companion to the Sonnet*, edited by A. D. Cousins and Peter Howarth. Cambridge: Cambridge University Press, 2011.
Crandall, Charles H. *Representative Sonnets by American Poets*. Boston: Houghton Mifflin, 1891.

Crew, Harvey W. *History of Dayton, Ohio: With Portraits and Biographical Sketches of Some of Its Pioneer and Prominent Citizens*. Dayton, Ohio: United Brethren Publishing House, 1889.

Cromwell, Otelia, Lorenzo Dow Turner, and Eva B. Dykes, eds. *Readings from Negro Authors for Schools and Colleges*. New York: Harcourt Brace, 1931.

Cullen, Countee. *The Black Christ and Other Poems*. New York: Harper, 1929.

———, ed. *Caroling Dusk: An Anthology of Verse by Negro Poets*. New York: Harper & Brothers, 1927.

———. *Color*. New York: Harper & Brothers, 1925.

———. "Dark Tower." *Opportunity*, April 1927.

———. *My Soul's High Song: The Collected Writings of Countee Cullen, Voice of the Harlem Renaissance*. Edited by Gerald Early. New York: Anchor Books, 1991.

———. "Yet Do I Marvel." *Century* 109 (November 1924).

Cummings, Allison. "Public Subjects: Race and the Critical Reception of Gwendolyn Brooks, Erica Hunt, and Harryette Mullen." *Frontiers: A Journal of Women Studies* 26, no. 2 (2005): 3–36.

cummings, e. e. "Maison." *Liberator*, July 1921.

Cunard, Nancy, ed. *Negro: An Anthology*. New York: Continuum, 1934.

Cunningham, James. "Review: 'The Treehouse and Other Poems.'" *Negro Digest*, January 1969.

Damroch, David, ed. *The Longman Anthology of British Literature: The Romantics and Their Contemporaries*. London: Longman, 1999.

Davis, Arthur P. *From the Dark Tower: Afro-American Writers, 1900 to 1960*. Washington, D.C.: Howard University Press, 1974.

Davis, Arthur P., and Saunders Redding, eds. *Cavalcade: Negro American Writing from 1760 to the Present*. Boston: Houghton Mifflin, 1971.

Dawson, Michael. "Foundational Myths: Recovering and Reconciling Narratives of Resistance." Chapter 1 from *Blacks In and Out of the Left*. Cambridge, Mass.: Harvard University Press, 2013.

DeLombard, Jeannine. *In the Shadow of the Gallows: Race, Crime, and American Civic Identity*. Philadelphia: University of Pennsylvania Press, 2012.

Dent, Tom. "Marcus B. Christian: A Reminiscence and an Appreciation." *Black American Literature Forum* 18, no. 1 (Spring 1984): 22–26.

Dickey, James. Introduction to *Selected Poems*, by Edward Arlington Robinson, edited by Morton Dauwen Zabel. New York: Macmillan, 1965.

Dion. "Glances at Our Condition; No. 1: Our Literature." *Frederick Douglass's Paper*, September 23, 1853.

Distiller, Natasha. *Desire and Gender in the Sonnet Tradition*. New York: Palgrave Macmillan, 2008.

Dodge, Mabel. *Movers and Shakers*. Albuquerque: University of New Mexico Press, 1936.

Dodson, Owen. "Countee Cullen (1903–1946)." *Phylon* 7, no. 1 (1st Qtr., 1946).

Donne, John. *The Complete English Poems*. London: Penguin Books, 1970.

Doreski, C. K. *Writing America Black: Race Rhetoric in the Public Sphere*. Cambridge: Cambridge University Press, 1998.

Dreer, Herman, ed. *American Literature by Negro Authors*. New York: Macmillan, 1950.

Du Bois, W. E. B. *The Autobiography of W. E. B. Du Bois: A Soliloquy on Viewing My Life from the Last Decade of Its First Century*. New York: International Publishers, 1968.

———. "The Criteria of Negro Art." *Crisis* 32, no. 6 (October 1926).

———. *The Souls of Black Folk*. Chicago: McClurg, 1903.

———. "Speech Given on July 21, 1930, at the Annual Meeting of the Alumni of Searles High School." *Berkshire Courier*, July 31, 1930.

———. "Strivings of the Negro People." *Atlantic Monthly*, August 1897, 194–198.

———. "Triumph." *Crisis* 2, no. 5 (September 1911).

Duckett, Alfred A. "Sonnet." *Twice a Year*, nos. 14–15 (1947).

Dunbar, Paul Laurence. "Bade Him Farewell." *Chicago Inter Ocean*, December 5, 1893.

———. *The Collected Poems of Paul Laurence Dunbar*. Edited by Joanne Braxton. Charlottesville: University of Virginia Press, 1993.

———. "Harriet Beecher Stowe." *Century*, November 1898.

———. Letter to Alice Moore, January 28, 1898 [letter 128]. *The Letters of Paul and Alice Dunbar: A Private History*. Edited by Eugene Wesley Metcalf. Berkeley: University of California Press, 1973.

———. *Lyrics of Love and Laughter*. New York: Dodd, Mead, 1903.

———. *Lyrics of Lowly Life*. New York: Dodd, Mead, 1909.

———. *Lyrics of the Hearthside*. New York: Dodd, Mead, 1899.

———. "Recession Never: Negro and the White Man." *Toledo Journal* 18 (December 1898).

———. "Robert Gould Shaw." *Atlantic Monthly* 86, no. 516 (October 1900).

Dunbar-Nelson, Alice. Review of Georgia Douglas Johnson's *Bronze: A Book of Verse*. *Messenger*, May 1923.

Dunn, Waldo H. "To Paul Lawrence Dunbar [sic]." *Voice of the Negro* 3–4 (1906–1907): 437.

Dykes, Eva Beatrice. *The Negro in English Romantic Thought; Or, a Study of Sympathy for the Oppressed*. Washington, D.C.: Associated Publishers, 1942.

Easthope, Anthony. *Poetry as Discourse*. New York: Routledge, 2013.

Eliot, T. S. "Philip Massinger." In *The Sacred Wood*, by T. S. Eliot. London: Methuen, 1921.

Ellison, Ralph. "The World and the Jug." In *Shadow and Act*. New York: Random House, 1964.

Emanuel, James A. "Renaissance Sonneteers: Their Contributions to the Seventies." *Black World* 24 (September 1975).

Emerson, Ralph Waldo. Review of Sonnets and Other Poems, by William Lloyd Garrison. *Dial* 4 (1844): 134.

Engberg, Kathrynn Seidler. *The Right to Write: The Literary Politics of Anne Bradstreet and Phillis Wheatley*. Lanham, Md.: University Press of America, 2009.

Falbo, Bianca. "Henry Reed and William Wordsworth: An Editor-Author Relationship and the Production of British Romantic Discourse." *Romantic Textualities: Literature and Print Culture, 1780–1840* 15 (Winter 2005).

Fauset, Jessie Redmon. Review of *The Heart of a Woman and Other Poems*. *Journal of Negro History* 4, no. 4 (October 1919).

———. "What to Read." *Crisis* 4, no. 4 (August 1912).

Feldman, Paula R., and Daniel Robinson, eds. *A Century of Sonnets: The Romantic-Era Revival, 1750–1850*. New York: Oxford University Press, 2002.

Flint, Allen. "Black Response to Colonel Shaw." *Phylon* 45, no. 3 (3rd Qtr., 1984): 210–219.

Ford, Karen Jackson. "The Sonnets of Satin-Legs Brooks." *Contemporary Literature* 48, no. 3 (Fall 2007): 345–73.

Francini, Antonella. "Sonnet vs. Sonnet: The Fourteen Lines in African American Poetry." *RSA Journal* 14 (2003): 37–66. http://www.aisna.net/sites/default/files/rsa/rsa14/14francini.pdf.

Fuller, Hoyt. "The Critics Will Learn." *Negro Digest*, November 1968.

Fussell, Paul. *Poetic Meter and Poetic Form*. New York: McGraw-Hill, 1965.

Gabbin, Joanna. *Sterling Brown: Building the Black Aesthetic Tradition*. Charlottesville: University of Virginia Press, 1985.

Gandhi, Nilay. "On 'The Lynching.'" *Modern American Poetry*, November 18, 2004.

Gannon, Thomas C. *Skylark Meets Meadowlark: Reimagining the Bird in British Romantic and Contemporary Native American Literature*. Lincoln: University of Nebraska Press, 2009.

Garrison, William Lloyd. *Sonnets and Other Poems*. Boston: O. Johnson, 1843.

Gascoigne, George. *Certayne Notes of Instruction Concerning the Making of Verfe or Ryme in Englifh, Written at the Requefl of Mafler Edouardo Donati*. Edited by Edward Arber. London: Bloomsbury, 1869.

Gates, Henry Louis, Jr. *Loose Canons: Notes on the Culture Wars*. New York: Oxford University Press, 1992.

———. *The Signifying Monkey: A Theory of African American Literary Criticism*. New York: Oxford University Press, 2014.

Gayle, Addison, Jr., ed. *The Black Aesthetic*. Garden City, N.Y.: Doubleday, 1971.

———. "Cultural Strangulation: Black Literature and the White Aesthetic." *Negro Digest*, July 1969.

———. "The Harlem Renaissance: Toward a Black Aesthetic." *American Studies* 11, no. 2 (Fall 1970).

———. "Making Beauty from Racial Anxiety." *New York Times*, June 2, 1972.

Gilroy, Paul. *The Black Atlantic: Modernity and Double Consciousness*. Cambridge, Mass.: Harvard University Press, 1993.

Giovanni, Nikki. "Black Poems, Poseurs and Power." *Negro Digest*, June 1969, 34.

———. "The Rocks Cry Out." *Negro Digest*, August 1969, 97–98.

Giovannitti, Arturo. *Arrows in the Gale*. Riverside, Conn.: Hillacre Bookhouse, 1914.

Girard, Melissa. "'Jeweled Bindings': Modernist Women's Poetry and the Limits of Sentimentality." In *Oxford Handbook of Modern and Contemporary American Poetry*, edited by Cary Nelson. New York: Oxford University Press, 2012.

———. "J. Saunders Redding and the 'Surrender' of African American Women's Poetry." *PMLA* 132, no. 2 (2017).

Goldsby, Jacqueline. *A Spectacular Secret: Lynching in American Life and Literature*. Chicago: University of Chicago Press, 2006.

Goldstein, Laurence, and Robert Chrisman, eds. *Robert Hayden: Essays on the Poetry*. Ann Arbor: University of Michigan Press, 2001.

Graham, Maryemma, ed. *Fields Watered in Blood: Critical Essays on Margaret Walker*. Athens: University of Georgia Press, 2001.

Gray, Thomas. "Elegy Written in a Country Churchyard." 1751. In *Gray's Poems*. London: Macmillan, 1891.

Greene, Roland. *Unrequited Conquests: Love and Empire in the Colonial Americas*. Chicago: University of Chicago Press, 1999.

Gregory, Horace, and Marya Zaturenska, eds. *A History of American Poetry: 1900–1940*. New York: Harcourt Brace, 1946.

Griffin, Martin. *Ashes of the Mind: War and Memory in Northern Literature, 1865–1900*. Amherst: University of Massachusetts Press, 2003.

Grimké, Angelina Weld. "To the Dunbar High School: A Sonnet." *Crisis*, March 1917, 222.

Hammond, Jupiter. *An Address to Miss Phillis Wheatly, Ethiopian Poetess, in Boston, Who Came from Africa at Eight Years of Age, and Soon Became Acquainted with the Gospel of Jesus Christ*. Hartford, Conn.: Watson & Goodwin, 1778.

Hanson, Michael. "Elegy, Ode, and the Eighteenth-Century Sonnet Revival: The Case of Charles Emily." *Literary Imagination* 12, no. 3 (November 2010).

Harper, Michael S., and Anthony Walton, eds. *The Vintage Book of African American Poetry*. New York: Vintage, 2000.

Harris, Joel Chandler. *Uncle Remus, His Songs and His Sayings: The Folk-lore of the Old Plantation*. New York: D. Appleton, 1881.

Hayden, Robert. *Collected Poems*. London: Liveright, 1972.

———. *Heart-Shape in the Dust: Poems by Robert Hayden*. Detroit: Falcon Press, 1940.

Hayes, Terrance. "Sonnet." In *Hip Logic*, by Terrance Hayes. New York: Penguin, 2002.

Henderson, Stephen. *Understanding the New Black Poetry: Black Speech and Black Music as Poetic References*. New York: Morrow, 1973.

Hentz, Caroline. *The Planter's Northern Bride*. Philadelphia: T. B. Peterson, 1854.

Hill, Herbert, ed. *Soon, One Morning: New Writing by American Negroes, 1940–1962.* New York: Knopf, 1963.

Hill, Leslie Pinckney. "Vision of a Lyncher." *Crisis*, January 1912.

———. "What the Negro Wants and How to Get It: The Inward Power of the Masses." In *What the Negro Wants*, edited by Rayford W. Logan. Chapel Hill: University of North Carolina Press, 1944.

———. *The Wings of Oppression.* Boston: Stratford, 1921.

Hillyer, Robert. *First Principles of Verse.* Boston: The Writer, Inc. Publishers, 1938.

Hollander, John. *Melodious Guile: Fictive Pattern in Poetic Language.* New Haven, Conn.: Yale University Press, 1990.

———. *The Work of Poetry.* New York: Columbia University Press, 1997.

hooks, bell. *Yearning: Race, Gender, and Cultural Politics.* Boston: South End Press, 1990.

Hopson, James O. "Book Review." *Crisis*, October 1935.

Horton, George Moses. *The Poetical Works of George M. Horton, the Colored Bard of North Carolina, to Which Is Prefixed the Life of the Author, Written by Himself.* Hillsborough, N.C.: Heartt, 1845.

———. "Slavery." *Freedom's Journal*, July 18, 1828.

———. "Slavery." *Liberator*, March 19, 1834.

———. "Slavery and Liberty." *Lancaster Gazette*, April 8, 1829.

Howells, William Dean. "Life and Letters." *Harper's Weekly*, June 27, 1896.

———. *Modern Italian Poets.* New York: Harper & Brothers, 1887.

———. "The New Poetry." *North American Review* 168 (May 1899).

———. "Review: Leigh Hunt, 'The Book of The Sonnet.'" *North American Review* 215 (April 1867).

Huggins, Nathan Irvin. *Harlem Renaissance.* Updated ed. New York: Oxford University Press, 2007.

Hughes, Langston. "The Bread and Butter Side." In "Problems of the Negro Writer," *Saturday Review*, April 20, 1963.

———. *The Collected Poems of Langston Hughes.* Edited by Arnold Rampersad and David Roessel. New York: Knopf, 1994.

———. "The Negro Artist and the Racial Mountain." *Nation*, June 23, 1926.

———. *New Negro Poets U.S.A.* Bloomington: Indiana University Press, 1964.

———. "Says Race Leaders, Including Preachers, Flock to Harlem Cabarets." *Pittsburgh Courier*, April 16, 1927, 8.

Hughes, Langston, and Arna Wendell Bontemps, eds. *The Poetry of the Negro, 1746–1949.* New York: Doubleday, 1949.

Hughes, Merrit Y., ed. *A Variorum Commentary on the Poems of John Milton.* 6 vols. New York: Columbia University Press, 1970.

Hull, Gloria T. *Color, Sex, and Poetry: Three Women Writers of the Harlem Renaissance.* Bloomington: Indiana University Press, 1987.

Hunt, Leigh. "The Book of the Sonnet." *North American Review* 215 (April 1867).

Hurston, Zora Neale. "Characteristics of Negro Expression." In *Negro: An Anthology*, edited by Nancy Cunard. London: Wishart & Co., 1934.

J. G. W. "The Slave Poet of North Carolina." *National Era*, November 23, 1848.

Jackson, Angela. *A Surprised Queenhood in the New Black Sun: The Life and Legacy of Gwendolyn Brooks*. Boston: Beacon Press, 2017.

Jackson, Blyden. "From One 'New Negro' to Another, 1923–1972." In *Black Poetry in America: Two Essays in Historical Interpretation*, edited by Blyden Jackson and Louis Rubin, Jr. Baton Rouge: Louisiana State University Press, 1974.

———. *A History of Afro-American Literature*. Vol. 1. Baton Rouge: Louisiana State University Press, 1989.

Jackson, Blyden, and Louis D. Rubin, Jr. *Black Poetry in America: Two Essays in Historical Interpretation*. Baton Rouge: Louisiana State University Press, 1974.

Jaji, Tsitsi. *Mother Tongues: Poems*. Evanston, Ill.: Northwestern University Press, 2019.

James, C. L. R. *Beyond a Boundary*. Durham, N.C.: Duke University Press, 2013.

———. "The Bloomsbury Atmosphere." *Letters from London: Seven Essays*. London: Signal Books, 2003.

Jarrett, Gene Andrew. *Representing the Race: A New Political History of African American Literature*. New York: New York University Press, 2011.

Jay-Z. *Decoded*. New York: Random House, 2011.

Jenkins, Lee M. "'If We Must Die': Winston Churchill and Claude McKay." *Notes and Queries* 50, no. 3 (September 2003).

Johnson, Abby Arthur, and Ronald Maberry Johnson. *Propaganda and Aesthetics: The Literary Politics of Afro-American Magazines in the Twentieth Century*. Amherst: University of Massachusetts Press, 1979.

Johnson, Charles Bertram. "A Shell." *Colored American*, February 1905.

Johnson, Charles S. "An Address to the Graduating Classes of Virginia Union University and Hartshorn College." June 6, 1928. Fisk University Library, Johnson Papers, 9–10.

———, ed. *Ebony and Topaz: A Collectanea*. Manchester, N.H.: Ayer, 1927.

Johnson, Georgia Douglas. "A Sonnet: To the Mantled!" *Crisis*, May 1917; rpt., *Phylon Quarterly* 3, no. 2 (2nd Qtr., 1942): 116.

Johnson, James Weldon. *Along This Way*. New York: Penguin Classics, 2008.

———. *Black Manhattan*. New York: Da Capo Press, 1930.

———. *The Book of American Negro Poetry*. New York: Harcourt Brace, 1922.

———. "Placido." *Crisis* 23, no. 2 (January 1922).

Jones, LeRoi. "Black Art." *Liberator*, January 1966.

———. "How You Sound?" In *New American Poetry*, edited by Donald M. Allen. New York: New Grove Press, 1960.

———. "The Myth of a 'Negro Literature.'" In "Problems of the Negro Writer," *Saturday Review*, April 20, 1963.

———. *Preface to a Twenty Volume Suicide Note*. New York: Totem Press, 1961.

Jones, LeRoi, and Larry Neal, eds. *Black Fire: An Anthology of Afro-American Writing*. New York: William Morrow, 1968.

Jones, Sharon Lynette. "The Poetry of the Harlem Renaissance." In *Cambridge Companion to Modernist Poetry*, edited by Alex Davis and Lee M. Jenkins. Cambridge: Cambridge University Press, 2007.

Jordan, June. "The Difficult Miracle of Black Poetry in America; Or, Something Like a Sonnet for Phillis Wheatley." *Massachusetts Review* 27, no. 2 (1986): 252–262.

———, ed. *Soulscript: Afro-American Poetry*. New York: Zenith Books / Doubleday, 1970.

Jules-Rosette, Bennetta. *Black Paris: The African Writers' Landscape*. Champaign: University of Illinois Press, 2000.

Karenga, Ron. "Black Cultural Nationalism." In *The Black Aesthetic*, edited by Addison Gayle Jr., 31–37. New York: Anchor Press, 1971.

Keats, John. *The Complete Poetical Works of John Keats*. New York: Thomas Crowell, 1895.

Kent, George E. *A Life of Gwendolyn Brooks*. Lexington: University of Kentucky Press, 1990.

———. "Patterns of the Harlem Renaissance." *Black World*, June 1972.

Kerlin, Robert Thomas. *Negro Poets and Their Poems*. Washington, D.C.: Associated Publishers, 1923.

Kitson, P. J. "Fictions of Slave Resistance and Revolt: Robert Southey's 'Poems on the Slave Trade' (1797) and Charlotte Smith's 'The Story of Henrietta' (1800)." In *Race, Romanticism, and the Atlantic*, edited by Paul Youngquist. New York: Ashgate, 2013.

Lanz, Henry. "The Physical Basis of Rime." *Publications of the Modern Language Association of America* 41, no. 4 (December 1926): 1011–1023.

Leonard, Keith D. *Fettered Genius: The African American Bardic Poet from Slavery to Civil Rights*. Charlottesville: University of Virginia Press, 2006.

Lerner, Gerda. "Early Community Work of Black Club Women." *Journal of Negro History* 59, no. 2 (April 1974): 158–167.

Lewis, C. S. *The Allegory of Love: A Study in Medieval Tradition*. New York: Oxford University Press, 1936.

Lewis, David Levering. *W. E. B. Du Bois: A Biography*. New York: Macmillan, 2009.

Lide, Edwin S. "American Literature by Negro Authors: Herman Dreer." *School Review* 59, no. 1 (January 1951): 59–60.

Lilly, Octave. "Heritage." *Negro Digest*, September 1969, 42.

Locke, Alain, ed. *The New Negro*. New York: Simon & Schuster, 1925.

———. "Wisdom de Profundis: The Literature of the Negro, 1949. Part I." *Phylon* 11, no. 1 (1st Qtr., 1950): 5–14.

———. "Wisdom de Profundis: Review of The Literature of the Negro, 1949: Part II—The Social Literature." *Phylon* 11, no. 2 (2nd Qtr., 1950): 171–175.

Logan, Deborah Anna, ed. *Writings on Slavery and the American Civil War*. DeKalb: Northern Illinois University Press, 2002.

Logan, Rayford W. *The Negro in American Life and Thought: The Nadir, 1877–1901*. New York: Dial Press, 1954.

Loggins, Vernon. *The Negro Author: His Development in America to 1900*. Rpt., New York: Kennikat Press, 1964.

Looney, Dennis. "Dante Abolitionist and Nationalist in the Nineteenth Century: The Case of Cordelia Ray." In *Dante in the Long Nineteenth Century: Nationality, Identity, and Appropriation*, edited by Aida Audeh and Nick Havely. New York: Oxford University Press, 2012.

——. *Freedom Readers: The African American Reception of Dante Alighieri and the Divine Comedy*. Notre Dame, Ind.: University of Notre Dame Press, 2011.

Loranger, Carol S. "The Outcast Poetics of Paul Laurence Dunbar and Edwin Arlington Robinson." *Studies in American Naturalism* 10, no. 2 (Winter 2015).

Lowell, Amy. "A Consideration of Modern Poetry." *North American Review* 205, no. 734 (1917): 103–117.

——. *Tendencies in Modern American Poetry*. New York: Macmillan, 1917.

Madhubuti, Haki R. *Say That the River Turns*. Chicago: Third World Press, 1987.

Major, Clarence, ed. *The New Black Poetry*. New York: International Publishers, 1969.

Marius, Richard, and Keith From, eds. *The Columbia Book of Civil War Poetry*. New York: Columbia University Press, 1994.

Markus, Julia. *Dared and Done: The Marriage of Elizabeth Barrett and Robert Browning*. New York: Knopf, 1995.

Martin, Tony. *Literary Garveyism: Garvey, Black Arts, and the Harlem Renaissance*. Dover, Mass.: Majority Press, 1983.

Martineau, Harriet. *The Martyr Age of the United States with an Appeal on Behalf of the Oberlin Institute in Aid of the Abolition of Slavery*. Newcastle upon Tyne: Newcastle upon Tyne Emancipation and Aborigines Protection Society, 1840.

Mather, Frank L. *Who's Who of the Colored Race: A General Biographical Dictionary of Men and Women of African Descent*. Vol. 1. Chicago, 1915.

Maxwell, William. "Introduction: Claude McKay—Lyric Poetry in the Age of Cataclysm." In *Claude McKay, Complete Poems*, edited by William J. Maxwell. Champaign: University of Illinois Press, 2004.

McCall, James Edward. "The New Negro." *Opportunity*, July 1927.

McClellan, George. "A January Dandelion." In *The Path of Dreams*, by George McClellan. Louisville: J. P. Morton, 1916.

McGill, Meredith. "Frances Ellen Watkins Harper and the Circuits of Abolitionist Poetry." In *Early African American Print Culture*, edited by Lara Langer Cohen and Jordan Alexander Stein. Philadelphia: University of Pennsylvania Press, 2012.

McHenry, Elizabeth. *Forgotten Readers: Recovering the Lost History of African American Literary Societies*. Durham, N.C.: Duke University Press, 2002.

McKay, Claude. *Complete Poems*. Edited by William J. Maxwell. Champaign: University of Illinois Press, 2004.

———. *Harlem Shadows*. New York: Harcourt, Brace, 1922.

———. "Honeymoon." *Challenge*, March 1934.

———. *A Long Way from Home*. 1937; rpt., New Brunswick, N.J.: Rutgers University Press, 2007.

———. "Two Sonnets." *Seven Arts* 2 (October 1917): 741.

McLaren, Joseph. "African Diaspora Vernacular Traditions and the Dilemma of Identity." *African Literatures* 40, no. 1 (Spring 2009).

Melhem, D. H. *Gwendolyn Brooks: Poetry and the Heroic Voice*. Lexington: University Press of Kentucky, 1988.

Menard, J. W. *Lays in Summer Lands*. Edited by Larry Eugene Rivers, Richard Mathews, and Canter Brown, Jr. Florida: University of Tampa Press, 2002.

Mencken, H. L. *The American Language: A Preliminary Inquiry into the Development of English in the United States*. New York: Knopf, 1919.

Meredith, George. *Modern Love and Poems of the English Roadside, with Poems and Ballads*. New Haven, Conn.: Yale University Press, 2013.

Milnes, Richard Monckton, ed. *The Life and Letters of John Keats*. 1848; rpt., London: J. M. Dent and Sons, 1927.

Monroe, Harriet. "Reviews: Arrows in the Gale." *Poetry*, April 1, 1915.

Mootry, Maria K. "Creative Practice in War Sonnets." In *Reading Race in American Poetry: An Area of Act*, edited by Aldon Lynn Nielson. Champaign: University of Illinois Press, 2000, 146.

Morris, John T. "The History and Development of Negro Journalism." *A.M.E. Church Review* 6, no. 3 (January 1890).

Morrissette, Noelle. *James Weldon Johnson's Modern Soundscapes*. Iowa City: University of Iowa Press, 2013.

Morse, Heidi. "Black Classical Ruins and American Memory in the Poetry of H. Cordelia Ray." *Legacy* 34, no. 1 (2017).

Morton, Tim. *The Poetics of Spice: Romantic Consumerism and the Exotic*. Cambridge: Cambridge University Press, 2006.

Müller, Timo. *The African American Sonnet: A Literary History*. Jackson: University of Mississippi Press, 2018.

———. "James Weldon Johnson and the Genteel Tradition." *Arizona Quarterly* 68, no. 2 (Summer 2013): 85–102.

———. "The Vernacular Sonnet and the Resurgence of Afro-Modernism." *American Literature* 87, no. 2 (June 2015).

Murillo, John. "Renegades of Funk." In *Up Jump the Boogie*, by John Murillo. Berkeley, Calif.: Cypher Books, 2010.

Murphy, Beatrice, ed. *Ebony Rhythm: An Anthology of Contemporary Negro Verse*. New York: Exposition Press, 1948.

———, ed. *Negro Voices: An Anthology of Contemporary Verse*. New York: Henry Harrison, 1938.

Musa, Mark, ed. *Petrarch's Canzoniere*. Bloomington: Indiana University Press, 1996.

Myrdal, Gunnar. *An American Dilemma: The Negro Problem and Modern Democracy*. Twentieth anniversary ed. New York: Harper & Row, 1962.

Neal, Larry. "The Black Arts Movement." *Drama Review*, Summer 1968.

———. "Ellison's Zoot Suit." In *Ralph Ellison's Invisible Man: A Casebook*, edited by John F. Callahan. Oxford: Oxford University Press, 2004.

Nelson, Cary. *Repression and Recovery*. Madison: University of Wisconsin Press, 1989.

Nelson, J. H. "Brief Mention: American Literature by Negro Authors, Ed. Herman Dreer." *American Literature* 23, no. 2 (May 1951): 276-280.

Nelson, Marilyn. "Owning the Masters." In *After New Formalism: Poets on Form, Narrative, and Tradition*, edited by Annie Finch. Ashland, Oreg.: Story Line, 1999.

———. "A Wreath for Emmett Till." *Faster Than Light: New and Selected Poems, 1996-2011*. Baton Rouge: Louisiana State University Press, 2012.

Nielson, Aldon Lynn. *Reading Race: White American Poets and the Racial Discourse in the Twentieth Century*. Athens: University of Georgia Press, 1988.

North, Michael. *The Dialect of Modernism: Race, Language, and Twentieth-Century Literature*. New York: Oxford University Press, 1998.

Nwankwo, Ifeoma Kiddoe. "More than McKay and Guillén: The Caribbean in Hughes and Bontemps's *The Poetry of the Negro* (1949)." In *Publishing Blackness: Textual Constructions of Race since 1850*, edited by George Hutchinson and John K. Young. Ann Arbor: University of Michigan Press, 2013.

Oxley, Thomas L. G. "Survey of Negro Literature, 1760-1926." *Messenger*, January 1927.

Padgett, Rod. "Nothing in That Drawer." In *Great Balls of Fire*, by Rod Padgett. Minneapolis: Coffee House Press, 1990.

Parker, John W. "The Song of One Hundred Negro Poets: Review of *Ebony Rhythm* by Beatrice M. Murphy." *Phylon* 10, no. 3 (3rd Qtr., 1949): 288-290.

Parrington, Vernon Louis. *Main Currents in American Thought*. Vol. 3, *The Beginnings of Critical Realism in America, 1860-1920*. New York: Harcourt Brace, 1930.

Pearson, Ralph I. "Combatting Racism with Art: Charles S. Johnson and the Harlem Renaissance." *American Studies* 18, no. 1 (Spring 1977): 123-134.

Penn, Irvine Garland. *The Afro-American Press and Its Editors*. Springfield, Mass.: Willey, 1891.

Peppis, Paul. "Schools, Movements, Manifestos." In *Cambridge Companion to Modernist Poetry*, edited by Alex Davis and Lee M. Jenkins. Cambridge: Cambridge University Press, 2007.

Peterson, Carla L. "Commemorative Ceremonies and Invented Traditions: History, Memory, and Modernity in the 'New Negro' Novel of the Nadir." In *Post-Bellum, Pre-Harlem: African American Literature and Culture, 1877–1919*, edited by Barbara McCaskill and Caroline Gebhard. New York: NYU Press, 2006.

Phelan, Joseph. *The Nineteenth Century Sonnet*. Berlin: Springer, 2005.

Pigman, George W., III. "Versions of Imitation in the Renaissance." *Renaissance Quarterly* 33, no. 1 (1980).

Porter, Dorothy B. "The Organized Educational Activities of Negro Literary Societies, 1828–1846." *Journal of Negro Education* 5, no. 4 (October 1936): 555–576.

Potter, Vilma R. "Race and Poetry: Two Anthologies of the Twenties." *CLA Journal* 29, no. 3 (March 1986): 276–287.

Pound, Ezra. *The ABC of Reading*. 1951; rpt., London: Faber & Faber, 1979.

Price, Kenneth M. "Charles Chesnutt, *The Atlantic Monthly*, and the Intersection of African American Fiction and Elite Culture." In *Periodical Literature in Nineteenth-century America*, edited by Kenneth Price and Susan Belasco-Smith. Charlottesville: University of Virginia Press, 1995.

Quitslund, Jon A. "Spenser's Amoretti VIII and Platonic Commentaries on Petrarch." *Journal of the Warburg and Courtauld Institutes* 36 (1973).

Rambsy, Howard, II, and Mary Rose. Oral history interview with Eugene Redmond, March 12, 2012, Southern Illinois University Edwardsville Library and Information Services, EBR Oral History HR MR March 12, 2012.

Ramey, Lauri. *A History of African American Poetry*. Cambridge: Cambridge University Press, 2019.

Rampersad, Arnold. "Langston Hughes and Approaches to Modernism in the Harlem Renaissance." In *The Harlem Renaissance: Revaluations*, edited by Amritjit Singh, William S. Shiver, and Stanley Brodwin. New York: Garland, 1989.

———. *The Life of Langston Hughes*. Vol. 1, 1901–1941. 2nd ed. New York: Oxford University Press, 2002.

Randall, Dudley. *The Black Poets*. New York: Bantam, 1971.

———. *Roses and Revolutions: The Selected Writings of Dudley Randall*. Detroit: Wayne State University Press, 2009.

Ray, H. Cordelia. *Poems*. New York: Grafton Press, 1910.

———. *Sonnets*. New York: J. J. Little, 1893.

Reason, Charles Lewis. "Sonnet." *Colored American*, November 28, 1840.

Redding, Saunders. *To Make a Poet Black*. Ithaca, N.Y.: Cornell University Press, 1939.

Redmond, Eugene B. *Drumvoices: The Mission of Afro-American Poetry: A Critical History*. New York: Anchor Books, 1976.

———. "Sonnet Serenade/Soulo Beauty for Gwendolyn Brooks." *Songs from an Afro/Phone*. East Saint Louis, Ill.: Black River Writers, 1972.

Reed, Ishmael. "Can a Metronome Know the Thunder or Summon a God?" In *The Black Aesthetic*, edited by Addison Gayle, 406. New York: Anchor, 1972.

Reeves, Roger. "What Black Poets Are Doing to Poetry." In *Yet Do I Marvel*. Poetry Society of America. https://www.poetrysociety.org/psa/poetry/crossroads/yetdoimarvel/roger_reeves/.

Rezek, Joseph. "The Print Atlantic." In *Early African American Print Culture*, edited by Lara Langer Cohen and Jordan Alexander Stein. Philadelphia: University of Pennsylvania Press, 2012.

Richardson, Alan. "Darkness Visible? Race and Representation in Bristol Abolitionist Poetry, 1770-1810." In *Romanticism and Colonialism: Writing and Empire, 1780-1830*, edited by Tim Fulford and Peter J. Kitson. Cambridge: Cambridge University Press, 2005.

Ridge, Lola. "Electrocution." *Red Flag*. New York: Viking Press, 1927.

Riding, Laura, and Robert Graves, eds. *A Survey of Modernist Poetry*. New York: Haskell House, 1927.

Robinson, Edwin Arlington. *The Children of the Night: A Book of Poems*. New York: Charles Scribner's Sons, 1919.

Robinson, William Henry. *Black New England Letters*. Boston: Trustees of the Public Library of the City of Boston, 1977.

Rogers, Carolyn M. "Black Poetry—Where It's At." *Negro Digest*, September 1969, 7-16.

Rossetti, Dante Gabriel. *The Early Italian Poets from Ciullo D'Alcamo to Dante Alighieri (1100-1200-1300)*. London: Smith, Elder & Co., 1861.

Rubin, Louis D., Jr. "The Search for Language, 1746-1923." In *Black Poetry in America: Two Essays in Historical Interpretation*, by Louis D. Rubin, Jr. Baton Rouge: Louisiana State University Press, 1974.

Saintsbury, George. *A History of English Prosody from the Twelfth Century to the Present Day*. Vol. 1. New York: Macmillan, 1906.

Salas, Angela M. "'Flashbacks through the Heart': Yusef Komunyakaa and the Poetry of Self-Assertion." In *The Furious Flowering of African American Poetry*, edited by Joanne V. Gabbin, 298-309. Charlottesville: University of Virginia Press, 2004.

Sanders, Mark. *Afro-Modernist Aesthetics & the Poetry of Sterling A Brown*. Athens: University of Georgia Press, 1999.

Sandweiss, Martha. *Passing Strange: A Gilded Age Tale of Love and Deception Across the Color Line*. New York: Penguin, 2009.

Santayana, George, "The Genteel Tradition in American Philosophy." In *Winds of Doctrine: Studies in Contemporary Opinion*, by George Santayana, 186-215. New York, Charles Scribner & Sons, 1912.

———. "Shakespeare: Made in America." *New Republic*, February 27, 1915.

Sarudzai. "Pan Africa." *Negro Digest*, September 1969.

Sauer, Elizabeth. "Tolerationism, the Irish Crisis, and Milton's 'On the Late Massacre in Piemont.'" *Milton Studies* 44 (2005): 40-61.

Savoie, John. "Dunbar, Douglass, Milton: Authorial Agon and the Integrated Canon." *College Literature* 37, no. 2 (Spring 2010): 24-27.

Schomburg, Arthur. "Letter." *Amsterdam News,* July 30, 1927.

————. "The Negro Digs Up His Past." *Survey,* March 1, 1925.

Schuyler, George S. "Forty Years of *The Crisis.*" *Crisis,* March 1951, 163.

————. "The Negro-Art Hokum." *Nation,* June 16, 1926.

Sedgwick, Ellery. *"The Atlantic Monthly," 1857–1909: Yankee Humanism at High Tide and Ebb.* Amherst: University of Massachusetts Press, 1994.

Sharp, William, ed. *American Sonnets.* London: Walter Scott, Paternoster Square, 1910.

————, ed. *Sonnets of This Century.* London: W. Scott, 1886.

Sherman, Joan R. *The Black Bard of North Carolina: George Moses Horton and His Poetry.* Chapel Hill: University of North Carolina Press, 1997.

————. *Invisible Poets.* Champaign: University of Illinois Press, 1989.

Silver, Isadore. *The Intellectual Evolution of Ronsard.* Geneva: Library Droz, 1992.

Simmons, William J. *Men of Mark: Eminent, Progressive, and Rising.* Cleveland: George M. Rewell, 1887.

Smethurst, James. *The New Red Negro: The Literary Left and African American Poetry, 1930–1946.* New York: Oxford University Press, 1999.

Smith, Barbara Herrnstein. *Poetic Closure: A Study of How Poems End.* Chicago: University of Chicago Press, 1965.

Smith, Gary. "The Black Protest Sonnet." *American Poetry* 2, no. 1 (Fall 1984): 2–12.

Southey, Robert. *The Complete Poetical Works.* New York: D. Appleton, 1846.

————. *The Poetical Works, Collected by Himself.* London: Longman, 1837.

————. *The Poetical Works: Complete in One Volume.* London: Longman, 1844.

Sperry, Margaret. "Countee P Cullen, Negro Boy Poet, Tells His Story." *Brooklyn Daily Eagle,* February 10, 1924.

Spiller, Michael R. G. *The Development of the Sonnet: An Introduction.* New York: Routledge, 1992.

Spillers, Hortense J. "The Crisis of the Negro Intellectual: A Post-Date." *Boundary* 21, no. 3 (1994): 65–116.

Steffen, Therese. "Rooted Displacement in Form: Rita Dove's Sonnet Cycle Mother Love." In *The Furious Flowering of African American Poetry,* edited by Joanne V. Gabbin. Charlottesville: University of Virginia Press, 2004.

Sterner, Lewis. "General Survey of the American Sonnet." In Lewis Sterner, *The Sonnet in American Literature.* Philadelphia: University of Pennsylvania Press, 1930.

Stewart, Susan. *The Poet's Freedom: A Notebook on Making.* Chicago: University of Chicago Press, 2011.

Still, William. *The Underground Railroad: A Record of Facts, Authentic Narratives, Letters, &c., Narrating the Hardships, Hair-breadth Escapes and Death Struggles of the Slaves in Their Efforts for Freedom, as Related by Themselves and Others, or Witnessed by the Author; Together with Sketches of Some of the Largest Stock-*

holders, and Most Liberal Aiders and Advisers, of the Road. Philadelphia: People's Publishing, 1872.

Strong, Mary Louise. Review of *Readings from Negro Authors for Schools and Colleges* by Otelia Cromwell, Lorenzo Dow Turner, and Eva B. Dykes. *Journal of Negro History* 17, no. 3 (July 1932).

Tate, Claudia. *Black Women Writers at Work*. New York: Continuum, 1983.

———. *Domestic Allegories of Political Desire: The Black Heroine's Text at the Turn of the Century*. New York: Oxford University Press, 1996.

———. *Psychoanalysis and Black Novels: Desire and the Protocols of Race*. New York: Oxford University Press, 1998.

Taussig, Charlotte. "The New Negro as Revealed in His Poetry." *Opportunity*, April 1927.

Thomas, Lorenzo. *Chances Are Few*. Berkeley, Calif.: Blue Wind Press, 1979.

Thompson, Mark Christian. "What Will Be African-American Literature?" *American Literary History* 25, no. 4 (Winter 2013).

Thurman, Wallace, ed. *FIRE!!* New York: Negro Universities Press, 1926.

———. "Negro Poets and Their Poetry." *Bookman*, July 1928.

Tidwell, John Edgar, and Ted Genoways. "Two Lost Sonnets by Sterling A. Brown." *Callaloo* 21, no. 4 (1998): 741–744.

Tidwell, John Edgar, and Steven C. Tracy, eds. *After Winter: The Art and Life of Sterling A. Brown*. New York: Oxford University Press, 2009.

Tolson, Melvin B. "Claude McKay's Art." Review of *Selected Poems of Claude McKay*, by Claude McKay." *Poetry* 83, no. 5 (February 1954): 287–290.

———. *Libretto for the Republic of Liberia*. Woodbridge, Conn.: Twayne, 1953.

Untermeyer, Louis. *The New Era in American Poetry*. New York: Holt, 1919.

Voltaire. Letter to Baron Constant de Rebecq. In *Anti-Slavery Opinion in France during the Second Half of the Eighteenth Century*, vol. 10, by Edward D. Seeber. Baltimore: Johns Hopkins University Press, 1937.

Wagner, Jean. *Black Poets of the United States: From Paul Laurence Dunbar to Langston Hughes*. Champaign: University of Illinois Press, 1973.

Wagner, Jennifer Ann. *A Moment's Monument: Revisionary Poetics and the Nineteenth-Century English Sonnet*. Madison, N.J.: Fairleigh Dickinson University Press, 1996.

Walker, Margaret. "The Struggle Staggers Us." In *For My People*, by Margaret Walker. New Haven, Conn.: Yale University Press, 1942.

Walkowitz, Rebecca L. "Shakespeare in Harlem: The Norton Anthology, 'Propaganda,' Langston Hughes." *Modern Language Quarterly* 60, no. 4 (1999): 495–519.

Wallace, Les. "Charles Lenox Remond: The Lost Prince of Abolitionism." *Negro History Bulletin* 40 (1977): 696–701.

Walser, Richard Gaither. *The Black Poet: Being the Remarkable Story of George Moses Horton, a North Carolina Slave*. New York: Philosophical Library, 1966.

Wangara, Kofi. "The Fire This Time." *Black World*, January 1975, 48.

Ward, W. E. "Charles Lenox Remond: Black Abolitionist, 1838–1873." PhD dissertation, Clark University, 1977.

Warren, Kenneth. *What Was African American Literature?* Cambridge, Mass.: Harvard University Press, 2011.

Washington, Mary Helen. *The Other Blacklist: The African American Literary and Cultural Left of the 1950s.* New York: Columbia University Press, 2014.

Watkins, Lucian B. "Ballade to Paul Laurence Dunbar." *Crisis*, December 1918.

Watson, Bruce. *Bread and Roses: Mills, Migrants, and the Struggle for the American Dream.* New York: Viking, 2005.

Wells, Henry. *The American Way of Poetry.* New York: Columbia University Press, 1943.

Westover, Jess. "African American Sonnets: Voicing Justice and Personal Dignity." In *A Companion to Poetic Genre*, edited by Erik Martiny. Hoboken, N.J.: Wiley-Blackwell, 2011.

Wheatley, Phillis. *Poems on Various Subjects, Religious and Moral.* London: Bell, 1773.

White, Newman Ivey, and Walter Clinton Jackson, eds. *Anthology of Verse by American Negroes.* Durham, N.C.: Trinity College Press, 1924.

Whitfield, James M. "America." In *America and Other Poems*, by James M. Whitfield. Buffalo, N.Y.: James S. Leavitt, 1853.

———. *The Works of James M. Whitfield: America and Other Writings by a Nineteenth-Century African American Poet*, edited by Robert S. Levine and Ivy G. Wilson. Chapel Hill: University of North Carolina Press, 2011.

Whitman, Albery. *Not a Man and Yet a Man.* Springfield, Ohio: Republic, 1877.

———. *Twasinta's Seminoles, or The Rape of Florida.* St. Louis: Nixon-Jones, 1885.

Wilentz, Elias, ed. *The Beat Scene.* New York: Corinth Books, 1960.

William, Gladys Margaret. "Gwendolyn Brooks's Way with the Sonnet." *CLA Journal* 26, no. 2 (December 1982): 215–240.

Williams, Pontheolla T. *Robert Hayden: A Critical Analysis of His Poetry.* Champaign: University of Illinois Press, 1987.

Williams, William Carlos. "The Poem as a Field of Action." *Selected Essays of William Carlos Williams.* Cambridge, Mass.: New Directions, 1954.

———. *Something to Say: William Carlos Williams on Younger Poets.* Edited by James E. B. Breslin. Cambridge, Mass.: New Directions, 1985.

Wilson, Sondra Kathryn, ed. *The "Crisis" Reader: Stories, Poetry, and Essays from the NAACP's "Crisis" Magazine.* New York: Modern Library, 1999.

———, ed. *The Messenger Reader.* New York: Modern Library Harlem Renaissance, 2000.

Wolfson, Susan J. "Sonnets Then and Now: Fields of Play." *Literary Imagination* 12, no. 3 (2010): 261–265.

Wood, Marcus. *The Poetry of Slavery.* New York: Oxford University Press, 2003.

Woodson, Carter G. *The Mis-education of the Negro.* 1933; rpt., Trenton, N.J.: Africa World Press, 1990.

Woodson, Jon. *Anthems, Sonnets, and Chants: Recovering the African American Poetry of the 1930s.* Columbus: Ohio State University Press, 2011.

———. "Anti Lynching Poems in the 1930s." *Flashpoint.* http://www.flashpoint mag.com/Woodson_Anti_Lynching_Poems_in_the_1930s.htm.

Wordsworth, William. *The Collected Poems of William Wordsworth.* Ware, UK: Wordsworth Editions, 1994.

———. *Poems, in Two Volumes.* Edited by Richard Matlak. Peterborough, Ont.: Broadview Press, 2015.

Wormley, Beatrice F., and Charles W. Carter, eds. *An Anthology of Negro Poetry by Negroes and Others.* Washington, D.C.: Works Progress Administration, 1937.

Wright, Richard. "Blueprint for Negro Writing." *New Challenge: A Literary Quarterly* 2, no. 1 (Fall 1937).

Yerby, Frank. "You Are a Part of Me." *Fisk Herald,* December 1937.

Young, Alexander. "Before a Monument." *Pittsburgh Courier,* April 6, 1940.

PERMISSIONS CREDITS

INDEX

abolitionist presses, 83-88. *See also* black presses

abolitionist sonnets, 75-81, 85, 204n28

African American poetry: approaches to, 22-33, 96, 101-102, 164-165, 169-172, 175-180; scholarship on, 3-4, 14-19, 24-25, 42-43, 185-189

Aldrich, Thomas Bailey, 95-96

Alexander, Elizabeth, 54, 179-180

Alexander, Lewis, 149-150

"America" (McKay), 127-128

"America" (Whitfield), 90

American Literature by Negro Authors (Dreer, ed.), 161-162

American Negro Poetry (Bontemps, ed.), 162, 164

Amoretti (Spenser), 37

anarchist poetry, 66-67

anthologies: approaches to, 132-134, 140-142, 147-149, 151-155, 161-162; editors of, 138; listed, 134; poets regularly appearing in, 139; sonnets in, 135-138t, 167-168t

Anthology of American Negro Literature (Calverton, ed.), 148

Anthology of Verse by American Negroes (White and Jackson, eds.), 139-140, 141

Anxiety of Influence, The (Bloom), 4-5

Appiah, Anthony, 19

Arion, 82-83

Astrophil and Stella (Sidney), 37

Atlantic Monthly, 95, 207n1; literary magazines more generally, 105. *See also* black presses

Baker, Houston, 23, 62, 177-178, 180, 185-187, 188, 222n61

"Ballade to Paul Laurence Dunbar" (Watkins), 124-125

Baraka, Amiri, 4-5, 172, 174; "Epistrophe," 173-174; as LeRoi Jones, 165, 167; "The Turncoat," 172-173

Baugh, Edward, 36, 38, 42, 44, 184, 199n15

"Before a Monument" (Young), 152

Bibby, Michael, 18, 27

"Birth in a Narrow Room, The" (G. Brooks), 159

Black Arts movement, 7-8, 31, 169, 172, 180. *See also* African American poetry: approaches to

"Black Majesty" (Cullen), 166-167

black presses, 93-94, 103-105, 115, 123, 130-131; abolitionist presses, 83-88; Douglass and, 28, 91, 210n58; literacy and, 83; literary magazines more generally, 105, 207n1; perceived lack of African American poetic voices and, 89-93

"Black Recruit" (G. D. Johnson), 151-52

Blake, William, 61, 75, 128

Bloom, Harold, 4-5

Blount, Marcellus, 18, 61, 108, 179

Bontemps, Arna: *American Negro Poetry*

Bontemps, Arna (*continued*)
    (ed.), 162, 164; *The Poetry of the American
    Negro* (ed., with Hughes), 153–154, 161
"Booker T. Washington" (Dunbar), 108–
    109, 121, 122, 140
Book of American Negro Poetry (J. W. John-
    son, ed.), 130, 139
Braithwaite, William Stanley, 4, 14, 112,
    116, 147; "On the Death of Thomas Bai-
    ley Aldrich," 95–96
"Bread and Butter Side, The" (Hughes),
    219n96
Bromwich, David, 70–71, 188
Brooks, Gwendolyn, 6, 130, 155–156, 157–
    160, 169, 175–180, 196n8; protest tradi-
    tion and, 7, 50; sonnet tradition and, 9,
    27, 31; Trethewey and, 2, 8
—works of: "The Birth in a Narrow
    Room," 159; "Gay Chaps at the Bar," 179;
    "A Lovely Love," 44–45; "Mentors," 157–
    158; *New Negro Poets, USA*, foreword, 6,
    134, 174; "XIII / intermission: I / deep
    summer," 42, 173; "To a Winter Squir-
    rel," 53–54; "The White Troops," 178–179
Brooks, Rupert, 13
Brown, Sterling A., 146–147, 215n32,
    215n36; "Salutamus," 146
Browning, Elizabeth Barrett, 93
Bryant, William Cullen, 87–89
Byron, George Gordon, Lord, 86, 97, 98,
    128, 208n22

Calverton, V. F., 148
Campbell, Thomas, 78–79
canon formation, 132–134, 169–172
"Canticus Troili" (Chaucer), 36–37
"Canticus Troili" (Sonnet 132; Petrarch),
    36–37
Caroling Dusk (Cullen, ed.), 142, 147
Chaplin, Ralph, 65–66
Chaucer, Geoffrey, 36–37
Christian, Marcus B.: "The Craftsman,"
    60; "Southern Share-Cropper," 69–70;
    "Spring in the South," 149–150
Color (Cullen), 126, 142
Colored American, 83–84, 85
Cornish, Samuel, 81, 83–4
Corrothers, James David, 112–115; "Paul
    Laurence Dunbar," 113–114

Cotter, Joseph Seamon, Jr., 125
Cotter, Joseph Seamon, Sr., 101–102
courtly love, 35–36, 39–42, 44–45
"Craftsman, The" (Christian), 60
Crisis, 62, 120, 123–125, 211n67, 211n74
"Criteria of Negro Art" (Du Bois), 167
Cromwell, Otelia, 148–49
Cullen, Countee, 142–144, 214n18, 214n20,
    218n86; anthologies and, 132, 139, 141,
    148, 149; Gwendolyn Brooks and, 178,
    179, 180; Hughes and, 64, 138, 162, 213n6;
    as influence, 152, 155, 158, 162; influ-
    ences on, 16, 60, 186, 213n16; Keats and,
    52, 58; Millay and, 198n70
—works of: "Black Majesty," 166–167; *Car-
    oling Dusk* (ed.), 142, 147; *Color*, 126, 142;
    "From the Dark Tower," 51–52, 60, 140,
    146, 163, 183; "Yet Do I Marvel," 142–
    143, 152
cummings, e. e., 67, 178, 221n51; "Maison,"
    67

Dante (Alighieri), 33, 34–36, 116, 205n41;
    "Tanto gentile e tanto onesta pare," 35–
    36, 38
"Dely" (Dunbar), 41–42, 59–60
Dial, 61–62
dialect, 21, 22, 63–64, 101, 147, 155, 201n75,
    207n10, 208n13, 220n10; Dunbar and,
    21, 41–42, 59–60, 105, 106, 110, 112,
    114
"Dilemma, The" (Randall), 180–181
Donne, John, 45–46
double consciousness, 8, 23, 171–172
"Douglass" (Dunbar), 105, 107–108, 110, 112,
    146, 155, 205n43
Douglass, Frederick, 57, 83, 114, 117,
    209n37; black presses and, 28, 91,
    210n58; "Douglass" (Dunbar), 105, 107–
    108, 110, 112, 146, 205n43; "Frederick
    Douglass" (Hayden), 16, 101, 154–156,
    183, 216n56
Dreer, Herman, 161–162
Du Bois, W. E. B., 8, 21, 23, 24, 82–83,
    204n23; *Crisis* and, 62, 120, 123–125,
    211n74; "Heritage" (Lilly) and, 182;
    McKay and, 28, 127; Santayana and, 64;
    "Sonnet to the Mantled" (G. D. John-
    son) and, 119

—works of: "The Criteria of Negro Art,"
167; "Triumph," 13

Duckett, Alfred A., "Sonnet," 160-161

Dunbar, Paul Laurence, 27, 50, 61, 101, 102,
104-115, 120, 171, 186, 188, 207n11, 208n30;
anthologies and, 132, 139; Baraka and,
174; Gwendolyn Brooks and, 177, 179,
180; Brown and, 147, 215n32; *Crisis* and,
211n74; dialect and, 21, 41-42, 59-60,
63, 105, 106, 110, 112, 114; Hill and, 123;
Hughes and, 162; as influence, 16, 30,
118, 144; Keats and, 107; McKay and, 16,
129-130; Nelson and, 3; protest tradition and, 4, 7, 19, 29, 92, 11, 207n8; views
on sonnet, 19, 32; Watkins and, 124-125

—works of: "Booker T. Washington," 108-
109, 121, 122, 140; "Dely," 41-42, 59-60;
"Douglass," 105, 107-108, 110, 112, 146,
155, 205n43; "Harriet Beecher Stowe,"
109-110; "Nature and Art,"110; "Passion
and Love," 40-41; "Recession Never,"
207n8; "Robert Gould Shaw," 15, 105-
109, 112, 117-118, 147-148, 152, 205n43,
208n16, 208n33; "Slow through the
Dark," 111, 141, 143, 145, 146, 152, 166-167;
"Sonnet: On an Old Book with Uncut
Leaves," 59-60

Dunbar-Nelson, Alice Moore, 123-124

Dykes, Eva B., 148-49

Ebony and Topaz (C. S. Johnson, ed.), 147-
148

Ebony Rhythms (Murphy, ed.), 151, 152-153

"Electrocution" (Ridge), 66-67

Eliot, T. S., 12, 177, 178, 197n36

Emanuel, James A., 15, 16-17, 128, 144, 163,
170; "Freedom Rider," 46-47

"England in 1819" (Shelley), 50-51

"Enter the New Negro" (Locke), 141,
213n16

"Epistrophe" (Baraka), 173-174

"Eulogy" (Horton), 85-86

"Farewell to My Mother," (Placido, trans.
Bryant), 87-89, 205n37

Filicaja, Vincenzo da, 81-82, 203n22

Fire! (Thurman, ed.), 147-148

First International Conference of Black
Writers, 171-172

"For Malcolm X" (Walker), 182-183

"For Mary McLeod Bethune" (Walker), 156

Francini, Antonella, 18, 22, 68, 158, 176

"Frederick Douglass" (Hayden), 16, 101,
154-156, 183, 216n56

Freedom's Journal, 81-83

"Freedom of Mind" ("The Free Mind,"
"Freedom for the Mind"; Garrison),
80-81

"Freedom Rider" (Emanuel), 46-47

"From the Dark Tower" (Cullen), 51-52,
60, 140, 146, 163, 183

Frost, Robert, 67, 178, 215n32; "The Silken
Tent," 70-71

Garrison, William Lloyd, 83, 155, 203n21,
205n41; "Freedom of Mind" ("The Free
Mind," "Freedom for the Mind"), 80-
81

Gates, Henry Louis, Jr., 5, 8, 12, 123, 188

"Gay Chaps at the Bar" (G. Brooks), 179

"Ginger Bread Mama" (Long), 184

Giovannitti, Arturo, 65

global black sonnet tradition, 25-26

Gray, Thomas, 52, 74, 91-92, 119

"Harlem Dancer, The" (McKay), 38-39

Harlem Renaissance, 16, 62, 130, 133, 171,
211n68

Harper, Frances Watkins, 30, 82, 92-93,
101

"Harriet Beecher Stowe" (Dunbar), 109-
110

Hayden, Robert: "Frederick Douglass," 16,
101, 154-156, 183, 216n56; "The Reformers," 174-175

Hayes, Terrance, 23-24

"Heritage" (Lilly), 182-183

Hill, Leslie Pickney, 15, 120-123; "Jim
Crow," 120-121; "To a Caged Canary in a
Negro Restaurant," 55-56; "Tuskegee,"
121-122; "Vision of a Lynching," 122-123

"Honeymoon" (McKay), 39

Horton, George Moses, 85-87; "Eulogy,"
85-86; "Slavery and Liberty," 86

Howard, Henry, rhyme scheme and, 37

Howells, William Dean, 105, 107, 112, 115,
129, 203n22, 207nn9-10, 208n13

Hughes, Langston, 14, 16, 62, 155, 158, 165,

Hughes, Langston (*continued*)
172, 177, 213n4, 213n6; anthologies and,
138, 153–154, 162; sonnet form and, 9, 17,
63–64, 130, 186, 215n32, 217nn79–80
—works of: "The Bread and Butter Side,"
219n96; "I, Too," 213n16, 214n20; "The
Negro Artist and the Racial Mountain,"
164; "Pennsylvania Station," 162–163;
"Ph.D.," 151–152; *The Poetry of the American Negro* (ed. with Bontemps), 153–154,
161; "Search," 166

"I, Too" (Hughes), 213n16, 214n20
"If We Must Die" (McKay), 12–17, 22, 125,
146, 161, 183, 209n44

Jackson, Walter Clinton, 139–140, 141
Jaji, Tsitsi, 189
"January Dandelion, A" (McClellan), 91–
92
Jay-Z, 188–189
"Jim Crow" (Hill), 120–121
Jim Crow system, represented in poetry,
51–52, 55–57, 70–71, 101, 120–121
Johnson, Charles Bertram, 68–69
Johnson, Charles Spurgeon, 147–148
Johnson, Georgia Douglas, 118–120; "Black
Recruit," 151–52; "Sonnet to the Man-
tled," 119
Johnson, Helene, 140, 144–145
Johnson, James Weldon, 5, 88–89, 129,
201n75, 205n37; *Book of American Negro
Poetry* (ed.), 130, 139
Johnson, Samuel, 74
Jones, LeRoi, 165, 167. *See also* Baraka,
Amiri
Jordan, June, 10–12, 21, 175; "Something
Like a Sonnet for Phillis Miracle
Wheatley," 11–12

Keats, John, 16, 86, 147, 203n10, 207n2;
Gwendolyn Brooks and, 178; Cullen
and, 52, 58; Dunbar and, 107; Hill and,
123; McKay and, 128
—works of: "On the Sonnet" ("If by Dull
Rhymes"), 58–59, 174, 200n65
Kerlin, Richard, 139–140, 141

labor union poetry, 64–67

Lazarus, Emma, 24, 102
Leonard, Keith D., 18, 22, 23, 112, 120, 159,
178
"Like His Gouged Eye" (Nelson), 19–20
Lilly, Octave, Jr., 182–183
literary magazines, 105, 207n1; *Atlantic
Monthly*, 95. *See also* black presses
Locke, Alain, 141, 213n16
"London 1802" (Wordsworth), 114
Long, Doughtry, 184
Longfellow, Henry Wadsworth, 95, 99,
102, 143, 147, 205nn41–42, 208n14,
215n32
"Lovely Love, A" (G. Brooks), 44–45
Lowell, Amy, 61–62
Lowell, James Russell, 92, 204n28, 211n67
lynching, represented in poetry, 20, 48–
49, 65–66, 122–123; protest poetry and,
66; Southey and, 75, 77. *See also* racial
violence, represented in poetry
"Lynching, The" (McKay), 48–49, 182

Mackey, Nathaniel, 2–3
"Maison" (cummings), 67
McCall, James Edward, 145–146
McClellan, George, 91–92
McKay, Claude, 27–28, 30, 50, 125–130, 165,
178, 186, 187, 197n33, 197n46, 217–218n80;
anthologies and, 132, 139, 141, 150, 170;
Braithwaite and, 116; Cullen and, 143–
144; dialect and, 63; Du Bois and, 28; as
influence, 64, 67, 104–105, 147; influences on, 66, 186; lynching and, 49, 66;
Nelson and, 3; protest tradition and,
7, 12–13, 14, 29, 50, 61, 170, 176, 196n27,
212n94; Whitfield and, 90
—works of: "America," 127–128; "The Harlem Dancer," 38–39; "Honeymoon," 39;
"If We Must Die," 12–17, 22, 125, 146, 161,
183, 209n44; "The Lynching," 48–49,
182; "Outcast," 67–68, 182; "Russian Cathedral," 141, 163; "To the Intrenched
Classes," 213n15; "To the White Fiends,"
126–127
Menard, John Willis, 100
"Mentors" (G. Brooks), 157–158
metaphors: bondage, 43, 51, 60–62; confinement, 44, 51–56; slavery, 44–45, 56–
57; violence, 45–47

meter, 21–22, 33, 43–44. *See also* sonnet form
Millay, Edna St. Vincent, 52, 67, 130, 142, 155, 187, 198n70
Milton, John, 9, 61, 74, 87, 106, 108, 111, 114, 147, 203n9, 208n22, 210n53; protest tradition and, 29, 50, 78, 85, 92, 123, 127, 130 —works of: "On the Late Massacre in Piedmont," 47–48, 49; "To the Lord General Cromwell," 73
Mis-Education of the Negro, The (C. Woodson), 101
"MMDCCXIII½" (Thomas), 185
modernist poetry, 19, 21, 62–65, 67, 167, 178, 184, 187, 201n81
Monroe, Harriet, 65, 95, 210n45
Murillo, John, 20–21
Murphy, Beatrice, M., 151, 152–153

"Nature and Art" (Dunbar), 110
Neal, Larry, 6, 9
"Negro Artist and the Racial Mountain, The" (Hughes), 164
Negro Poets and Their Poems (Kerlin, ed.), 139–140, 141
Nelson, Marilyn, 3, 24–25; "Like His Gouged Eye," 19–20; "A Wreath for Emmett Till," 20
neoclassical poetic tradition, 74
New Negro (ideology), 140, 141, 144–146, 165
New Negro, The (Locke), 141, 213n16
"New Negro, The" (McCall), 145–146
"New Negro, The" (Watkins), 140
New Negro Poets, USA, foreword (G. Brooks), 6, 134, 174
newspapers. *See* black presses
North, Michael, 62
Not a Man and Yet a Man (A. A. Whitman), 99–100
"Nothing in That Drawer" (Padgett), 24
"Nuns fret not" (Wordsworth), 52–53, 121, 157

"Oliver Wendell Holmes" (Cotter Sr.), 101–102
"On the Death of Thomas Bailey Aldrich" (Braithwaite), 95–96

"On the Late Massacre in Piedmont" (Milton), 47–48, 49
"On the Papal Court at Avignon" (Petrarch), 199n33
"On the Sonnet" ("If by Dull Rhymes"; Keats), 58–59, 174, 200n65
Othello (Shakespeare), 11, 196n14
"Outcast" (McKay), 67–68, 182
"Ozymandias" (Shelley), 128, 145

Padgett, Ron, 24
"Pan Africa" (Sarudzai), 25–26
"Passion and Love" (Dunbar), 40–41
"Paul Laurence Dunbar" (Corrothers), 113–114
"Pennsylvania Station" (Hughes), 162–163
periodicals, 105, 207n1. *See also* black presses
Petrarch, Francis, 33–37, 48, 184, 186, 198n4; "On the Papal Court at Avignon," 199n33; Sonnet 76, 33–34; Sonnet 132 (trans. as "Canticus Troili"), 36–37
Petrarchan (Italian) sonnet form, 32–36
"Ph.D." (Hughes), 151–152
Phoenix Society, 83
Placido (Gabriel de la Concepción Valdes), 87–89, 205n37
Platonic thought, 34–35
"Pleasures of Hope, The" (Campbell), 78–79
"Poems Concerning the Slave Trade" (Southey), 75–78
Poetry of the American Negro, The (Hughes and Bontemps, eds.), 153–154, 161
Pound, Ezra, 63
"Prisoner's Bench, The" (Giovannitti), 65
protest tradition (in poetry), 9, 29, 47–51, 64–67, 78, 107, 123, 130; Gwendolyn Brooks and, 7, 50; Cullen and, 52; Dunbar and, 7, 29, 92, 111, 207n8; McKay and, 7, 12–13, 14, 29, 50, 61, 128, 212n94; Milton and, 29, 50, 78, 85, 92, 123, 127, 130; Wordsworth and, 50, 78

racial violence, represented in poetry, 12–13, 48–49, 56–57, 101, 105–107, 207n8; Emmett Till, 19–20. *See also* lynching, represented in poetry

Randall, Dudley, 180–181

Rape of Florida, The (A. A. Whitman), 97–98

Ray, Charles Bennett, 84

Ray, Henrietta Cordelia, 84, 104, 116–118, 210n54; "Robert G. Shaw," 117–118; *Sonnets*, 118

Readings from Negro Authors for Schools and Colleges (Cromwell, Turner, and Dykes, eds.), 148–149

Reason, Charles Lewis, 84

"Recession Never" (Dunbar), 207n8

Redmond, Eugene, 16, 18, 49, 140; "Sonnet Serenade," 181–182, 221n51

"Reformers, The" (Hayden), 174–175

"Renegades of Funk" (Murillo), 20–21

rhyme scheme, 33, 36–37. *See also* sonnet form

Ridge, Lola, 66–67

"Robert G. Shaw" (H. C. Ray), 117–118

"Robert Gould Shaw" (Dunbar), 15, 105–109, 112, 117–118, 147–148, 152, 205n43, 208n16, 208n33

Robinson, Edwin Arlington, 58, 62, 64, 68; "Sonnet," 56–57

Rosetti, Dante Gabriel, 35–36

"Russian Cathedral" (McKay), 141, 163

Russwurm, John, 81

"Salutamus" (Brown), 146

Santayana, George, 64, 67–68, 206n54

Sarudzai, 25–26

"Search" (Hughes), 166

Shakespeare, William, 27, 61, 213n4; Gwendolyn Brooks, 42; Christian and, 60; Cullen and, 143; Dunbar and, 41; Horton and, 86; McKay and, 13, 39, 126, 186; Nelson and, 20; Wheatley and, 11; Wordsworth and, 79

—works of: *Othello*, 11, 196n14; Sonnet 18, 37–38; Sonnet 29, 64, 67–68, 69; Sonnet 30, 84; Sonnet 127, 199n15

Shakespearean sonnet form, 38, 200n65

Shaw, Robert Gould, 15, 105–109, 117–118, 147–148, 152, 205n43

"Shell, A" (C. B. Johnson), 68–69

Shelley, Percy Bysshe, 16, 29, 52, 65, 92, 107, 111, 128; "England in 1819," 50–51; "Ozymandias," 128, 145

Sidney, Philip: *Astrophil and Stella*, 37; Sonnet 47, 44

"Silken Tent, The" (Frost), 70–71

"Slavery and Liberty" (Horton), 86

slave songs, 22–23

"Slow through the Dark" (Dunbar), 111, 141, 143, 145, 146, 152, 166–167

Smethurst, James, 43, 54–55, 152–153, 156, 176, 180, 184

"Soldier, The" (R. Brooks), 13

"Something Like a Sonnet for Phillis Miracle Wheatley" (Jordan), 11–12

"Sonnet" (Duckett), 160–161

"Sonnet" (Dunbar-Nelson), 123–124

"Sonnet" (Filicaja), 81–82, 203n22

"Sonnet" (Hayes), 23–24

"Sonnet" (Reason), 84

"Sonnet" (Robinson), 56–57

"Sonnet, A" (Menard), 100

"Sonnet XIV" (Donne), 45–46

Sonnet 18 (Shakespeare), 37–38

Sonnet 29 (Shakespeare), 64, 67–68, 69

Sonnet 30 (Shakespeare), 84

Sonnet 47 (Sidney), 44

Sonnet 76 (Petrarch), 33–34

Sonnet 127 (Shakespeare), 199n15

Sonnet 132 ("Canticus Troili"; Petrarch), 36–37

sonnet crown, 20

sonnet form, 32–33; courtly love in, 35–36, 39–42, 44–45; as "European" or white, 8–10, 130–131, 176; opposition to, 23–24, 63, 159–60, 172; Petrarchan (Italian), 32–36; popularity of, 24, 123, 202n5; rhyme scheme and, 36–37; Shakespearean, 38

"Sonnet: On an Old Book with Uncut Leaves" (Dunbar), 59–60

Sonnets (H. C. Ray), 118

"Sonnets on the Punishment of Death" (Wordsworth), 202n94

"Sonnet Serenade" (Redmond), 181–182, 221n51

"Sonnet—The Montenegrin" (A. A. Whitman), 98–99

"Sonnet to a Negro in Harlem" (H. Johnson), 140, 144–145

"Sonnet to Negro Soldiers" (Cotter Jr.), 125

"Sonnet—To the Housatonic" (Arion), 82–83
"Sonnet to the Mantled" (G. D. Johnson), 119
sonnet writing, represented in poetry, 58–60
"Southern Share-Cropper" (Christian), 69–70
southern United States, represented in poetry, 149–150
Southey, Robert, 20, 29, 50, 66, 72, 81, 203nn9–11; "Poems Concerning the Slave Trade," 75–78
"Southland" (L. Alexander), 149–150
Spenser, Edmund, 37
spoken performance, 43–44
"Spring in the South" (Christian), 149–150
Steffen, Therese, 18, 56, 186
Stevens, Wallace, 62, 63
Stowe, Harriet Beecher, 109–110, 112, 147, 155
"Struggle Staggers Us, The" (Walker), 43
"Surprised by Joy" (Wordsworth), 124, 158

"Tanto gentile e tanto onesta pare" (Dante; trans. Rosetti), 35–36, 38
"Tell Me Something Good" (Jaji), 189
"There Is a Bondage" (Wordsworth), 51
"There's a Brown Girl in the Ring" (Baugh), 36, 38, 42, 44, 184, 199n15
"XIII / intermission: I / deep summer" (G. Brooks), 42, 173
Thomas, Lorenzo, 185
Thurman, Wallace, 147–148
Till, Emmett, represented in poetry, 19–20. See also lynching, represented in poetry; racial violence, represented in poetry
"To a Caged Canary in a Negro Restaurant" (Hill), 55–56
"To a Winter Squirrel" (G. Brooks), 53–54
"To the Intrenched Classes" (McKay), 213n15
"To the King's Most Excellent Majesty" (Wheatley), 73–74, 79, 84
"To the Lord General Cromwell" (Milton), 73
"To the White Fiends" (McKay), 126–127

"To Toussaint L'Ouverture" (Wordsworth), 79–80, 154
Trethewey, Natasha, 1–2, 6, 8, 9, 187
"Triumph" (Du Bois), 13
"Turncoat, The" (Baraka), 172–173
Turner, Lorenzo Dow, 148–49
"Tuskegee" (Hill), 121–122
"MMDCCXIII½" (Thomas), 185

"Vision of a Lynching" (Hill), 122–123

Walker, Margaret, 156–157; "For Malcolm X," 182–183; "For Mary McLeod Bethune," 156; "The Struggle Staggers Us," 43
Washington, Booker T., 101, 108–109, 121, 140, 147
Watkins, Lucian B.: "Ballade to Paul Laurence Dunbar," 124–125; "The New Negro," 140
"Wesley Everest" (Chaplin), 65–66
Wheatley, Phillis, 3, 4, 10–12, 25, 29, 72–75, 91, 100, 149, 165, 202n5, 203n6; "To the King's Most Excellent Majesty," 73–74, 79, 84
White, Newman Ivey, and Walter Clinton Jackson, 139–140, 141
"White Troops, The" (G. Brooks), 178–179
Whitfield, James Monroe, 90
Whitman, Albery Allson, 96–100, 101, 206n61; Not a Man and Yet a Man, 99–100; The Rape of Florida, 97–98; "Sonnet—The Montenegrin," 98–99
Whitman, Walt, 43, 201n75
Whittier, John Greenleaf, 87, 89, 90
Woodson, Carter, 101
Woodson, Jon, 18, 49, 70, 120, 123, 130, 203n10
Wordsworth, William, 16, 29, 54, 104, 107, 200n47; abolitionist poetry and, 72, 75, 81, 85, 204n28; protest tradition and, 50, 78
—works of: "London 1802," 114; "Nuns fret not," 52–53, 121, 157; "Sonnets on the Punishment of Death," 202n94; "Surprised by Joy," 124, 158; "There Is a Bondage," 51; "To Toussaint L'Ouverture," 79–80, 154

World War I, 12, 29, 125, 152; poets of, 66, 160–161

World War II, 7, 152, 161

"Wreath for Emmett Till, A" (Nelson), 20

Wyatt, Thomas, rhyme scheme and, 37

"XIII / intermission: I / deep summer" (G. Brooks), 42, 173

Yerby, Frank, 163–164

"Yet Do I Marvel" (Cullen), 142–143, 152

"You Are a Part of Me" (Yerby), 163–164

Young, Alexander, 152